Revolutions in Development Inquiry

To the memory of
Jimmy Mascarenhas

Revolutions in Development Inquiry

Robert Chambers

publishing for a sustainable future

London • Sterling, VA

First published by Earthscan in the UK and USA in 2008

ISBN-13: 978-1-84407-624-6

Typeset by JS Typesetting Ltd, Porthcawl, Mid Glamorgan
Printed and bound in the UK by Antony Rowe, Chippenham
Cover design by Susanne Harris

For a full list of publications please contact:

Earthscan
Dunstan House
14a St Cross St
London, EC1N 8XA, UK
Tel: +44 (0)20 7841 1930
Fax: +44 (0)20 7242 1474
Email: earthinfo@earthscan.co.uk
Web: **www.earthscan.co.uk**

22883 Quicksilver Drive, Sterling, VA 20166-2012, USA

Earthscan publishes in association with the International Institute for Environment and
Development

A catalogue record for this book is available from the British Library

Library of Congress Cataloging-in-Publication Data

Chambers, Robert, 1932-
  Revolutions in development inquiry / by Robert Chambers.
    p. cm.
  ISBN 978-1-84407-624-6 (hardback) – ISBN 978-1-84407-625-3 (pbk.) 1. Rural
development. I. Title.
  HN46.C6C53 2008
  307.1'4120723–dc22

                                                                        2008017441

The paper used for this book is FSC-certified and totally
chlorine-free. FSC (the Forest Stewardship Council) is an
international network to promote responsible management
of the world's forests.

Contents

List of Figures, Tables and Boxes

Figures

Tables

Boxes

Preface

I think we are lucky, and that this is a brilliantly exciting time to be alive and working as development professionals. So much is changing, and changing so fast, and new potentials are continually opening up. If we are to do well this means massive and radical learning and unlearning. It means personal, professional and institutional change as a way of life. For some this is a threat; for others a wonderful and exhilarating challenge opening up new worlds of experience.

Participatory methodologies – approaches, methods and attitudes, behaviours and relationships – are one part of this ... They are different each time. They improvise and innovate. They fit our world of accelerating change. It is not easy to keep up to date. I keep on having to revise these notes, and do it sometimes twice a year. If you see them and they are more than six months old, please remember that. Much may have changed. And anyway, I am behind the game. It is creative and reflective practitioners in the field who are making the running and from whom those of us not in the field have continuously to learn.

Spirit and orientation

These are the opening words in my notes for *Whose Reality Counts?* workshops in 2008. I am starting with them because they express the spirit of this book. Change in our times accelerates in many dimensions. Those that are more obvious – political, economic, social, cultural and, above all, communications – receive recognition and attention and are much researched and written about. But changes in how we inquire and find out, especially in development practice, are relatively neglected. Methodologies is not a subject in its own right. Yet recent decades have witnessed not one but many revolutionary innovations in development inquiry.

The title of the book has itself been subject to accelerating change. It has progressed through *Finding Out in Development* and *Revealing Realities?* before daring to settle on its present title. Jethro Pettit and others have helped it on its way. *Revolutions* has two senses: revolutions that are upending and transformative; and revolutions like a wheel going round to revisit former positions. *Development inquiry* refers mainly to approaches and methods for finding out about local (sometimes described as 'field') conditions and individual, group and community realities.

Most of the innovations, practice and experience on which I draw is from non-OECD (Organisation for Economic Co-operation and Development) countries, but their applications in OECD countries have been, and will be, many. Almost all the transfer of technology has been from non-OECD to OECD, reversing what earlier had been the normal direction.

On orientation, three points need to be made.

First, with revolution in the sense of a wheel going round, much remains of enduring value in the approaches and methods of the past. The transient fashions of development manifest not only in policies, words and concepts, but also in methodologies. The frenetic search for new fashions abandons and buries a lot that has lasting value. The succession of acronyms RRA (rapid rural appraisal), PRA (participatory rural appraisal) and PLA (participatory learning and action) has misled some into supposing that what had come earlier had been superseded. Parts of Chapters 1 to 5 draw on lessons from earlier decades that seem to me as valid today as ever.

Much that matters has slid out of sight. Thus as PRA and PLA (Chapter 5) became fashionable, so it became rare for attention to be paid to the art of observation and noticing small things like microenvironments (Chapter 3), or to the other key skills of RRA (Chapter 4), like semi-structured interviewing. Activities once seen as state of the art became rare in training, crowded out by the more trendy, visible and photogenic diagrams and maps of PRA. But observation and RRA are not second bests in inquiry. They are overdue for rehabilitation and restoration to their proper places in the professional repertoire.

Second, new methodologies and their applications continuously open up. RRA (Chapter 4) led on to PRA (Chapter 5) with its visuals and analyses by groups, which in turn gave rise to participatory approaches and methods for generating numbers (Chapter 6) and participatory spatial analysis (Chapter 7). All these innovations raised anew, and sometimes more acutely, issues of ethics in inquiry, and questions of who found out what, for what purpose, and for whom (Chapter 8). And this is the beginning, not the end, of innovation and excitement, with potentials for branching out in many directions, cross-fertilizing, and opening up many frontiers (Chapter 9). With methods of inquiry, especially those that are taught, there is a tempting illusion that we have arrived. Chapters 8 and 9 challenge any such view, considering the traps we are caught in and how to escape them, and then proposing innovation of modes of inquiry as a permanent part of professional practice.

Third, methodological pluralism has been and has to remain the way forward. My ideology, my fundamentalism almost, is that fundamentalisms are flawed. Monocultures of methods misfit much of our complex, diverse and dynamic world. This can apply to questionnaires, or RRA, or PRA, or any other methodology. Each of these in its time was a revolution. Now many good new modes of inquiry are hybrids or mixtures; many are improvised adaptations; many are inventions. As Chapter 9 concludes, critical eclectic pluralism, ever combining, ever experimenting, ever innovating, and ever learning and unlearning, is the key to good practice. It can even lead to discovering that what was thought to be undoable and unknowable can now be done and known.

So in this book I seek to describe some of the practical experience and theory of these revolutions, to bring them up to date with developments in the latter 2000s, and to outline potentials for the future. In doing this, I try to give some sense of history, of what things were like and how they were done and seen in the past. I have been astonished at myself when recollecting, as this book has forced me to, how differently I saw and did things in the 1960s, 70s, 80s and even 90s, believing at each time that we were at a methodological frontier beyond which discovery would diminish. Every time I failed to imagine what was to come. The lesson from this reflection back into the frames and mindsets of earlier decades is to recognize that now in the latter 2000s, we are still, perhaps even more, in a state of transition; that this is a lasting part of the human and professional condition; and that when those who are still around in 2020, 2030 or 2040 look back on the latter 2000s, they similarly will marvel at how we too, once again, had not imagined what was to come.

Limitations

A first limitation is about scope. Much of this book is about one stream of methodological revolutions. The main subject matter is the sequence and family of approaches and methods which includes agroecosystem analysis (Gypmantasiri et al, 1980; Conway, 1985), RRA, PRA and PLA. This stream is only one among many which mingle now more and more in a whole river. Among these are Naturalistic Inquiry (Lincoln and Guba, 1985; Guba and Lincoln, 1989), action research and participatory action research (Greenwood and Levin, 1998; Bradbury and Reason, 2001), action learning (Taylor et al, 1997), Appreciative Inquiry (Hammond and Royal, 1998; Elliott, 1999), Planning for Real (Gibson, 1996), Stepping Stones (Welbourn, 1995, 2007) and Reflect (Archer and Newman, 2003; Archer and Nandago, 2004). There is no pretence of balanced or comprehensive coverage in this book. The best I can do is provide references to some of the main sources for some of the more widespread and promising of other approaches, remembering and warning the reader that there is much, much more out there that I do not know about or refer to.

A second limitation is more personal. The book began with the fond fantasy of republishing some earlier papers. I soon realized that they would have to be brought up to date. At the same time colleagues urged me, twisting my somewhat compliant arm, to cover some parts of my personal journey. So these chapters represent one person's fallible view. It has been a privilege to have been alive and around during this period, when so many have been pioneering. I have had the freedom and time to visit some of the innovators and to watch, listen, learn and write. It is part of the injustice of our world that someone like myself from the North can gain credit by writing and publishing about the work of colleagues in the South who then pass unrecognized. They are many, too numerous to name, but I wish to acknowledge them and thank them, and also to note that with their greater field experience, they and others are likely to disagree with or wish to qualify some of the views expressed.

Let me warn the reader about some of my predispositions and biases. I have been fascinated by evidence, myth and realities since studying history, notably the *Risorgimento* – the unification of Italy. Scepticism about evidence carried over into research in Kenya where I was exposed to the limitations and inefficiencies of questionnaire surveys. This was reinforced by experience as one of a research team in India and Sri Lanka. These and later experiences made me not just a happy sceptic about traditional modes of inquiry, but prejudiced against them, vulnerable to glee when finding errors, and an enthusiastic companion to those who were evolving alternatives. I am also biased from having been an intermittent participant–observer in the revolutions of RRA and PRA and PLA. I have often been wrong, and am surely wrong about some of the assertions in this book. It is in all our interests that it be read through a critical lens, and its errors and omissions identified and corrected.

Overview

The first five chapters are about those parts of the stream where I have found myself being carried along. The last four chapters – on participation and numbers, participation and space, traps and liberations, and eclectic pluralism for the future – are largely new. They suggest that change is accelerating. They could not have been written five years ago. The rate of innovation, and of evolving new applications in new domains, shows no sign of slowing. For those concerned, the challenges and excitement do not diminish; the frontiers continue to expand; the revolutions, it seems, will keep on coming.

These revolutions have been, but should not have been, quiet. For many they have been imperceptible and unperceived. This book does not set out to shout from the rooftops. But what has been happening is important, inspiring and exhilarating. More people should know about it. More professionals need to embrace new ways of finding out, and to become innovators themselves. Participatory inquiry takes us into new spaces. What began as a search for cost-effectiveness has evolved into a movement carrying with it the seeds of social transformation. This, then, is about more than modes of inquiry. It comes to be about ways of living and being.

Robert Chambers
April 2008

Acknowledgements

Colleagues and friends from whom I have learnt on my journey are too numerous to name. They include those who undertook evaluation research on the Kenya Government's Special Rural Development Programme (SRDP) (1969–71), co-researchers on the project on agrarian change in South India and Sri Lanka (1973–74), many who developed RRA in the 1970s and 1980s, innovators and collaborators in the International Institute for Environment and Development (IIED) and in India, Kenya and many other countries who developed the approaches and methods of PRA from 1988 onwards, colleagues working on participation and reflective practice at the Institute of Development Studies (IDS) (over the past decade and a half), and most recently pioneers with participatory numbers and Participatory Geographic Information Systems (PGIS).

For constructive criticism, comments and suggestions which led to re-organizing and rewriting the book I thank Rosalind Eyben, John Gaventa and Jethro Pettit. Others who have made useful comments on drafts of chapters and related papers at different stages include Carlos Barahona, Andrea Cornwall, Colette Harris, Dee Jupp, Henry Lucas, Joy Moncrieffe, Zander Navarro, Peter Reason, Cathy Shutt and Bill Torbert. Other ideas, information and advice have come from Laura Cornish, Leslie Groves, Renwick Irvine, Penny Lawrence, Sonya Ruparel, Koy Thomson and many others.

For help with the production of this book and related papers I am grateful to Birte Bromby, Dee Donlan, Samantha Finn, Jeanne Grant, Alison Norwood, Georgina Powell-Stevens, Patsy Tayler and Sinnet Weber. I thank them all, both those who have given sustained and detailed support and those who have cheerfully stepped into the breach at short notice. They have all made my life easier and the production of the book quicker and more enjoyable.

My greatest debt is to Jenny without whom this would never have been written.

Chapters 1–7 include some text that has already been published. This is indicated by the date of earlier publication given in brackets at the head of the text, with new text preceded by (2008). Chapters 8 and 9 are new. Permission from the publishers to reproduce the source papers in whole or part is gratefully acknowledged, as follows:

Chapter 1: The republished text is from Chapter 3 of *Rural Development:Putting the Last First*, Longman, Harlow (now Pearson Scientific) 1983 pp49–55.

Chapter 2: The republished text is from Chapter 1 of *Rural Development: Putting the Last First*, Longman, Harlow (now Pearson Scientific) 1983 pp7–27. The second section updates and adds from subsequent experience.

Chapter 3: The first section is abridged from 'Microenvironments unobserved' in R. P. Singh (ed) *Proceedings of the International Symposium on Natural Resources Management for a Sustainable Agriculture*, 6–10 February 1990, New Delhi, republished edited by Jules Pretty with the same title as *Gatekeeper Series* SA22, International Institute for Environment and Development, London 1990.

Chapter 4 is in part *Rapid Rural Appraisal: Rationale and Repertoire*, Discussion Paper 155, IDS, Brighton 1981 republished in *Public Administration and Development*, vol 2, no 2, pp95–106, 1981.

Chapter 5 includes material from a chapter written for the second edition (2008) of *Handbook of Action Research: Participative Inquiry and Practice*, edited by Peter Reason and Hilary Bradbury, Sage Publications.

Chapter 6: 'Who Counts? Participation and Numbers' is updated and expanded as the latest of several incarnations, including *Who Counts? The Quiet Revolution of Participation and Numbers*, IDS Working Paper 296, December 2007, 'The best of both worlds' in Ravi Kanbur (ed) *Q-Squared: Qualitative and Quantitative Methods of Poverty Appraisal*, Permanent Black, New Delhi, 2003, pp35–45 and 'Participation and numbers', *PLA Notes*, vol 47, August 2003 pp6–12.

Chapter 7: 'Whose Space? Mapping, Power and Ethics' is an expanded version of *Participatory Mapping for Change*, a paper written for the International Conference on Participatory Spatial Information Management and Communication: 'Mapping for Change', held in the Kenya College of Communication and Technology, Nairobi, 7–10 September 2005.

List of Acronyms and Abbreviations

AAI	ActionAid International, Johannesburg
ABC	attitude and behaviour change
AI	Appreciative Inquiry
AKF	Aga Khan Foundation, Geneva
AKRSP	Aga Khan Rural Support Programme (India) (Pakistan)
ALPS	Accountability, Learning and Planning System of AAI
CBCRM	Community-Based Coastal Resource Management
CDD	Community-Driven Development
CDRA	Community Development Resource Association, Cape Town
CGIAR	Consultative Group for International Agricultural Research
CLTS	Community-Led Total Sanitation
cPPIPs	cumulative Prioritized Problem Indices of Poor
DFID	Department for International Development, London
EDP	Exposure and Dialogue Programme, Bonn
ERR	egocentric reminiscence ratio
FAO	Food and Agriculture Organization, Rome
GDP	gross domestic product
GIS	Geographic Information Systems
GIT & S	Geographic Information Technology and Systems
GPS	Global Positioning Systems
ICRISAT	International Crops Research Institute for the Semi-arid Tropics, Patancheru, Hyderabad (CGIAR)
IDRC	International Development Research Centre, Ottawa
IDS	Institute of Development Studies, Sussex, UK
IFPRI	International Food Policy Research Institute, Washington DC
IIED	International Institute for Environment and Development, London
ILAC	Institutional Learning and Change (CGIAR)
ILS	Internal Learning System
INGO	international non-governmental organization
IPM	integrated pest management
ITK	indigenous technical knowledge
KKU	Khon Kaen University, Thailand
M and E	monitoring and evaluation
MDG	Millennium Development Goal

ME	microenvironment
MISR	Makerere Institute of Social Research, Kampala
MYRADA	MYRADA, Bangalore
NCAER	National Council for Applied Economic Research, Delhi
NESA	New Entity for Social Action, Bangalore
NGO	non-governmental organization
NOVIB	NOVIB, Netherlands, now Oxfam Novib
NRI	Natural Resources Institute, Chatham, UK
NSO	National Statistical Office, Malawi
ODA	Overseas Development Administration (now DFID), London
ODI	Overseas Development Institute, London
OECD	Organisation for Economic Co-operation and Development
PALS	Participatory Action Learning System
PC	personal computer
PE	participatory epidemiology
PGIS	Participatory Geographic Information Systems
PIA	Participatory Impact Assessment
PLA	participatory learning and action
PLWHA	Person Living With HIV and AIDS
PM and E	participatory monitoring and evaluation
PM	participatory methodology
PPA	Participatory Poverty Assessment
PPI	Participatory Poverty Index
PRA	participatory rural appraisal
Pradan	Professional Assistance for Development Action
PRGA	Participatory Research and Gender Analysis programme
PRSP	Poverty Reduction Strategy Paper
PTD	Participatory Technology Development
R & D	research and development
RAP	Rapid Assessment Process/Procedures
RCT	randomized control trial
REFLECT	now Reflect, originally Regenerated Freirian Literacy through Empowering Community Techniques
RRA	rapid rural appraisal
RRA1	Paper to the Workshop on Rapid Rural Appraisal, 26–27 October 1978 at the IDS, Sussex
RRA2	Paper to the Conference on Rapid Rural Appraisal, 4–7 December 1979 at the IDS, Sussex
SARAR	Self esteem, Associative strength, Resourcefulness, Action planning and Responsibility
SCF	Save the Children Fund, London
SDC	Swiss Agency for Development and Cooperation, Bern
SEWA	Self Employed Women's Association, Ahmedabad
SIDA	now Sida. Swedish International Development Agency, Stockholm
SIT	spatial information technology
SOSOTEC	self-organizing systems on the edge of chaos

SPSS	Statistical Package for the Social Sciences
SRDP	Special Rural Development Programme, Kenya
SS	Stepping Stones
SSC	Social Science Council, UK
STAR	Stepping Stones and Reflect
TIP	Targeted Inputs Programme (Malawi)
TOT	transfer of technology
UNDP	United Nations Development Programme, New York
UNHCR	United Nations High Commissioner for Refugees
UNHS	Uganda National Household Survey
UNICEF	United Nations Children's Fund, New York
UPPAP	Uganda Participatory Poverty Assessment Process
USAID	United States Agency for International Development, Washington DC
VERC	Village Educational Resource Centre, Bangladesh
WCED	World Commission on Environment and Development
WSP	Water and Sanitation Program, World Bank, Washington DC

1

The Provocation: Dinosaurs

In late Cretaceous times the mammals were developing at a rapid rate... As contrasted to the mammals, the dinosaurs were virtual walking automatons. (Colbert, 1951, p116)

Abstract

Experiences in the 1970s, in Kenya, India and Sri Lanka, sparked critiques of the use of large-scale multi-subject questionnaires (the dinosaurs) for rural research. They were ponderous, costly and vulnerable to many errors. Of these, investigator effects appeared as serious as they were overlooked. Such surveys placed heavy burdens on researchers whom they trapped and enslaved. And even with the best efforts they tended to generate data that were bad, unusable and unused. All data are artefacts, or fabricata, but those from large-scale multi-subject questionnaires especially so through their preset categories and structured interactions.

Large-scale questionnaire investigations have proved robustly sustainable. Three types are: large-scale time series surveys like censuses; surveys that seek to find out about topics and context; and surveys that apply an experimental design of treatment and controls. Classical scientific methodology with treatment and controls fits for research with large numbers, standard treatments, uniform receiving environments, measurable outcomes and plausible causal linkages. At high cost they have been made to work with standard social treatments as with a study of the effects of women's groups in Nepal on neonatal mortality. With Community-Driven Development, this approach, embraced, propagated and sponsored by the World Bank has been a costly and ineffective way of trying to learn.

Other approaches and methods are needed for finding out about complexity. The issues are paradigmatic, and basic to this book.

The dinosaurs that provoke are large-scale multi-subject questionnaire surveys. Starting with the dinosaur analogy, I first called this chapter 'Jurassic Park'. But the dinosaurs in Stephen Spielberg's film are not survivors from the past, but clones from the bellies of fossilized mosquitoes. Nor are dinosaur questionnaires confined in a park, but spread worldwide And rather than the Jurassic, the late Cretaceous was more apposite and reflected my wishful thinking, for by then the dinosaurs were in decline and the early mammals, small, nimble and more intelligent, were at their feet.

The provocation is both personal and paradigmatic. The personal reasons are my own experiences with these dinosaurs and with the search, on which so many have been engaged, for better modes of inquiry. Paradigmatically, the provocation is that many powerful professionals are trapped in the mindsets and methods of a deductive paradigm of things, standardized blueprints like questionnaires, and reductionism, when for many purposes we can find out and learn better through an inductive paradigm of people, diverse processes and methodologies, and holism.

Experiences

Starting the journey (2008)

Let me describe where I am coming from[1] and describe some of my biases.

Research experiences in the early 1970s in Kenya and in South Asia exposed me to large-scale multi-subject questionnaire surveys. In Kenya I was involved in coordinating evaluation for the Kenya Government's Special Rural Development Programme (SRDP) in six sub-districts. The results of a major survey for the SRDP were long delayed and emerged in a large report delivered long after it was due. I do not think it had much influence. On top of this, Jon Moris wrote a comprehensive critique of multi-subject surveys (1970) which sadly was never published. He listed 40 such surveys. He had taken some part in 14 of them himself. His long list of defects indicated major flaws and cast doubt on many 'findings'.

I went on from Kenya to become assistant director for a research programme on technology and change in rice-growing areas of Sri Lanka and Tamil Nadu (Farmer, 1977). We were a multidisciplinary and international team. That we would use a questionnaire was never questioned. Meeting in Cambridge (UK), we drew up a long list of questions, covering our varied disciplinary and research concerns. Each of us added questions. None of us wanted to challenge the questions of others. With hindsight it is easy to see that this was an error and arrogant. But unlike many of the East African surveys reviewed by Moris, this one was conducted well in the field. My colleagues were highly professional, committed and well qualified. The investigators, as they were called, were well selected, well trained, and conscientious. Internal checks were followed up when they showed inconsistencies. Through Herculean efforts, the data were collected, processed and analysed, and findings were indeed derived from the survey. But nagging questions would not go away: was such a gargantuan effort really needed to learn what we wanted to learn? How much of the mass of data was unused? How timely was the analysis and presentation? How much of what we came to know was derived from the survey? How reliable were the findings? And then there was the 'so what?' question – what difference did it make?[2] Who were the main beneficiaries of the survey? Was it the people among whom we worked, or was it us, the researchers, because it gave us processed data for our academic papers?

Thus, both the Kenya and the India/Sri Lanka projects included the large-scale application of lengthy questionnaires. I was a free-rider, privileged not to be engaged directly in the management or analysis of either. This gave me space to follow up on unexpected leads,[3] and to observe what the surveys entailed. For those involved, the surveys themselves were irreversibly committing, and exacting and demoralizing. They generated mountains of data, much of it of doubtful value, and demanded much time, money, diligence and patience – far more than anticipated[4] – to process and analyse.

These experiences were the beginning of the journey, the threads of which weave through this book. They also conditioned me so strongly that I have carried with me biases and preconceptions, some might say prejudices, that predispose me to 'four legs good, two legs bad' dichotomies in which large multi-subject questionnaires have two legs and almost anything else four. In criticizing them, I recognize the danger of being out of touch and out of date. I am grateful to those who, in correspondence and conversation, have corrected errors and updated insights. There have been improvements in questionnaire survey methodology. Nevertheless, normal pathology persists. These dinosaurs of inquiry may be overdue for extinction but continue to reproduce and flourish.

Large-scale multi-subject questionnaire surveys observed

During the India and Sri Lanka fieldwork and after it, I watched the stress and agony of my colleagues who were to varying degrees engaged in the survey and its analysis. I then wrote about some of the many drawbacks I had observed. But these large-scale questionnaire surveys seemed to be immune to any radical challenge. Heresies like mine were not well received. The institution and rituals of surveys were preserved and performed with something close to reverence. Many researchers were socialized into them, trained to carry them out, and seemed willing to be enslaved by them.

Investigator effects

Whatever their weaknesses, these surveys were well protected, as a story against myself can illustrate. In the Tamil Nadu research we had eight investigators for 12 villages: four of them had two villages each, and four had only one. I analysed the findings on agricultural extension, and drafted a paper. Something was wrong but I could not put my finger on it. Then I matched the findings for each of the pairs of villages with the same investigator. The similarities in the pairs, one might say twins, were so striking that it was difficult to avoid the conclusion that the investigator was the main explanatory variable. So I wrote a paper entitled 'Up the garden path'. However, it so upset some in our team that I never sent it for publication and now it is lost. So I never passed the warning on to others. Loyalty and friendship took precedence over sharing with others what I believed I had learnt.

I am not alone in this finding and this delinquency. Gerry Gill, in his penetrating critique *O.K., the Data's Lousy, But It's All We've Got (Being a Critique of Conventional Methods)* quotes a colleague who told him that in a situation:

> ...*where the coefficients were 'all over the place', he ran an analysis of variance on a randomly selected subset of the data, using the enumerators' identification numbers as the independent variable. He was alarmed, if not totally surprised, to find that the values of the F statistics were consistently so high as to be 'off the end of the scale'! He did not, for some reason, try to publish his findings.*
> (Gill, 1993, p9)

After the South Asia survey experience, I twice challenged the National Council for Applied Economic Research (NCAER), one of the largest survey organizations in India, to analyse their data treating the enumerator as an independent variable. On both occasions the director of the time agreed to do so. But to my knowledge it was never done, or if done, never published. There are standards of rigour associated with sampling and sample size, and it is normal practice to make these transparent. Arguably, there should equally be standards of rigour for enumerator effects and it should be normal good professional practice to publish tables of enumerator variance. If this is not done, it raises suspicions that those who manage and analyse data are as guilty as I was of withholding discordant information. The analysis is not technically difficult and publishing the results ought to add to overall credibility. The NCAER, National Sample Surveys in various countries, and the research departments and Independent Evaluation Group of the World Bank could set examples.[5]

Pressures on researchers

Participant observation in the Sri Lanka and Tamil Nadu research showed that pressures on senior researchers could be almost intolerable.[6] While they were conducting, managing, processing and analysing a survey, their domestic life cycles with children at school and the stage of their career with teaching and administrative as well as research responsibilities, placed almost insufferable demands on their time and energy. On top of all this, they faced pressures and temptations to take on extra research and other work, leading to pathological overcommitment. This imposed a paradoxical urban bias on rural research as senior researchers had more and more to do in town, and less and less time for the field. Office working conditions also exposed them to endless interruptions. Under such time pressures, senior researchers were trapped in the inescapable and necessary activities of managing the survey process instead of themselves conducting research and themselves learning. They too, like the field staff, were enslaved.

Ten years after these experiences, and drawing also on other sources, I wrote a book *Rural Development: Putting the Last First*, from which the following extracts are taken. The two cultures referred to are those of negative academics and positive practitioners (Chambers, 1983, pp29–35).

Convergence on questionnaires (1983)

The most common method of formal rural research is the questionnaire survey. The purpose of outsiders may be to find out about subjects as diverse as farming practices, family planning, agricultural extension, child care, nutrition, medical knowledge, household income, literacy, or use of the media, but whatever the purpose the reflex is the same. A questionnaire is drawn up, a sample selected, and the questionnaire applied.

Several forces combine to promote these questionnaire surveys. The strongest bridge between the two cultures, of practitioners and academic social scientists, has been the rubric and reality of 'planning'. To academics, planning is an acceptable activity, being concerned less with instant nuts and bolts and more with policy in the medium or longer term. But planning, whether national or local, requires 'data' about rural people which can be aggregated to give an overall view. What other mechanisms for obtaining such data than surveys? Again, agencies concerned about the effectiveness of projects they have funded want to know what they have or have not achieved. What better than a benchmark survey of the project area and of a control, with follow-up surveys later? Then, many non-social scientists, and especially natural scientists, have a mathematical training, a reverence for hypothesis-formulation and testing, and a belief that the social sciences should strive for a rigour similar to that of the natural sciences. Questionnaire surveys subject to statistical analysis seem to meet these requirements. Another factor is professional predispositions in economics and statistics. Economists are better able than those in most other disciplines to straddle between practitioners and academics. They therefore unduly influence the nature and style of collaboration. Statisticians, for their part, whether in ministries or research institutes, must justify their existence; and to do this they need numbers. So economists and statisticians, both numerate, both acceptable to both cultures, and both required in 'planning', demand surveys and the statistical data which they generate, and which allow them both to consummate their professional skills and to be, or at least appear to be, useful.

Convenience, class, prestige and power also play their part in promoting surveys. The analysis of survey data can be done safely and comfortably in an urban office without rural exposure. It reinforces what M. N. Srinivas has described as 'The division of labour between the theoretician-analyst and the fact-gatherer', the latter constituting a 'helot class' which does the rural work of investigation and enumeration, allowing the analyst to work away without the inconvenience of contact with the reality (Srinivas, 1975, pp1389–1390). The manipulation of figures is a clean, tidy and unpolluting activity. Arcane mathematical mystery allows its high priests to criticize, veto or amend the research of others; and it demands sophisticated computers for its devotees.

These forces help to explain why an urban-based industry of rural social surveys has mushroomed, financed by national governments, research councils and foundations, and following the changing fashions of topics – the diffusion of innovations, family planning, the green revolution, agricultural practices, cooperatives, credit, rural industries, employment, self-help, baseline or bench-mark surveys for projects and programmes, and the plight of women. Surveys are a respectable reflex. It is scarcely surprising that a 1974 Conference on field data collection in the social sciences concerned itself mostly with data collection through surveys and little with other techniques (Kearl, 1976). In the minds of some, rural research is surveys.

But questionnaire surveys have many well-known shortcomings. Unless careful appraisal precedes drawing up a questionnaire, the survey will embody the concepts and categories of outsiders rather than those of rural people, and thus impose meanings on the social reality. The misfit between the concepts of urban professionals and those of poor rural people is likely to be substantial, and the questions asked may construct artificial chunks of 'knowledge' which distort or mutilate the reality which poor people experience. Nor are questionnaire surveys on their own good ways of identifying causal relationships – a correlation alone tells us nothing definite about cause – or of exploring social relationships such as reciprocity, dependence, exploitation and so on. Their penetration is usually shallow, concentrating on what is measurable, answerable, and acceptable as a question, rather than probing less tangible and more qualitative aspects of society. For many reasons – fear, prudence, ignorance, exhaustion, hostility, hope of benefit – poor people give information which is slanted or false.

For these and many other reasons, conventional questionnaire surveys have many drawbacks if the aim is to gain insight into the lives and conditions of the poorer rural people. Other methods are required, either alone, or together with surveys. But extensive questionnaire surveys pre-empt resources, capturing staff and finance, and preventing other approaches. Let us examine this phenomenon more closely.

Survey slavery (1983)

The costs and inefficiencies of rural surveys are often high: human costs for the researchers; opportunity costs for research capacity that might have been better used; and inefficiencies in misleading 'findings'.

Thousands, perhaps tens of thousands, of researchers have surrendered their freedom to surveys; and if field workers are helots, their masters can also be slaves. For preparing, conducting, analysing and writing up a rural survey are heavily committing activities, the demands of which are habitually ignored or underestimated, and the duration of which almost always exceeds that planned.

Commitment to surveys is all too easily and willingly accepted. It is not just that statisticians, economists and others have professional preferences. Research institutions and universities need to obtain funds; once they have conducted some surveys, there are pressures and obligations to find further employment for field staff, who then go from project to project for years; and funding sponsors are prepared to pay for surveys because they feel that they will get at least something, an identifiable and justifiable product, for their money. Commitment then deepens. The more complicated, extensive and expensive the survey, so the more sophisticated will be its data processing (more marks for computers, programming, tapes and printouts than for anything as primitive as hand tabulation),[7] the greater the prestige for the senior researchers, and the more time required. There is also a 'because it's there' element, a sense that until social scientists have conducted their surveys and struggled with their computers, they have not climbed their Everests. And like attempts to climb Everest, extensive surveys require much administrative and logistical support, cost a lot, and often fail.

The pathology of rural surveys follows common paths. Its demands are not properly estimated. At the planning stage, it is easy and tempting to expand the geographical area to be covered, the numbers in the sample, and the questions to be asked. Where a team is involved, with each member contributing ideas, the questionnaire grows. The more multi-disciplinary the team, the greater is the questionnaire's potential for growth: the more disciplines, the more questions. It is also easier to admit a new question than to argue with a colleague in another discipline (and with whom one has to work for months or years to come) that his or her question is unnecessary. Short-term peace in the team is bought at the cost of long-term liabilities. The outcome is excessive data to collect and therefore less likelihood that the data will be well collected or that they will be checked, coded, punched, processed, and analysed, and less chance of the distant consummation of the survey being written up, let alone read and acted on. And on top of this there are the administrative demands of recruiting and training enumerators, the logistics in the field, and the thousand and one technical and practical problems of implementation.

Whatever the problems, commitment to completing a survey is irreversible, often from the start; there is no going back. Under pressure of the immediate need to keep the survey running, its objectives slide out of sight; the means – the collection of information – become the end. There is neither time, energy, nor resources to explore new questions or to notice the unexpected. Urban bias grows with unkind irony, as administrative and logistical demands tie senior researchers to urban areas and confine their brief field activities to administrative matters – housing and allowances for investigators, supplies of schedules, pay. The survey becomes a juggernaut pushed by and pulling its researcher slaves, and sometimes crushing them as it goes.

As data collection is completed, processing begins. Coding, punching and some simple programming present formidable problems. Consistency checks are too much to contemplate. Funds begin to run out because the costs of this stage have been underestimated. Reports are due before data are ready. There has been an overkill in data collection; there is enough information for a dozen Ph.D. theses but no one to use it. Much of the material remains unprocessed, or if processed, unanalysed, or if analysed, not written up, or if written up, not read, or if read, not remembered, or if remembered, not used or acted upon. Only a miniscule proportion, if any, of the findings affect policy and they are usually a few simple totals. These totals have often been identified early on through physical counting of questionnaires or coding sheets and communicated verbally, independently of the main data processing.

A report is required. It has to be written late, by dispirited and exhausted researchers who have already begun new tasks. Their families do not thank them for their absences, late nights, and short tempers. They stare at printouts and tables. Under pressure for 'findings', they take figures as facts. They have neither time nor inclination to reflect that these are aggregates of what has emerged from fallible programming of fallible punching of fallible coding of responses which are what investigators wrote down as their interpretation of their instructions as to how they were to write down what they believed respondents said to them, which was only what respondents were prepared to say to them in reply to the investigators' rendering of their understanding of a question and the respondent's understanding of the way they asked it; always assuming that an interview took place at all and that the answers were not more congenially compiled under a tree or in a teashop or bar, without the tiresome complication of a respondent. The distortions are legion. But mercifully, however spurious their precision, 'findings' printed out by a computer have a comforting authority. The machine launders out the pollutions of the field and delivers a clean product, which looks even cleaner and more comfortingly accurate when transferred to tables and text. These 'findings' are artefacts, a partial, cloudy and distorted view of the real rural world. But in the report they are, they have to be, facts.

Writing the report, then, demands casuistry. Conclusions have indeed been arrived at, but they are based on anecdote, common sense, observations incidental to the survey, 'I-once-met-a-farmer-who-' statistics, and the opinions of local people and officials. But the report-writer feels obliged to derive them from the survey's formal statistical output. Cosmetic surgery on the body of data improves appearances; sloppy syntax slurs non-sequiturs; concluding paragraphs assert that the data showed, or proved, what careful reading would show they did not show, or prove, but which may be true nonetheless. As it is, no one will read the report in enough detail to notice this, for the writers have compulsively crammed it with almost raw data. They have felt that all, or most of, the data must be presented, lest all that awful effort should have been in vain. It must all, surely, have some value sometime to someone somewhere. And indeed, it has. It is there, undigested and unabsorbed. It is not read, because it has been written in execrable style: jerky, unmemorable and ugly. Tables, statistics and turgid prose cloy the reader's critical faculties. So either the text goes unread; or if read, not understood; or if understood, not remembered. This serves the report well, investing it with authority; for who can challenge the conclusions without being sure that they are not supported somewhere in the document or its appendices? Dull survey data badly written up present a background against which other information stands out; and what stand out and may be remembered are those simple conclusions gained outside the survey which, happily, are more likely to combine truth with usefulness.

Finally, after the report or the book, evaluation of the survey process is unthinkable. It has taken so long that the main actors are exhausted or have moved on. The staff in the funding agencies who sponsored the survey are now in other jobs, and their successors have other surveys planned or in progress. There is an (unread) report as a monument or tombstone for the project. At least this is something to show for the money. And in any case evaluation might be damaging because of what it would reveal, if, that is, it was more accurate than the survey itself. Honest self-criticism is neither easy, rewarded, nor popular. There is no Journal of Misleading Findings. To describe the muddle, shortcuts, and fudging might destroy the survey in the eyes of colleagues, peers and sponsors. Too much is at stake: the reputation of the institution, the career of the researcher, the chances of future contracts and jobs; or so it is believed. Criticism is not put in writing; or if it is, it is the first victim of the editor's pencil. It would be damaging in the report; or the publishers demand that the book be shortened, and since none of the findings in the chapters by individual authors can easily be cut, the section on methodology suffers most.[8] And honesty loses friends and may be disloyal. To criticise one's own shortcomings is one thing; let the solitary social anthropologists with their disarming candour by all means continue to tell stories against themselves. But to criticise the shortcomings of a team is to impugn colleagues, perhaps friends. Better, it will seem, to remain silent. And so it is that myth masquerades as fact, unchallenged, to two places of decimals, and new innocents plunge unwarned into the morass.

Data as *Fabricata* (2008)[9]

This 1983 critique has been described as 'withering' (Holland and Campbell, 2005, p8). I am human and confess that it was fun to write. Perhaps it exaggerates. The reader will judge. It reflected my experience at the time I wrote it. What I did not realize was that I was missing a whole dimension of criticism and weakness. In his incisive review of data sources, Gerry Gill (1993, p1) considered that the large-scale customized survey (his phrase) had to a large extent been discredited. It had characteristics of inappropriate technology. And he added additional disadvantages when applied in developing, compared with developed, countries. These, listed in Table 1.1, are what I had missed.

These, especially the first, may apply less in the latter 2000s than they did in the early 1990s. They do, though, present a checklist for reflection on what actually takes place in any survey and add to the other actual or potential weaknesses.

Of these divergences, enumerator–respondent differences – of literacy, language, gender, demeanour, power – and their relationship in the interview situation, have perhaps been the most serious. Social anthropologists may reflect critically on what goes on between individuals in interviews, and how this co-constructs a reality, how prudence, presentation of the self, saying what is expected, refraining from sharing information that would be personally shameful – how these can distort. With questionnaire surveys they are neither seen nor reflected on. Though cases should exist, I have never seen them discussed in a survey write-up.

A questionnaire survey in the Maheshwaram watershed in Andhra Pradesh, recorded only one farmer among 272 (0.4 per cent) as cross ploughing (a practice officially frowned upon) but group discussions generated a figure of 28 per cent, itself also, from casual observation, probably an understatement (Sitapathi Rao pers. comm.). Farmers who were uncooperative had been penalized by being

Table 1.1 *Questionnaire surveys in developed and developing countries:*
Divergences in environment and design

Developed Country	Developing Country
1. Questionnaire generally designed by specialist with appropriate training	1. Questionnaire often designed by persons with no specialist training in questionnaire design
2. Questionnaire written in language in which it will be administered	2. Questionnaire normally written in another language and translated, either beforehand or during the interview
3. Respondents normally familiar with the general purpose of surveys	3. Respondents unfamiliar with rationale behind surveys; often apprehensive as to use of data
4. Restricted scope, simple issues addressed, short questions; usually 'opinion type' surveys	4. Complex issues; information often sensitive; long questionnaires; wide scope; need for many 'open-minded' questions
5. Built-in reliability checks	5. Often little scope to check reliability of findings
6. Repeat surveys routine if trend information required	6. One-shot, cross-sectional; trend estimation very difficult
7. Respondents tend either to give a flat refusal or else cooperate fully	7. 'Conspiracy of courtesy': tendency to give answers respondent thinks are wanted
8. Little if any systematic gender bias	8. Enumerators usually men; often severe problems in interviewing women respondents
9. Literate respondents	9. Respondents either non-literate or unrepresentative
10. Enumerators from roughly the same socio-economic background as respondents	10. Enumerators often from very different socio-economic background from respondents
11. Respondents can understand what enumerator is writing; can correct errors	11. Non-literate respondents cannot correct any mistakes or misunderstandings

Source: Gill, 1993, p10

denied inputs. On their own with an interviewer with clipboard, they knew what not to admit to. And the interviewers may have known not to record it. Anonymous and more secure in a group of colleagues, the farmers were more open.

Other distorting effects are suggested in the results of the Nepal Fertility Survey (Campbell et al, 1979, p5). These purported to show that people were ignorant of family planning. However, a field investigation found that 80 per cent of the sample respondents were unable fully to understand the questions asked. So their apparent ignorance was a fabrication of the questionnaire and the nature and context of the interview. When social anthropologists, on a small and different sample, asked the same questions the positive responses were much higher. When they checked again with those who had given negative responses, the total positive were all over 90 per cent (but one may ask whether the social anthropologists scored an own goal here, when people remembered they had been asked the day before).

Table 1.2 *Rural people's knowledge of family planning*

	Per cent of positive responses according to Nepal Fertility Survey (national sample)	Per cent positive according to the study survey N=76	Per cent positive after cross-checking N=76
Heard of pills	12	63	97
Heard of loop	6	56	91
Heard of condom	5	45	95
Heard of vasectomy	16	58	95
Heard of abortion	5	64	100

Source: Campbell et al (1979, p5). Percentages rounded to whole numbers.

This example dramatizes the extent to which poor people's 'ignorance' can be an artefact, a construction of survey interaction and context. Such an extreme case may be rare. But it is a warning to all researchers. Data are 'things given' in the Latin. But data are a social product (Herring, 2003). In training sessions, Henry Lucas (pers. comm.) refers not to data collection but data production. When data result from interviews, as above, they are better described as *fabricata*, 'things made'.[10]

Review and reflection (2008)

One danger in development practice is being out of touch and out of date. People who are considered to have passed their youthful prime are especially vulnerable. In what follows, I struggle to be informed and fair. The question is, since the 1970s and 1980s, what has changed and what more can be said?

Thomas Henry Huxley's dictum is a warning here, 'It is the customary fate of new truths to begin as heresies and to end as superstitions.' I have asked myself whether the critiques of questionnaires in the 1970s, which seemed new truths then, may by now have become superstitions held on my part. In writing this chapter evidence has made me qualify my critical view in a few respects, not least because of improvements in the practice of surveys. Many professionals struggle through their careers to do large-scale questionnaires better, to modernize the dinosaurs. Despite this, pathology seems still common, perhaps still the norm. If much has changed, that has not been indicated by examples which have come my way in the 2000s.

A questionnaire survey with 10,000 respondents proposed in 2007 in South Africa, aimed to 'empower marginalised communities with necessary capacities to access services and resources that will enable them to improve and sustain their livelihood status'; yet the long questionnaire was anything but empowering. In another recent case I inquired about the findings of a survey sponsored by the World Bank in India. I was met first with no response, then later with 'the data are still being cleaned' and finally with the silence of the grave. One can ask how often 'cleaning the data' is code for 'please spare us the embarrassment, don't press us, have the decency to let us abandon our terminal care and bury our patient in privacy and peace, and at all costs please don't exhume the corpse'. Contamination, morbidity and the death rates would seem to remain high. There are no mortality statistics for failed or abandoned questionnaire surveys. There are no death certificates to be registered and counted. They are abandoned and laid to rest quietly, furtively even. Those who have been involved in them hope that questions will not be asked, that senior staff or those who commissioned the research will move on, and that their successors will either not know about or will tacitly and tactfully overlook the costly non-event. All of which means that nothing will be learnt and nothing will change.

At one level, the issues are paradigmatic and basic to this book, contrasting top–down standardized reductionism which has preset categories with bottom–up diverse complexity and emergence. Between these paradigms, it is not an absolute case of either/or but of an optimal balance and mix. This is hard to achieve when top–down has the power, the funds, the patronage, and the learning disabilities of 'all power deceives'.[11] As we shall see in Chapters 4–9, there are many alternatives to the standardized long questionnaire approach, especially with sequences, improvisation and innovation, but these are not part, even now, of dominant normal professionalism.

Types of large-scale survey

Three families of large-scale questionnaire surveys can be distinguished:

1   Large-scale repeated time series censuses and surveys.
2   Surveys which seek to find out about a topic or context.
3   Surveys which apply a 'scientific' experimental design.

Let us consider the first two together, and the third separately since it has controversial interest which leads in to the rest of the book.

I Large-scale time series censuses and surveys

Large-scale time series surveys like national censuses, the National Sample Survey in India, and Living Standards Measurement Surveys (LSMSs) in many countries, and panel studies present many problems and are often much less accurate than they appear. Careful cross-checking of the official Malawi census suggested an undercount of the rural population of the order of 35 per cent (Barahona and Levy, 2003, pp4–9) (see page 119). At the same time, expensive and inaccurate though they may be, such censuses and surveys can and usually do add value in insights into totals, proportions and changes, especially if they are in comparable time series and there is extensive triangulation and cross-checking. Most of them should be improved, not abandoned.

2 Large-scale surveys to find out about a topic or context

In the 1970s and 1980s, these surveys were in high demand in African and Asian countries. The Kenya SRDP and Tamil Nadu and Sri Lanka surveys were examples. Though big and clumsy, such surveys still survive and remain vulnerable to systematic error, especially misleadingly positive evaluations. A well documented and researched example is Jean Dreze's (1990) devastating critique of evaluations of the Indian Government's flagship anti-poverty Integrated Rural Development Programme. Not all such surveys may produce such biased results, but over-favourable findings resulting from factors like deference and prudence in the interview interaction are likely to remain widespread.

Sustainability, evolution and resilience

Apart from utility and cost-effectiveness, or the lack of these, the survival of these two families of large-scale surveys into the 21st century can be in part understood in terms of five factors: demand, utility, routine reproduction and supply; more timely processing – with shorter gestation periods; mixed methods with qual–quant sequences; failure to perceive alternatives; and power and pathology.

First, *demand, utility, routine reproduction and supply.* Large questionnaire surveys continue to flourish through sustained demand. Census and other time series studies embed themselves in statistical series which cry out to be continued. While these are expensive and can mislead, the state needs, in James Scott's (1998) term, to 'see like a state': to have a sense of numbers of people, their location, characteristics, living standards and so on. For their part, ad hoc studies are repeatedly sought for many topics and contexts. And there is routine reproduction of people to provide the supply. University and training college courses teach questionnaire surveys and the statistics that go with them. Teachers repeat courses year after year with less and less effort, and little or no incentive to change. Textbooks are handed on or sold second-hand by one generation of students to another. A steady flow of trained, one might say conditioned or indoctrinated, professionals feeds the machine.

Second, *shorter gestation.* Timeliness has improved. In 1983 I wrote:

> *The worldwide acceptance of late submission of post-graduate theses teaches academics early in their careers not to take writing deadlines seriously. The secure tenure of many university posts is relaxing. Priority goes to immediate*

demands of lecturing, teaching, administration and university politics. The culture of university life is detached and reflective compared with government departments or voluntary agencies. The inability of most academics to manage a personal work programme pushes research again and again to the end of the queue. Finally, respectable rural research methodology requires either extensive surveys or long residence in the field, and both of these take much time. For all these reasons tension over getting results on time is almost universal between agencies which commission research and university departments or institutes which carry it out.

Since then several factors have contributed to more timely delivery.

One is the discipline of the market and the decline in the security of university tenure. These combine as incentives. For all its defects, competitive bidding for research projects, now common in many countries, has played a part. University researchers are less feather-bedded with core grants, more dependent on projects, and more reliant on consultancies to augment their incomes. They have been driven to become more efficient and prompt in delivery.

Another is the numbers of firms of consultants, in North and South, that now conduct research. In the 1970s and 1980s, it was more universities and institutes that did this. More than for university staff, who have a basic assured income, the livelihoods of the staff of consultant organizations and their reputations depend on doing what is required and delivering a product on time.

Yet another factor is ease of processing: now that computers are fast, portable and widespread, analysis has speeded up, and become easier, more versatile and less risk-prone. Something has been lost from the more tactile and legible (usually) days of punched cards when it was exciting to thread needles through, lift them out and read the richness of detail, sparking hypotheses, insights, and 'ahhas!' But anyone less than a Luddite has to recognize that the gains in speed outweigh the losses in fun and serendipity. And with very short surveys, a different genus altogether, analysis is sometimes conducted in the field and can even be done overnight in a village on a laptop.[12] Going even further, with handheld computers data can be recorded during an interview, easily aggregated and quickly analysed.

Third, *mixed methods and qual–quant sequences.* This is the most significant improvement. The combinations and sequences of methods in research have received increasing attention. The Department for International Development (DFID) commissioned a report in 1998 'Participation and Combined Methods in African Poverty Assessment: Renewing the agenda' (Booth et al, 1998) which opened up some of the issues. A DFID-funded research project led in March 2001 to the collection 'Combining Quantitative and Qualitative Survey Work: Methodological framework, practical issues, and case studies' (NRI, DFID and SSC, 2001). A Cornell workshop in 2001 led to the publication of 'Q-Squared: Combining qualitative and quantitative methods in poverty appraisal' (Kanbur, nd, c. 2003). A conference at the University of Wales, Swansea in 2002 led to 'Methods in Development Research: Combining qualitative and quantitative approaches' (Holland and Campbell, 2005). Particular research projects in which a large-scale questionnaire survey is a component have increasingly mixed and sought synergies between qualitative and quantitative methods. A study of poverty and vulnerability in Uttar Pradesh and Bihar used qualitative methods both before and after a questionnaire survey (Parker and Kozel, 2007). A study of destitution in Ethiopia used qualitative and quantitative methods and included participatory visuals (pile sorting) in the interview (for example, Sharp et al, 2003). Sequences and mixes like these, when used, can enhance the relevance and accuracy of a questionnaire.

Fourth, *unrecognized alternatives*. With the imagery of dinosaurs, ponderous surveys may (or may not) be gradually declining in numbers, but no exterminating meteors are on the horizon. Other new modes of inquiry, like the little mammals at their feet, are often ignored, trampled on or brushed aside. Alternatives are not considered rigorous. They are on wavelengths outside the normal spectrum of scientific sight. Early participatory alternatives to questionnaires (for example ActionAid-Nepal, 1992; and Eldridge, 1995, 1998, 2001) were peripheral, evanescent eddies bypassed by the mainstream. But this has been changing. To inquire into changes over time, for example, participatory trend and change diagramming (International HIV/AIDS Alliance, 2006b, pp80–81, 178–179; Jones, 1996), and innovations like those of Anirudh Krishna (2004, 2005, 2006), have many advantages over large-scale surveys – speed, low cost, range of insight, emergent categories, cross-checking and debate between participants, identification of key events, sense of trends, and opportunities to interview the diagrams and learn more. As we shall see (Chapters 4–7) there are now many better modes of inquiry and learning – cheaper, faster, more insightful, and with at the same time scope to empower local people.

Fifth, *power and pathology*. The dinosaurs of long, detailed multi-subject questionnaire surveys may have evolved slightly but they remain archetypically lumbering, clumsy, slow and inefficient. But they are far from endangered as species. And they have a safe haven in the World Bank (henceforth the Bank).

This is not surprising. The biggest users of questionnaire data or *fabricata* are economists. The Bank is dominated by economists: they are the great majority of its staff. The Bank has also become 'the largest center of development research in the world' (Broad, 2006, p388). In early 2007, of the 83 full-time staff under the Development Economics Vice-Presidency which is responsible for research, all but 4 were economists[13] (Rao and Woolcock, 2007). Economists, and perhaps especially macroeconomists, live off numerical data and their analysis.[14] Questionnaires, however unreliable their outputs, are reliable in supplying them. And however unreliable and inaccurate the data are, they can be used. So large-scale surveys with long questionnaires continue to be widely commissioned by the Development Economics Vice-Presidency, the Independent Evaluation Group (formerly the Operations Evaluation Department) and field offices. Through its international status and muscle, the Bank sets standards and norms for much development practice, including research methodology. It sponsors research in many countries, and researchers have plenty of incentives to obtain and supply the data in the traditional manner and on the scale expected or required.

The system is self-referential and incestuous. The 20 members of a team that evaluated the research of the Bank were all development economists! (Rao and Woolcock, 2007). Damning though much of their evaluation report was, it does not appear to have considered field research methodology.[15] That, one may surmise, was not perceived as a problem because the evaluators were themselves economists. The epistemological concerns of the team focused on the analysis and interpretation of data, not their genesis and quality.

Were the Bank like Arthur Conan Doyle's *Lost World*, an isolated plateau with its own primeval fauna and ecosystem, cut off from the rest of the world by high cliffs, this would be of little concern. Unfortunately, lost world or not, it is highly connected and influential, and at the same time unaware of its learning disability. Despite the alternative methods that have been evolved over the past three decades (Chapters 4–7),[16] the Bank has to my knowledge little used them or commissioned their use. Methodologically out of touch and out of date, it is stuck in its Jurassic.[17]

3 Scientific experimental method, controls and causality

The pathology of method is most marked with inappropriate attempts to apply 'rigorous' scientific methodology. The model is experimental. The large-scale survey with long questionnaire is used to compare effects on a population receiving an intervention with a matched control population without the intervention.

Let me start with confession. In about 1970, when I was working on the SRDP in Kenya, a well-informed doctor shot down my proposal for a follow-up questionnaire survey, with a classic treatment and control structure, to identify benefits from the Zaina water scheme in Nyeri District. I was upset. This was the first gravity-reticulated water scheme in Africa. It seemed to me important to know what effects it was having. A baseline survey had been carried out in the area, together with a neighbouring control area. A repeat survey was crying out to be done. It did not help that I was almost inarticulate with passion in my advocacy. The doctor countered calmly that the quality and content of the original survey were so poor, the control and treatment areas so different, the causality of impacts so imponderable, and the difficulties of inferring cause–effect relationships so great, that whatever the 'findings' it was unlikely that any useful conclusions could be drawn. This shook me, coming moreover as it did from a medical doctor for whom experimental method with treatment and controls might be considered a norm. I was deflated. The follow-up survey never took place. The original survey had been a waste of time and resources. And I believe the doctor was right.

The scientific and medical model has standards of rigour. What I had to learn was where these could be applied, and where not. I had to learn that I was proposing to extend the method beyond its limits into a realm where those forms of rigour could not apply.

Here is my best understanding now. Favourable conditions for the experimental method with intervention and controls are:

- a standard, uniform, measurable and verifiable treatment
- conditions closely similar in both treatment and controls
- a standard and measurable effect or effects
- size of treatment and control populations sufficient to test for statistical significance with randomized samples (unless total populations are involved)
- a plausible hypothesized causal link between treatment and effect
- means of investigating potential confounding (e.g. covariant) factors and verifying the causal link.

Hypotheses can then be tested. Often this is comparing treatment with control, with random sampling, the method being known as randomized control trials, often referred to simply as RCTs. When these conditions are met and in other respects an experiment is conducted well, the results can be valid according to conventional scientific and statistical canons.

This is well applied in some medical research. An example is giving vitamin A supplements to large numbers of under-five-year-old children and measuring their mortality. Such research has usually shown a significant decline in mortality in the treatment group compared with the control. The causality is credible because these conditions are met:

- A standard uniform input. The process of treatment is one-off, observable and clearly yes–no (taking vitamin A pills).
- The receiving environment (the inside of the human body) is standardized within narrow tolerances in both treatment and control groups.
- An impact can be counted (fewer child deaths) and being common knowledge can be cross-checked.
- Large numbers of children provide the basis for statistically significant findings.
- (I presume) a plausible hypothesized causal link.

In these conditions, credible findings can result from statistical rigour with large randomized samples and experimental rigour with controls, placebos and a double-blind methodology (meaning that not even the researchers know who receives the treatment and who the placebo).[18]

Confirming these points, the examples of experimental method to identify associations and causality laid out authoritatively in a classic textbook of the 1970s – Moser and Kalton's (1971) *Survey Methods in Social Investigation* – are mostly close to this medical model. In the chapter 'Experiments and Invest-igations' the hypothetical and actual illustrations to which more space is given include:[19] drinking methylated spirits as a cause of hallucinations; the effective-ness of a film in changing attitudes to drinking and driving; vaccinating children against polio; smoking and cancer of the lung; the effect of alcohol on the ability of subjects to solve problems; and the effect of an educational film on children. How to find out about all of these is discussed in terms of variants of conventional scientific experimental design. These and the other examples used in the book can be classed as medical or educational. They have single standard treatments, large populations of similar subjects, effects hypothesized which are measureable and usually single, plausible causal linkages between treatment and effect, and scope for quite short questionnaires. Conventional scientific rigour is a credible aspiration.

The boundaries of this scientific and medical approach have been extended, albeit at great cost, to a participatory intervention with women's groups in Nepal (Manandhar et al, 2004; Morrow and Dawodu, 2004). In this case the intervention and the receiving environment were more variable: the intervention was facilitation and the immediate receiving environment was women's groups identifying perinatal problems. The women's groups were in matched pairs of geopolitical clusters, one treatment and one control, and the impacts – neonatal and maternal mortality, could again, as with vitamin A, be counted. The research was a major enterprise, and at the same time an impressive application of the exacting methodological and ethical standards required by medical research to assess the impact of a participatory intervention. The cost of achieving conventional credibility was very high. Unlike vitamin A trials, the impact numbers were small but the results considered credible. Neonatal deaths were 30 per cent lower in the treatment. Reported maternal mortality also reduced, though the numbers were tiny (11 in the control, as against 2 in the treatment). The cost of a similar research project in progress in Malawi has been withheld, possibly because it is embarrassingly high.

It is in trying to go further, into more complexity, diversity, dynamism and multiple causality, that we run into deep, even terminal, trouble. Some in the Bank, aspiring to the high status rigour of the scientific experimental method, have sought credibility by trying to apply randomized control trial methods to Community-Driven Development (CDD). These are conditions where there are:

- different interventions (roads, schools, clinics, markets, water supply, sanitation, micro-credit, other infrastructure ... moreover differing within each type), unlike, say vitamin A supplements
- complex variable environments (Chambers and Harriss, 1977), making matching problematical to say the least
- multiple hypothesized effects (income, nutritional status, social capital)
- relatively small populations (where the unit is the community, ruling out the large numbers of a medical trial)
- indeterminate multiple causality for impacts
- factors which vary seasonally and between years
- externalities – a new facility may inflict costs elsewhere as staff and other resources are diverted to it
- (possibly) systemic differences (in access, political influence etc.) between treatment and control communities.

Any one or even two of these on its own might be manageable: the Nepal study of women's groups faced the problem of matching communities, but controlled much else. But when all or almost all these factors combine, as they do with CDD, there is so much 'noise' – variance, diversity and complexity – combined with the normal difficulties and distortions of survey methodology, that seeking this form of conventional scientific rigour makes no sense. Communities are not like human bodies: bodies have skin boundaries, identical internal structures, and homeostatic controls with narrow tolerances; communities are porous, idiosyncratic, with many varying and interlinked social, economic, political and cultural variables. Put starkly, bodies are bounded and alike; communities are permeable and differ. And to try to overcome these intractable incompatibilities by increasing the sample size may do little more than raise costs, delay processing, and amplify noise, quite apart from ethical considerations of taking more of people's time and raising their expectations. Rigour is unrigorous.

There is a cruel irony with such studies. The more complex the reality and multiple the causality, the longer the questionnaire becomes and the more prone it is to fabricating garbage, to longer processing, and to inconclusive findings. Difficulties are compounded when a long questionnaire is to be applied to a random sample of respondents who have then to be found and persuaded to be interviewed. Were the methodology participatory, with local analysis of causes and effects (including unanticipated effects) credible insights might be gained (Chapters 5 and 6). But in the pursuit of scientific rigour, the reflex is not to go deeper but wider, with ever larger samples. In a proposed evaluation of CDD in Indonesia, for example, a comparison was to be made between 160 communities which had had CDD interventions and 100 control communities which had not. The mind boggles at the scale and cost of the effort required, the many professional years to be devoted, the probability of great struggles to 'clean the data', and the likelihood, as with the early 1970s survey in South India and Sri Lanka, that many of the most useful (and timely) insights would be gained by the enumerators not through the questionnaire at all but coincidentally through their presence and casual encounters and conversations in the communities.

The three approaches are compared in Table 1.3.

Questionnaires, complexity and participation

A common view has been that the more complex and variable the phenomena and relationships, the more inclusive and comprehensive the questionnaire should be.

Leaving aside questions of data accuracy, this is a paradigmatic misfit for complexity (see Chapters 8 and 9). Despite pilot testing, large questionnaires are liable to be preset, top–down, imposing fixed categories on realities, in contrast with learning processes which are iterative, interactive and emergent. Put differently, these surveys belong to a paradigm of things rather than a paradigm of people. Also they ask mainly 'what?' questions, and much less the complementary 'how?' and 'why?' questions which illuminate 'what?' findings.

My own journey has been further than I realized. I have been astonished and appalled to read that in 1972 I wrote:

Table 1.3 *Treatment and control: Three applications compared*

	Vitamin A Over 10 studies	Women's groups Nepal	Proposed CDD impact Studies questionnaire
Experimental intervention	Vitamin A tablets	Facilitation of women's groups	Road, clinic, school, water, sanitation, micro-credit etc.
Treatment sample size	Typically thousands	Approx 54 women's groups and 14,884 women – 3190 pregnancies	160 communities
Control sample size	Typically thousands	14,047 women – 3524 pregnancies	100 communities
Receiving environment	Bodies of under-five-year-old children Uniform, homeostatically controlled, predictable	Women's groups and pregnant women Intermediate	Communities Varied, uncontrolled, unpredictable
Double-blind placebo control	In some cases, considered	No	No
Impacts measured	Child deaths	Neonatal and maternal deaths	Various
Hypothesized causal link	Physiological effects of Vitamin A on the body	Facilitated groups improve care and conditions	Apparently not made explicit
Credible rigour of causal inferences	Very high where well conducted	High	Low
Cost of research	High	High	High
Learning	High	High	Low
Participatory alternatives	None developed	Was participatory, combined with conventional rigour	See Chapters 4–7

Large-scale surveys still have a place, particularly when little is known about rural conditions, where issues are being investigated which have complex inter-relations with many aspects of rural life and economy, and where the intention is to exploit economies of scale by investigating several themes simultaneously.

I could scarcely have been more wrong. There are many alternatives and complements to questionnaire surveys, as we shall see in Chapters 4 (rapid rural appraisal) and 5 (participatory rural appraisal) as modes of inquiry, in Chapter 6 for ways of generating numbers, and in Chapter 9 for working with complex causality. There can be a case for lean ad hoc questionnaires with checklists, complementing and triangulating with other methods, as in the Malawi rural population study (p119). But large-scale multi-subject questionnaire surveys remain a trap. Unless informed and qualified by face-to-face fieldwork, they invite misleading reductionism in analysis. The longer the questionnaire, the larger the sample, and the more questionnaire length and sample size combine, the more vulnerable the research is to inflexibility, superficiality, distortion, invention without interviews, inadequate supervision, low motivation, the projection and mirroring back of researchers' categories and perspectives, failures to achieve timely analysis, laborious cleaning of data, dilemmas of analysis and interpretation, and rejection of bad data. And the more complex the issues and causality, the harder they are to unravel and understand through the crude standardized template of a questionnaire and correlations.

When Carlos Barahona, a professional statistician and pioneer of combining participatory generation of numbers and statistical methods and rigour, reviewed the research methods used in the 'Malawi Starter Pack' studies, he noted that the choice of a (questionnaire-based) survey 'imposed a constraint on the complexity of the questions that could be asked' (Barahona, 2005, p80). In his view (Barahona, 2005, p82)

> *Complex questions demand the use of sophisticated methods of enquiry such as participatory methods...*

Let the last words come from a Ugandan researcher in a letter dated 6 September 1993. This starts with conventional approaches, and then flips into another paradigm, here characterized as participatory rural appraisal (PRA). It is a cameo and foretaste of much that the rest of this book is about:

> *Being a statistician by profession and now working as a research associate with Makerere Institute of Social Research (MISR) I first came across PRA in a workshop organised by 'Forests, Trees and People Programmes' in Uganda, where I was nominated to represent my institute in the training.*
>
> *I had quite extensively used traditional questionnaire method in ground water resource management, socio-economic study funded by the International Development Research Centre and always remained cursing the limitations of these questions in the questionnaire. We designed them in the office, pre-tested and re-designed. Yet whenever we got to the actual fieldwork they seemed*

to have needed re-designing again. So we had to accept, just to work to an approximation.

...our respondents kept on asking us ... 'You have asked us all these questions, so what next?' Or intervened to say 'But you have asked us that question what about this and that, don't you think it is also useful, since it is connected to water?' Yet others surprisingly requested that they also wanted to be availed with the final report of the study findings, since they had contributed their answers.

In the course of the interview, many would crowd around and try to guide the interviewee. But I would kindly request them to allow one respondent at a time participate and avoid prejudice, and in the name of confidentiality – Was this not against participation? Yet we wanted to work out a community participatory ground water resource management strategy to be implemented by the Uganda Government for rural water supply programmes in the country.

I personally kept being defeated by this traditional method. In carrying out the analysis back in the office, we got all the beautiful statistics, with the SPSS software computer package and with our intellectual knowledge, sat down to interpret, analyse and write a report.

I would always look at the report and feel offended! Can we say statistics mean this? ... How do I get together with the poor and plan. I would sit down to think! ... Just as I was wondering whether my efforts had not been frustrated, like a 'saviour', I met Mr Shah Parmesh and John Devavaram – our trainers in PRA.

...after this ten days of intensive training, I got back and trained some of my fellow researchers at MISR. They were so impressed. What an overwhelming methodology – 'PRA is the only way forward.' one of them expressed. 'With PRA you will not get it wrong.' yet another said.

I redesigned my methodology for the next field work on ground water research.

It was fantasy in the field:

- *Mapping was applauded by the local people.*
- *The local people excelled in the analysis of water related diseases with the aid of seasonal calendars.*
- *Gender income/expenditure differentials came out quite clearly.*
- *To mention but not least, the setting up of water committee, local by-laws, educational campaigns on use of clean water, suggestions for financial contribution for minor repairs, spontaneously evolved from the community itself.*

...here you are, the rural people had done these themselves. I am now to tell the government that water committees are set up, the community is financing minor repairs [with] an enabling economic environment to sustain the peoples' ability to manage their own water supply systems ...

Yours sincerely,
Orone Patrick (Research Associate)

Notes

1   Older men have a notorious and lamentable tendency to talk about themselves and their experiences. There are five hypotheses about the ERR – the egocentric reminiscence ratio – the proportion of a person's speech devoted to their past: that it is higher among men than women, rises with age, on retirement leaps to a new upward-sloping plateau, is higher in the evening than the morning and rises sharply with the consumption of alcohol. My excuse or explanation for the egocentric thread that runs through this book is that I am driven by the first three, but only occasionally, and not at the time of writing, by the last two.

2   For the main findings see Farmer (1977).

3   This led to a paper 'Opportunism in rural research' (Chambers, 1974b) in which I puzzled about what I had actually been doing.

4   Jon Moris, on the basis of his review of 40 large questionnaire surveys, concluded that a reasonable rule of thumb was that processing, analysis and writing up would take twice as long and cost twice as much as budgeted.

5   Jean-Louis Arcand (pers. comm. 22 Aug 2006) reports that the use of handheld PCs in a paperless survey in Senegal made it easy to track the performance of enumerators. The inclusion of enumerator-specific effects contributed nothing to the results, but led to the firing of one of them. There must surely be cases of published tables of enumerator effects, but I do not know of any. I shall be indebted to any reader who can draw any to my attention.

6   This paragraph is summarized from 'Practices in Social Science Research: Some heresies', paper to a workshop at the Agrarian Research and Training Institute, Colombo (Chambers, 1973).

7   I have not edited out these brackets because they are a marker of how far we have come, and how rapid has been the development of survey data processing.

8   The B. H. Farmer (ed) 1977 *Green Revolution?* book published the results of Sri Lanka and South India study. It was precisely the methodology chapter that was shortened.

9   For more detailed analysis and examples, see Chambers (1997) pp93–97, the section on 'Confirmation by Questionnaire'.

10 Fabricate *vb* (*tr*). 1, to make, build, or construct; 2, to devise, invent or concoct (a story, lie etc.); 3, to fake or forge [C15 from Latin *fabricare* to build, make, from *fabrica* workshop ...] (*Collins English Dictionary*, Seventh Edition, 2005). I have a photograph on my office door of the sign outside a rural workshop in Kerala QUALITY FORGINGS AND FABRICATIONS. To what extent there are forgings and fabrications, and of what quality, in this book is for readers to judge.

11 For evidence and elaboration of the theme 'All power deceives' see Chapter 5 of Chambers (1997) *Whose Reality Counts?*

12 Analysis overnight on a laptop is done 'by us'. A better alternative is likely to be analysis 'by them', in which case they will be empowered, will learn for themselves (for example a relationship between source of water and episodes of diarrhoea) and will be more likely to act.

13 Rao and Woolcock do not give the number of four for non-economists. I have inferred it from two percentages given in their paper.

14 It is beyond the scope of this chapter or book to consider other mutually reinforcing links between methodology and ideology in the World Bank. For an example of how alarming these can be see Rodriguez (2007) 'Policy-makers Beware: The use and misuse of regressions in explaining economic growth'. I thank Henry Lucas for bringing this to my attention.

15 For a summary review of the evaluation of World Bank research www.brettonwoodsproject.org/art.shtml?x=549070

16 A two-hour presentation I gave in the World Bank in 2005 on numbers from participatory approaches and methods did not as far as I know make any significant impression or lead to any change.

17 My better judgement tells me that I should delete this purple paragraph but mischievous fun has got the better of me.

18 For a review of 12 studies conducted 1966 to 1992 see Fawzi et al, (1993) 'Vitamin A supplementation and child mortality: A meta-analysis', *Journal of the American Medical Association*, 17 February, vol 269, no 7, pp878–903. For debate over the rigour of methodologies used see Reddy, V. and Vijayaraghavan, K., (1991) letter to *Lancet*, 26 January, vol 337, no 8735, p232. In UNICEF's view '…Vitamin A Supplementation can save over a quarter of a million lives a year', www.unicef.org/mdg/childmortality.html (accessed 4 January 2008).

19 I have not included whether psychotherapy improves the mental health of neurotic patients because I am sceptical of the credible feasibility of such studies. Others to which less space is devoted include effects of fluoride in water on tooth decay, and a speed of reaction test after living in a cold climate.

2

Rural Development Tourism: Poverty Unperceived

What the eye does not see, the heart does not grieve about. (Old English proverb)

Abstract

With the priority of poverty reduction and with accelerating change in many dimensions, up-to-date and realistically informed perceptions of the lives and conditions of people living in poverty have come to matter more than ever. At the same time, new pressures and incentives increasingly trap decision-makers in headquarters and capital cities, reinforcing earlier (1983) analysis of the attraction of urban 'cores' and the neglect of rural 'peripheries'. These trends make decision-makers' learning about poverty and from people living in poverty rarer and ever more important. One common means has been rural development tourism, the phenomenon of the brief rural visit from an urban centre. In 1983, six biases of such visits – spatial, project, person, seasonal, diplomatic and professional – against seeing, meeting and learning from the poorer people, were identified and described.

In the mid 2000s, these biases persist, and security considerations have emerged as another factor. It is now more accepted and expected that visitors will want to meet poor people. In offsetting the biases, critical awareness is a key factor.

Genesis and rationale (2008)

The wonderful freedom and opportunities I had in India and Sri Lanka gave space for many short rural visits, and then reflection on these, on what I was seeing and not seeing, whom I was meeting and not meeting, what I was learning and not learning. Some of the visits were with government staff. Some with colleagues. Some simply with an interpreter. One series was when Benny Farmer, the director of the project, came out for a visit. We all began to realize how such visits were slanted, and how they reinforced selective perceptions and misperceptions. This provoked, in a 1974 paper on Opportunism in Rural Research (Chambers, 1974b):

The most important injunction of all is to sustain a very high degree of scepticism about the information derived verbally from such visits. It is alarming how quickly, through notes, writing and conversation, some small piece of verbal information about which one is initially very sceptical, becomes transformed into an established 'fact'. The rural development tourist may be trying to jump to conclusions, lacking time to take a more leisurely and certain path; but he [sic!] must try to retain a high degree of self-doubt and self-critical appreciation of the selective and uncertain nature of his perceptions.

Later, in the Institute of Development Studies (IDS), a day's brainstorming with Ian Carruthers, Scarlett Epstein, Richard Longhurst and others covered the walls of a room with lists of features of these visits, and the biases of rural development tourism – the phenomenon of the brief rural visit by the urban-based outsider – were named.

The theme of this chapter is that because of these biases rural poverty has been largely unperceived. Part of Chapter 1 'Rural Poverty Unperceived' of *Rural Development: Putting the Last First* (1983) is reprinted to raise questions about contemporary relevance. This is then qualified and updated with other experience, and the newly recognized security bias added.

My conclusion is that the biases are all alive and well, but they have tended to slip out of sight and off the agenda. In the otherwise useful book *Finding Out Fast* (Thomas et al, 1998) the biases of rural development tourism receive only one mention (p151) and that does not say what they are. If even the authors of a book like that do not describe the biases, few development professionals may now be aware of them. Further, in the mid-2000s, the core or urban trap appears tighter than it was. Road travel may generally have become easier, but rural visits, especially by aid agency staff, are widely acknowledged and agreed to have become less common. The quality of such visits therefore matters more now than ever. Finally and as indicated in Chapter 8 (pp156–158) the biases can be offset.

Rural poverty unperceived (1983)[1]

The urban trap

...the international system of knowledge and prestige, with its rewards and incentives ... draws professionals away from rural areas and up through the hierarchy of urban and international centres. They are also attracted and held fast by better houses, hospitals, schools, communications, consumer goods, recreation, social services, facilities for work, salaries and career prospects. In third world countries as elsewhere, academics, bureaucrats, foreigners and journalists are all drawn to towns or based in them. All are victims, though usually willing victims, of the urban trap. Let us consider them in turn.

For academics, it is cheaper, safer and more cost-effective in terms of academic output, to do urban rather than rural research. If rural work is to be done, then peri-urban is preferable to work in remoter areas. Rural research is carried out mainly by the young and inexperienced. For them, rural fieldwork is a rite of passage, an initiation which earns them the right to do no more, giving them a ticket to stay in the town. But the fieldwork must first be performed in the correct manner as prescribed by custom. The social anthropologist has to spend a year or so in the village, the sociologist to prepare, apply, analyse and write up a questionnaire survey. The ritual successfully completed, the researcher is appointed and promoted. Marriage and children follow. For women, pregnancy and child care may then dislocate a career and prevent further rural exposure.[2] For men, family responsibilities tie less, but still restrain. Promotion means responsibility and time taken with teaching, supervising, administration, and university or institutional politics. The stage of the domestic cycle with small children means accumulation of responsibilities – driving children to school and picking them up again, family occasions, careful financial management to make ends meet, moonlighting and consultancies to supplement a meagre salary – all of which take time.

The researcher has now learnt enough to make a contribution to rural research. He or she has the confidence and wit to explore new ideas and to pursue the unexpected. There is evidence enough of this in the books by social anthropologists who have undertaken second and subsequent spells of fieldwork. But it is precisely at this time that the able academic is chained to desk, lectern and home. If the university rewards ability, then the more able persons are likely to be most trapped. Ageing, ability, promotion and the domestic cycle conspire to prevent further rural contact.

The amalgam which glues these forces together and finally immobilises the would-be rural researcher in mid-career is over-commitment. It is a mystery why so many of the presumably intelligent people who do research are so miserably incompetent at managing their own lives. Academics can be found who are simultaneously supervising half a dozen theses (if their students can get near them), managing a major research project (actually managed by a junior administrator and by field staff), lecturing (from old notes or off-the-cuff), sitting on a dozen committees (or sending in, or failing to send in, apologies for absence), writing a couple of books (or adding notes to the draft by the junior author), developing a new curriculum or course (which for lack of time ends up much like a previous one), and carrying out a consultancy for an aid agency (which, for inescapable financial reasons, takes priority over all else). To judge from a limited and scattered sample, I suspect a positive correlation between over-commitment at work and size of family, though whether this reflects a lack of restraint and planning in both domains may be an idle speculation. But for such people, over-commitment is an addiction. In extreme cases, they take on more and more and complete less and less, complete it less and less well and, as they become more eminent, are less and less likely to be told their work is bad. Needless to say, there is also less and less time for any direct rural exposure; for the demands of students, researchers, administrators, committees, new curricula, books and consultancies all require presence in town. Ambition, inefficiency, and an inability to say no, tie the academic down, as an urban prisoner. Parole is rare and brief; rural contact is restricted to hectic excursions from the urban centre where the university or institute is sited.

For government staff, there are similar pressures and patterns. On first appointment, when ignorant and inexperienced, technical or administrative officers are posted to the poorer, remoter, and politically less significant areas. Those who are less able, less noticed, or less influential, remain there longer. The more able, and those who come favourably to attention or who have friends in headquarters, are soon transferred to more accessible or more prosperous rural areas, or to urban centres.

Administration is, anyway, an urban-based and urban-biased activity. So with promotion, contact with rural areas, especially the remoter ones, recedes. If a serious error is committed, or a powerful politician offended, the officer may earn a 'penal posting', to serve out punishment time in some place with poor facilities – a pastoral area, an area without irrigation, an area distant from the capital, an area which is hot and unhealthy – in short, a place where poorer people will be found. But the pull of urban life will remain; children's education, chances of promotion, congenial company, consumer goods, cinemas, libraries, hospitals, and quite simply power; all drawing bureaucrats away from rural areas and towards the major urban and administrative centres.

Once established in offices in the capital city, or in the regional or provincial headquarters, bureaucrats too are trapped. Unless they are idle and incompetent, or exceptionally able and well supported, they are quickly over-committed. They are tied down by committees, subcommittees, memoranda, reports, urgent papers, personnel problems, financial management, and the professional substance of their work. There are political demands to which they must be able to react swiftly and efficiently. There are times of the year, during the budget cycle, when they cannot contemplate leaving their desks. The very emphasis on agricultural and rural development creates work, which holds them in their offices.

If the government is inactive, they may be relatively free. But the more the government tries to do, so the more paperwork is generated, the more co-ordination and integration are called for, the more reports have to be written and read, and the more inter-ministerial and inter-departmental coordination and liaison committees are set up. The more important these committees become, so the more members they have, the longer their meetings take, and the longer their minutes grow. The demands of aid agencies are a final straw, requiring data, justifications, reports, evaluations, visits by missions, and meetings with ministers. More activity, more aid, more projects, more coordination – all these mean more time in the office and less in the field.

Foreigners are also urban-based and urban-biased. Foreigners in third world countries who are concerned with rural development and rural poverty include staff in voluntary agencies and aid organisations, technical cooperation personnel of various sorts, and consultants. Many voluntary agency workers and a few technical cooperation staff do live in rural areas. But most of these foreigners are also urban-based, many of them in capital cities, and have the familiar problems of paperwork, meetings and political and family pressures which tie them there. In addition, their rural movements may be restricted by a suspicious government, or smothered in protocol. Their perceptions vary from the acute and correct to the naive and mistaken. They often labour under the notorious difficulties and distortions of having to rely on interpreters, of being taken on conducted tours, and of misleading responses from those met.

A final group, neglected yet vital for the formation of opinion about rural life, are journalists. They combine the most direct access to mass media with the severest constraints on rural exposure. Journalists who wish to visit a rural area have three problems. First, they must persuade their editor that the visit is worthwhile. This is difficult. In terms of news, it is almost always quicker and cheaper to look for and write up an urban story; moreover a disproportion of newspaper readers are urban dwellers interested in urban news. Second, journalists must be sure to get a story. This usually means a visit either in special company (for example, the Prime Minister's visit to a region) with an official entourage and all that goes with it, or to an atypical rural place where there is either a project or a disaster. Third, journalists cannot hang around. They must find out what they want quickly and write it up quickly. Checking information is difficult, and with rural people who are unlikely to read what is written let alone sue, the incentive to check it is low. It is the one-off rushed and unconfirmed interview which appears in quotation marks in the newspaper article. Like academics, bureaucrats and foreigners, journalists are both actors and victims in the brief rural visit.

Rural development tourism[3]

For all these urban-based professionals, the major source of direct experience of rural conditions is, then, rural development tourism, the phenomenon of the brief rural visit. This influences and is part of almost all other sources of information. It is extremely widespread, with perhaps tens of thousands of cases daily in third world countries. In spite of its prevalence, it has not, to my knowledge, been seriously analysed. This omission is astonishing until one reflects on the reasons. For academic analysis, rural development tourism is too dispersed and ephemeral for convenient rigour, not neatly in any disciplinary domain, and barely conceivable as the topic for a thesis. For practical professionals engaged in rural development, it is perhaps too near the end of the nose to be in focus. Rural development tourism is, moreover, a subject of anecdote and an object of shame. It generates stories for bar gossip rather than factors for comparative study, and evokes memories of personal follies one prefers not to expose to public ridicule. In any case, self-critical introspection is not one of the more prominent characteristics of rural developers. Yet it is through this rural development tourism, if at all, that 'core' (urban based, professional, powerful) visitors see and meet those who are 'peripheral' (rural, uneducated, weak). The brief rural visits by 'core' personnel can scarcely fail to play a key part in forming their impressions and beliefs and influencing their decisions and actions.

Let us examine the phenomenon. The visits may be for one day or for several. The 'tourists' or visitors may come from a foreign country, a capital city, a seat of regional or provincial government, a district headquarters, or some smaller urban place. Most commonly, they are government officials – administrators, health staff, agriculturalists, veterinarians, animal husbandry staff, educators, community developers, engineers, foresters, or inspectors of this and that – but they may also be private technical specialists, academic researchers, the staff of voluntary agencies, journalists, diplomats, politicians, consultants, or the staff of aid agencies. Differing widely in race, nationality, religion, profession, age, sex, language, interests, prejudices, conditioning and experience, these visitors nevertheless usually have three things in common: they come from urban areas; they want to find something out; and they are short of time.

Rural development tourism has many purposes and many styles. Technical specialists concerned with physical resources may in practice have little contact with rural people, and there may be little formality about their visits. Others – those concerned with administration and human development in its various forms – may in contrast be involved in many meetings with rural people. It is with these kinds of visits that we are primarily concerned. It is tempting to caricature, and exaggeration is built into any process of induction from anecdotes which are repeated and remembered because they make good stories. There are also differences between cultures, environments and individual tourists. But it may hold generally that the older, more senior, more important, and more involved with policy the tourist is, so the larger will be the urban centre from which he[4] leaves, and the more likely his visit is to be selective and formally structured. The more powerful professionals are, the less chance they have of informal learning.

A sketch can illustrate the problems[5] of such visits by the powerful, important, and distinguished. The visitor sets out late, delayed by last minute business, by colleagues, by subordinates or superiors anxious for decisions or actions before his departure, by a family crisis, by a cable or telephone call, by others taking part in the same visit, by mechanical or administrative problems with vehicles, by urban traffic jams, or by any one of a hundred forms of human error. Even if the way is not lost, there is enough fuel, and there are no breakdowns, the programme runs behind schedule. The visitor is encapsulated, first in a limousine, Land Rover, Jeep or car and later in a moving entourage of officials and local notables – headmen, chairmen of village committees, village accountants, progressive farmers, traders, and the like.

Whatever their private feelings (indifferent, suspicious, amused, anxious, irritated, or enthusiastic), the rural people put on their best face and receive the visitor well. According to ecology, economy and culture, he is given goats, garlands, coconut milk, coca-cola, coffee, tea or milk. Speeches are made. Schoolchildren sing or clap. Photographs are taken. Buildings, machines, construction works, new crops, exotic animals, the clinic, the school, the new road, are all inspected. A self-conscious group (the self-help committee, the women's handicraft class), dressed in their best clothes, are seen and spoken to. They nervously respond in ways which they hope will bring benefits and avoid penalties. There are tensions between the visitor's questions and curiosity, the officials' desire to select what is to be seen, and the mixed motives of different rural groups and individuals who have to live with the officials and with each other after the visitor has left. Time and an overloaded programme nevertheless are on the officials' side. As the day wears on and heats up, the visitor becomes less inquisitive, asks fewer questions, and is finally glad to retire, exhausted and bemused, to the circuit bungalow, the rest house, the guest house, the host official's residence, or back to an urban home or hotel. The village returns to normal, no longer wearing its special face. When darkness falls and people talk more freely, the visitor is not there.

Shortage of time, the importance of the visitor, and the desire for information separately or together influence what is perceived. Lack of time drives out the open-ended question; the visitor imposes meanings through what is asked. Checking is impossible, and prudent, hopeful, or otherwise self-serving lies become accepted as facts. Individually or in groups, people are neglected while formal actions and physical objects receive attention. Refugees in a rural camp in Tanzania said of UN and government officials that 'They come, and they sign the book, and they go', and 'They only talk with the buildings'. A villager in Senegal said to Adrian Adams concerning visitors: 'Ils ne savent pas qu'il y a ici des gens vivants'.[6] (Adams, 1979, p477). Above all, on such visits, it is the poorer people who tend not to be seen, far less to be met.

Rural poverty unperceived: The six biases

Many biases impede outsiders' contact with rural poverty in general, and with the deepest poverty in particular. These apply not only to rural development tourists, but also to rural researchers and local-level staff who live and work in rural areas. Six sets of biases stand out:

Spatial biases: Urban, tarmac and roadside

Most learning about rural conditions is mediated by vehicles. Starting and ending in urban centres, visits follow networks of roads. With rural development tourism, the hazards of dirt roads, the comfort of the visitor, the location of places to visit and places for spending the night, and shortages of both time and fuel dictate a preference for tarmac roads and for travel close to urban centres. The result is overlapping urban, tarmac and roadside biases.

Urban bias concentrates rural visits near towns and especially near capital cities and large administrative centres. But the regional distribution of the poorest rural people often shows a concentration in remoter areas – north-eastern Brazil, Zambia away from the line of rail, lower Ukambani in Kenya, the Tribal Districts of Central India, the hills of Nepal. In much of the developing world, some of the poorest people are being driven from those densely populated areas better served with communications and are being forced, in order to survive, to colonise less accessible areas, especially the savannahs and forests. Hard to reach from the urban centres, they remain largely unseen.

Tarmac and roadside biases also direct attention towards those who are less poor and away from those who are poorer. Visible development follows main roads. Factories, offices, shops and official markets all tend to be at the sides of main roads. Even agricultural development has a roadside bias: in Tamil Nadu agricultural demonstrations of new seeds and fertilisers have often been sited beside main roads; and on irrigation systems, roads follow canals so that the farms seen are those of the topenders who receive more water and not those of the tailenders who receive less or none. Services along roadsides are also better. An improved tarmac or all-weather surface can bring buses, electricity, telephone, piped water supply, and better access to markets, health facilities and schools. Services near main roads are better staffed and equipped; Edward Henevald found that two schools near a main highway in Sumatra had more than their quota of teachers, while a school one kilometre off the road had less than its quota.

When roads are built, land values rise and those who are wealthier and more influential often move in if they can. In Liberia, new rural roads were followed by speculators rushing to acquire deeds and to buy or to displace local farmers (Cobb et al, 1980, pp12–16). For part of western Kenya, Joseph Ssennyonga had described a similar tendency for the wealthier and more influential to buy up roadside plots, creating an 'elite roadside ecology' (1976, p9). So the poorer people shift away out of sight. The visitor then sees those who are better-off and their houses, gardens, and services, and not those who are poorer and theirs. Ribbon development along roadsides gives a false impression in many countries. The better the road, the nearer the urban centre, and the heavier the traffic, so the more pronounced is the roadside development and the more likely visitors are to see it and be misled.

Nor does spatial bias apply only to main roads. Within villages, the poorer people may be hidden from the main streets and the places where people meet. M. P. Moore and G. Wickremesinghe, reporting on a study of three villages in the Low Country of Sri Lanka, have this to say about 'hidden poverty':

> In retrospect at least, one of the most obvious aspects of poverty in the study villages is the extent to which it is concealed from view ... the proportion of 'poor' households ... varies from 14 per cent in Wattegama to 41 per cent in Weligalagoda. Yet one could drive along all the motorable roads in the villages and scarcely see a single 'poor' house. Here, as in most of rural Sri Lanka, wealthier households use their social and economic power to obtain roadside homestead sites. Not only do these confer easier access to such tangible services as buses, electricity connections or hawkers, but they provide such intangible benefits as better information and gossip from passers-by. Equally, the roadside dweller has a potential site for opening a small shop, especially if located near the all-important road junctions, which provide the focus of commercial and social life in almost all rural areas. **To even see the houses of the poor one often has to leave the road. Many visitors, including public officers, appear not to do so very often.** (1980, p59; emphasis added)

The same can be said of Harijan colonies in or near villages in South India, and of Basarwa (Bushmen) in or outside the villages of the Kalahari. Peripheral residence is almost universal with the rural poor.

It is not just the movements of officials that are guided by these spatial biases of rural development tourism. Social science researchers are far from immune.

There are honourable exceptions, but urban and tarmac biases are sometimes evident in choices of villages to study. Of all specialists, social anthropologists are perhaps the least susceptible, but even they sometimes succumb: as they have grown, Bangalore and Bangkok have each swallowed up a social anthropologist's village.[7] Again, when Indian institutions were urged to adopt villages, two research and training organisations in Bangalore, unknown to each other, included the same village: it can scarcely be a coincidence that it was close to the main Bangalore-Mysore road, a decent but convenient distance from Bangalore itself. Within villages, too, the central, more prosperous, core is likely to attract researchers.

Moore, again describing three villages in Sri Lanka, writes:

> *Apart from the roadside issue, the core can exercise a great pull on the outsider who decides to do a few days' or a week's fieldwork. Apart from the facilities and the sense of being at the strategic hub of local affairs, it can claim a sense of history and tradition, to which sociologists especially appear vulnerable.*
> (1981, p48)

He considers that sociologists writing on Sri Lanka have mostly focussed on core areas and completely ignored the peripheries. One may speculate about how generally the location of good informants and of facilities at the cores of villages prevent perception by social scientists of the peripheral poor.

Urban bias is further accentuated by fuel shortages and costs. When fuel costs rise dramatically, as they have done in recent years, the effect is especially marked in those poor countries which are without oil and also short of foreign exchange. The recurrent budgets of government departments are cut. Staff are difficult to shed, so the cuts fall disproportionately on other items. Transport votes are a favourite. Rural visits, research and projects shrink back from more distant, often poorer areas to those which are closer, more prosperous, and cheaper to visit.[8]

In Zambia, the travel votes of the Ministry of Agriculture and Water Development could buy in 1980 only one fifth of the petrol they could buy in 1973 (ILO, 1981, p74) and senior agricultural extension staff were virtually office bound. In Bangladesh, similarly, district agricultural officers have been severely restricted in their use of vehicles. In India, cuts have occurred in transport allocations for staff responsible for supervising canal irrigation: the likely effects include less supervision leading to less water reaching the already deprived areas and less staff awareness of what is happening there. Every rise in oil prices impoverishes the remoter, poorer people by tilting the urban–rural terms of trade against them, and at the same time reduces the chances of that deprivation being known. Visits, attention and projects are concentrated more and more on the more accessible and more favoured areas near towns.

Project bias

Rural development tourism and rural research have a project bias. Those concerned with rural development and with rural research become linked to networks of urban–rural contacts. They are then pointed to those rural places where it is known that something is being done – where money is being spent, staff are stationed, a project is in hand. Ministries, departments, district staff, and voluntary agencies all pay special attention to projects and channel visitors towards them. Contact and learning are then with tiny atypical islands of activity which attract repeated and mutually reinforcing attention.

Project bias is most marked with the showpiece: the nicely groomed pet project or model village, specially staffed and supported, with well briefed members who know what to say and which is sited a reasonable but not excessive distance from the urban headquarters.[9] Governments in capital cities need such projects for foreign visitors; district and sub district staff need them too, for visits by their senior officers. Such projects provide a quick and simple reflex to solve the problem of what to do with visitors or senior staff on inspection. Once again, they direct attention away from the poorer people.

The better known cases concern those rural development projects which have attracted international attention. Any roll of honour would include the Anand Dairy Cooperatives in India; the Chilalo Agricultural Development Unit in Ethiopia; the Comilla Project in Bangladesh; the Gezira Scheme in Sudan; the Intensive Agricultural Districts Programme (IADP) in India; Lilongwe in Malawi; the Muda Irrigation Project in Malaysia; the Mwea Irrigation Settlement in Kenya; and some ujamaa villages in Tanzania. These have been much visited and much studied. Students seeking doctorates have read about them and then sought to do their fieldwork on them.[10]

Research generates more research; and investment by donors draws research after it and funds it. In India, the IADP, a programme designed to increase production sharply in a few districts which were well endowed with water, exercised a powerful attraction to research compared to the rest of India. An analysis (Harriss, 1977, pp30–34) of rural social science research published in the *Bombay Economic* and *Political Weekly* showed an astonishing concentration in IADP districts, and an almost total neglect of the very poor areas of central India. In a different way, the Comilla Project may also have misled, since Comilla District has the lowest proportion of landless of any district in Bangladesh. Research on ujamaa in Tanzanian in the clusters of villages (the Ruvuma Development Association, Mbambara and Upper Kitete) which were among the very few in the whole country with substantial communal agricultural production, sustained the myth that such production was widespread. Research, reports and publications have given all these atypical projects high profiles, and these in turn have generated more interest, more visitors, and yet more research, reports and publications.

Fame forces project managers into public relations. More and more of their time has to be spent showing visitors around. Inundated by the celebrated, the curious, and the crass – prime ministers, graduate students, women's clubs, farmers' groups, aid missions, evaluation teams, school parties, committees and directors of this and that – managers set up public relations units and develop a public relations style. Visitors then get the treatment. A fluent guide follows a standard route and a standard routine. The same people are met, the same buildings entered,[11] the same books signed, the same polite praise inscribed in the book against the visitors' names. Questions are drowned in statistics; doubts inhibited by handouts. Inquisitive visitors depart loaded with research papers, technical evaluations, and annual reports which they will probably never read. They leave with a sense of guilt at the unworthy scepticism which promoted their probing questions, with memories of some of those who are better-off in the special project, and impressed by the charisma of the exceptional leader or manager who has created it. They write their journey reports, evaluations and articles on the basis of these impressions.

For their part, the project staff have reinforced through repetition the beliefs which sustain their morale; and their projects take off into self-sustaining myth. But in the myth is the seed of tragedy, as projects are driven down this path which leads, step-by-step to self-deception, pride, defensiveness, and ultimately debunking.

Person bias

The persons with whom rural development tourists, local-level officials, and rural researchers have contact, and from whom they obtain impressions and information, are biased against poorer people.

Elite bias

'Elite' is used here to describe those rural people who are less poor and more influential. They typically include progressive farmers, village leaders, headmen, traders, religious leaders, teachers, and paraprofessionals. They are the main sources of information for rural development tourists, for local-level officials, and even for rural researchers. They are the most fluent informants. It is they who receive and speak to the visitors; they who articulate 'the village's' interests and wishes; their concerns which emerge as 'the village's' priorities for development. It is they who entertain visitors, generously providing the expected beast or beverage. It is they who receive the lion's share of attention, advice and services from agricultural extension staff (Chambers, 1974a, p58; Leonard, 1977, ch 9). It is they who show visitors the progressive practices in their fields. It is they too, who, at least at first, monopolise the time and attention of the visitor.

Conversely, the poor do not speak up. With those of higher status, they may even decline to sit down. Weak, powerless and isolated, they are often reluctant to push themselves forward. In Paul Devitt's words:

> *The poor are often inconspicuous, inarticulate and unorganised. Their voices may not be heard at public meetings in communities where it is customary for only the big men to put their views. It is rare to find a body or institution that adequately represents the poor in a certain community or area. Outsiders and government officials invariably find it more profitable and congenial to converse with local influentials than with the uncommunicative poor.* (1977, p23)

The poor are a residual, the last in the line, the most difficult to find, and the hardest to learn from: 'Unless paupers and poverty are deliberately and persistently sought, they tend to remain effectively screened from outside inquirers' (Devitt, 1977, p23).[12]

Male bias

Most local-level government staff, researchers and other rural visitors are men. Most rural people with whom they establish contact are men. Female farmers are neglected by male agricultural extension workers. In most societies women have inferior status and are subordinate to men. There are variations and exceptions, but quite often women are shy of speaking to male visitors. And yet poor rural women are a poor and deprived class within a class. They often work very long hours, and they are usually paid less than men. Rural single women, female heads of households, and widows include many of the most wretched and unseen people in the world.

User and adopter biases

Where visits are concerned with facilities or innovations, the users of services and the adopters of new practices are more likely to be seen than are non-users and non-adopters. This bias applies to visitors who have a professional interest in, say, education, health or agriculture, to local-level officials, and to researchers. They tend to visit buildings and places where activity is concentrated, easily visible, and hence easy to study. Children in school are more likely to be seen and questioned than children who are not in school; those who use the health clinic more than those who are too sick, too poor, or too distant to use it; those who come to market because they have goods to sell or money with which to buy, more than those who stay at home because they have neither; members of the cooperative more than those who are too poor or powerless to join it; those who have adopted new agricultural, health or family planning practices more than those who have not.

Active, present and living biases

Those who are active are more visible than those who are not. Fit, happy, children gather round the Jeep or Land Rover, not those who are apathetic, weak and miserable. Dead children are rarely seen. The sick lie in their huts. Inactive old people are often out of sight; a social anthropologist has recorded how he spent some time camping outside a village in Uganda before he realised that old people were starving (Turnbull, 1973, p102). Those who are absent or dead cannot be met, but those who have migrated and those who have died include many of the most deprived. Much of the worst poverty is hidden by its removal.

Dry season biases

Most of the poor rural people in the world live in areas of marked wet–dry tropical seasons. For the majority whose livelihoods depend on cultivation the most difficult time of the year is usually the wet season, especially before the first harvest. Food is short, food prices are high, work is hard, and infections are prevalent. Malnutrition, morbidity and mortality all rise, while body weights decline. The poorer people, women and children are particularly vulnerable. Birth weights drop and infant mortality rises. Child care is inadequate. Desperate people get indebted. This is both the hungry season and the sick season. It is also the season of poverty ratchet effects, that is, of irreversible downward movements into poverty through the sale or mortgaging of assets, the time when poor people are most likely to become poorer.

The wet season is also the unseen season. Rural visits by the urban-based have their own seasonality.

> Nutritionists take care to plan
> To do their surveys when they can
> be sure the weather's fine and dry,
> the harvest in, food intake high.

> Then students seeking Ph.D's
> Believe that everyone agrees
> that rains don't do for rural study
> – suits get wet and shoes get muddy

> And bureaucrats, that urban type,
> wait prudently till crops are ripe,
> before they venture to the field
> to put their question: 'What's the yield?'

For monsoonal Asia, which has its major crop towards the end of the calendar year, it is also relevant that:

> The international experts' flights
> have other seasons; winter nights
> In London, Washington and Rome
> are what drive them, in flocks, from home

since they then descend on India and other countries north of the equator in January and February at precisely the time of least poverty and when marriages and celebrations are to be seen and heard. Some opposite tendencies, however, deserve to be noted:

> And northern academics too
> are seasonal in their global view
> For they are found in third world nations
> mainly during long vacations.

North of the equator this means visits at the bad time of the monsoon in much of Asia and of the rains of West Africa. There are also professionals like agriculturalists and epidemiologists whose work demands rural travel during the rains, for that is when crops grow and bugs and bacteria breed.

But the disincentives and difficulties are strong. The rains are a bad time for rural travel because of the inconveniences or worse of floods, mud, landslides, broken bridges; and getting stuck, damaging vehicles, losing time, and enduring discomfort. In some places roads are officially closed. In the South Sudan, there is a period of about two months after the onset of the rains when roads are impassable but when there is not yet enough water in the rivers for travel by boat. Many rural areas, especially those which are remote and poor, are quite simply inaccessible by vehicle during the rains. The worst times of the year for the poorer people are thus those that are the least perceived by urban-based outsiders.

Once the rains are over such visitors can however travel more freely. It is in the dry season, when disease is diminishing, the harvest in, food stocks adequate, body weights rising, ceremonies in full swing, and people at their least deprived, that there is most contact between urban-based professionals and the rural poor. Not just rural development tourism, but rural appraisal generally is susceptible to a dry season bias. A manual for assessing rural needs warns of an experience when 'Once, the jeeps needed for transporting the interviewers were recalled for a month during the **few** precious months of the dry season' (Ashe, 1979, p26; my emphasis). Whole institutes concentrate their field research in the dry seasons; the rains are for data analysis and writing up with a good roof over one's head. Concern to avoid inconveniencing respondents when they are busy and exhausted with agricultural activities provides a neat justification, both practical and moral, for avoiding research during the rains. Many factors thus conspire to ensure that the poorest people are most seen at precisely those times when they are least deprived; and least seen when things are at their worst.

Diplomatic biases: Politeness and timidity

Urban-based visitors are often deterred by combinations of politeness and timidity from approaching, meeting, and listening to and learning from the poorer people. Poverty in any country can be a subject of indifference or shame, something to be shut out, something polluting, something, in the psychological sense, to be repressed. If honestly confronted, it can also be profoundly disturbing. Those who make contact with it may offend those who are influential. The notables who generously offer hospitality to the visitor may not welcome or may be thought not to welcome, searching questions about the poorer people. Senior officials visiting junior officials may not wish to examine or expose failures of programmes intended to benefit the poor. Politeness and prudence variously inhibit the awkward question, the walk into the poorer quarter of the village, the discussion with the working women, the interviews with Harijans. Courtesy and cowardice combine to keep tourists and the poorest apart.

Professional biases

Finally, professional training, values and interests present problems. Sometimes they focus attention on the less poor: agricultural extension staff trained to advise on cash crops or to prepare farm plans are drawn to the more 'progressive' farmers; historians, sociologists and administrators, especially when short of time, can best satisfy their interests and curiosity through informants among the better-educated or less poor; those engaged in family welfare and family planning work find that bases for the adoption of any new practices can most readily be established with better-off, better-educated families. But sometimes, in addition, professional training, values and interests do focus attention directly on the poor. This is especially so in the fields of nutrition and health, where those wishing to examine and to work with pathological conditions will tend to be drawn to those who are poorer.

More generally, specialisation, for all its advantages, makes it hard for observers to understand the linkages of deprivation. Rural deprivation is a web in which poverty (lack of assets, inadequate stocks and flows of food and income), physical weakness and sickness, isolation, vulnerability to contingencies, and powerlessness all mesh and interlock. But professionals are trained to look for and see much less. They are programmed by their education and experience to examine what shows up in a bright but slender beam which blinds them to what lies outside it.

Knowing what they want to know, and short of time to find it out, professionals in rural areas become even more narrowly single-minded. They do their own thing and only their own thing. They look for and find what fits their ideas. There is neither inclination nor time for the open-ended question or for other ways of perceiving people, events and things. 'He that seeketh, findeth.' Visiting the same village, a hydrologist enquires about the water table, a soils scientist examines soil fertility, an agronomist investigates yields, an economist asks about wages and prices, a sociologist looks into patron–client relations, an administrator examines the tax collection record, a doctor investigates hygiene and health, a nutritionist studies diets, and a family planner tries to find out about attitudes to numbers of children. Some of these visiting professionals may be sensitive to the integrated nature of deprivation, but none is likely to fit all the pieces together, nor to be aware of all the negative factors affecting poorer people.

Specialisation prevents the case study which sees life from the point of view of the rural poor themselves; but where such case studies are written (e.g. Gulati, 1981; Howes, 1980; Ledesma, 1977; Lewis, 1959) their broader spread helps understanding and points to interventions which specialists miss. In contrast, narrow professionalism of whatever persuasion leads to diagnoses and prescriptions which underestimate deprivation by recognising and confronting only a part of the problem.

The unseen and the unknown

The argument must not be overstated. To all of these biases, exceptions can be found. There are government programmes, voluntary organisations, and research projects that seek out those who are more remote and poorer. Some projects and programmes, such as those for the weaker sections and vulnerable classes in rural India, have an anti-poverty focus. Person biases can work the other way: women's groups and women's programmes attract attention; doctors see those who are sick; nutritionists concentrate on the malnourished; agriculturalists and epidemiologists alike may have professional reasons for travel during the rains; and during an agricultural season, a daytime visit to a village may provide encounters with the sick, aged and very young, and not with the able-bodied who are out in the fields. Such exceptions must be noted. At the same time, there are dangers of underestimating the force of the biases by failing to see how they interlock and by underestimating their incidence.

The way in which spatial, project, person, dry season, politeness/timidity and professional biases interact can be seen by analysing almost any example of an urban-based outsider investigating rural conditions. With many 'insights' and beliefs about rural life, the several biases can and do reinforce each other. The prosperity after harvest of a male farmer on a project beside a main road close to a capital city may colour the perceptions of a succession of officials and dignitaries. The plight of a poor widow starving and sick in the wet season in a remote and inaccessible area may never in any way impinge on the consciousness of anyone outside her own community.

Nor are those professionals and rural staff who originate from rural areas, who have a home, second home, or farm there, or who live and work there, immune from these tendencies. Three examples can illustrate that their perceptions too can be powerfully distorted by the biases.

The first example is from a densely populated part of western Kenya. Junior agricultural extension staff and home economics workers were each given a random sample of hundred households to survey. The households were in the area where they worked. After the survey, those who had conducted it all considered that the sample had been unfairly weighted against the more progressive and better-educated households, over-representing those that were poorer. One of the agricultural staff complained that of his hundred households, only one had an exotic grade cow, and that there would have been several more if the sample had been truly representative. In reality, however, in that area there was only one exotic grade cow for every two hundred households, so each sample of hundred had only a fifty per cent chance of including one at all. A home economics worker said that she was appalled at the poverty she had encountered among her sample. On two occasions she had burst into tears at what she had found. She had not known that there was such misery in the area. 'These people,' she said, 'do not come to my meetings.'

For the same area, David Leonard (1977, p178) has documented the marked tendency for extension staff to visit progressive farmers and not to visit non-innovators (57 per cent of visits to the 10 per cent who were progressives and only 6 per cent to the 47 per cent who were non-innovators). Thus, it is not only outsiders who are affected by anti-poverty biases. Local-level rural staff are also affected, and unless there are strong countervailing incentives, they too will under-perceive deprivation in the very areas where they work.

The second example is from a study by Moore and Wickremesinghe (1980, p98) in Sri Lanka. After observing how the houses of the poor are physically hidden from the core of the villages they studied, and how public officers appear not to see them very often, Moore and Wickremesinghe noted:

Although most of the rural population ... are poor and dependent in part or whole on wage labour, one hears comments of the nature: 'Of course, most of the people around here have some job or little business in Colombo.'

The implication of such comments was that most people in the villages had other incomes and a modest well-being. This might be true of those who lived at the centres of the villages, who were better off and with whom there was contact; but it was unlikely to be true of many of those who lived on the peripheries, who were poorer, and with whom there was no contact.

In the third example, a senior official in a ministry in a capital city stated that in his rural home area no one ever went short of food. But a social anthropologist working in the area reported families seriously short of food during the annual hungry season; twice women were interviewed who said they had not eaten for three days. There was, however, food in the shops nearby, giving the impression that there was no reason for anyone to go hungry.

Perhaps this phenomenon is world-wide, as marked in rich urban as in poor rural agricultural society. Compared with others, the poor are unseen and unknown. Their deprivation is often worse than is recognised by those who are not poor.

Finally, we may note additional factors often missed by rural development tourists, local-level staff and even researchers. It is not just a case of the invisible poorer people. There are also other invisible dimensions: international influences on rural deprivation; social relations (patron–client, indebtedness, webs of obligation and exploitation); and trends over time. The very act of being in a rural area and trying to learn about it creates biases of insight and interpretation towards what can be seen; and the observer's specialisation increases the likelihood of one-sided diagnoses, explanations and prescriptions. Poor people on disaster courses may not be recognised. A nutritionist may see malnutrition but not the seasonal indebtedness, the high cost of medical treatment, the distress sales of land, and the local power structure which generate it. A doctor may see infant mortality but not the declining real wages which drive mothers to desperation, still less the causes of those declining real wages. Visibility and specialisation combine to show simple surface symptoms rather than deeper combinations of causes. The poor are little seen, and even less is the nature of their poverty understood.

The biases reviewed (2008)

The six biases – spatial, project, person, seasonal, diplomatic and professional – continue to manifest in many ways, and continue to interlock. To these can now be added a seventh, security bias. Whether there is a new urban bias is open to question. And to some degree offsetting all these is a new degree of understanding and acceptance that visitors may wish to visit poorer places and meet poorer people. To the original analysis there are now illustrations and qualifications; and readers will have more to contribute to what was, until the recent decline of rural visits, becoming a flourishing folklore.[13]

The biases continue to reinforce misperceptions. How this could happen was an ahha! moment in the early 1970s research in India. We were working in 12 villages. At different times, and separately, the four of us who were the main researchers – Barbara Harriss, John Harriss, Nanjamma Chinnappa and myself – visited each of the villages, often with the investigator working in that village. In conversation we discussed the villages' characteristics and built up an image of each. The 'ahha!' was when we realized that we had been taken to the same farmers and visited the same fields, and were reifying and generalizing from similar slanted experiences, reinforced through repetition and agreement.

Spatial bias

'Airport bias' eluded me in the early 1980s. It may have become more common. In the late 1980s, the chief executive of ActionAid issued an instruction that all ActionAid growth projects had to be within four hours' drive of an airport (pers. comm. Tom Thomas). Dr Reddy, the director of the Indian Institute of Public Administration, has noted that the location of airports is a determining factor in where research occurs (pers. comm. David Hulme). The existence of poverty and accessibility to airports interact to influence choice of location so that places which have high poverty or 'backward' indicators which are one or two hours from airports tend to get selected.

Airport and other spatial biases were evident around 1990 with the Maheshwaram watershed development programme in Andhra Pradesh, about an hour's drive from the Hyderabad International Airport. This was so much visited that the staff had routinized what they called a 'two-hour treatment' and a 'four-hour treatment' for visitors. The reality in the watershed was that on the sloping land the anti-erosion works created rather than prevented erosion: stone gully plugs intended to reduce erosion instead increased it as they were bypassed and water cut into the banks; and water built up behind the irregular contour earth bunds made by bulldozers and broke through to start new gullies. Farmers, moreover, were angry at the damage done to their land without their permission: one told me that he woke up one morning to find a bulldozer making these destructive bunds on his land but he felt unable to stop it, and did not want to get on bad terms with the government.

In this watershed, though, the route on which visitors were taken followed roads on the flat land of ridges where the erosion caused by the anti-erosion works was not visible, except in one place. As an important World Bank visitor passed this place on the way in, one of the government district staff pointed out something on the other side of the road. On the way out, the distraction was repeated as we passed it again. At no point during the four hours did the visitor see any of the extensive damage done by this World Bank-funded programme. He was, however, no naive newcomer to this sort of treatment, and repeatedly asked to meet a farmer. This proved embarrassing, time-consuming and difficult to arrange; perhaps farmers were fed up with visitors and refused to give their time, or perhaps officials judged there would be too much danger of the truth coming out, to the extent, that is, that they were themselves aware of it.

Some spatial biases, as I described them in 1983, need qualifying. 'Roadside bias' remains widespread. Those who are better off still speculate in buying roadside land, and build their houses there. But sometimes the poorest people are to be found at roadsides. In famines in Ethiopia, those who are desperate often migrate to the main roads in search of relief. In his *Rural Rides*, that pioneering and polemical rural development tourist, William Cobbett, describing his horse ride from Cricklade to Cirencester in England, observed:

> *The labourers seem miserably poor. Their dwellings are little better than pig-beds, and their looks indicate that their food is not nearly equal to that of a pig. Their wretched hovels are stuck upon little bits of ground* on the road side, *where the space has been wider than the road demanded … it seems as if they had been swept off the fields by a hurricane, and had dropped and found shelter under the banks on the road side!* (Morris, 1984, p21. Emphasis in the original)

Perhaps it was only on the public roadside that they could find any space to live on that was not private property. In the 1990s I noticed a similar phenomenon in the railway reserve between Mombasa and Nairobi where very poor looking huts had been constructed between the railway line and its boundary fence.

Within cities and villages, the biases of cores persist with the poorer people often at the peripheries. But poor people can also be seen in core places. Beggars are an example, when they are not driven away. And in India, landless labourers seeking work sometimes congregate in the centre of villages in early morning to wait for those who may employ them for the day.

Project bias

This is alive and well, even though among lenders and donors projects have fallen somewhat from grace. That said, the project subspecies *island of salvation* has proved resilient, and finds varied habitats. In the early 1980s, visiting Sukhomajri, the village in Haryana famous for its exceptionally equitable and sustainable natural resource management, I found myself in trouble because I had arrived ahead of a group of prominent visitors and taken the best guide. The plaques by the eucalyptus by the Sukhomajri school were a Who's Who of the agricultural establishment of India and of the World Bank who had planted them on their visits. In 2003, visiting Community-Led Total Sanitation in Bangladesh, the salvation was on a literal, if seasonal, island, exceptional for its isolation and cohesive minority population. I arrived by boat just as another boat was leaving with senior staff of an international non-governmental organization (INGO), and in due course signed my name after theirs in the visitors' book. More recently, the Millennium Villages in African countries have received so much special treatment and so much publicity that they must surely join the family of earlier islands of salvation, also much visited unless visitors are kept away.

Person bias

Person bias remains strong and serious. It has been reduced by the shift in gender awareness, and a weakening in some, perhaps most societies of the barriers to women talking to visitors, especially men, though in some these remain strong or almost overwhelming.[14] It has also been offset by changes in diplomatic bias (see below). Questions always remain about who is being left out, and these as ever often include old people and children.

Seasonal bias

This has not diminished except to the extent that many tarmac road networks are more extensive, and to some degree where helicopters are used. They are much maligned and mocked. Much can be misperceived on their short stops. For example, arriving by helicopter, it must be easy to overlook or underestimate the degree of seasonal isolation since this is not confronted or experienced through days of difficult travel on the ground. All the same, the access they can provide to places seasonally cut off can be remarkable.

The tendency for Northerners to flock from their cold winters to warmer climes continues and is recognized in Bangladesh by calling them *sheether pakhi* – winter birds who come in January to March. Seasonally there can, too, be questions of whose convenience counts? When the Select Committee on Overseas Aid of the British House of Commons wanted to visit India in the winter, the Indian authorities requested postponement; it was inconvenient to receive visitors so near the end of their financial year, which was 31 March. But the convenience of the MPs prevailed, and they too visited at what for many poor people in rural India was their least bad time of year – cool, dry, relatively healthy and after harvest.

From diplomatic to poverty bias

Diplomatic bias, not visiting or seeing poor people, is still there, but has to a degree been offset and even in places reversed. The widespread rhetoric on poverty has made it more acceptable in many countries and regions for a visitor to ask to go to the poorest villages or slums, or the poorest part of a village or slum or to meet poorer people. Even here, though, there can be a person bias, of a new sort; the poor people met may be practised, rehearsed and reliable performers, as I have experienced with at least one women's organization. And in one Indian village, it was the same Dalit, with the same milch buffalo supplied through the Integrated Rural Development Programme, who was paraded to a succession of visitors to whom he dutifully explained the benefits he and his family had gained from that misperceived and overrated programme.[15]

In some cases diplomatic bias has been turned on its head and replaced by a poverty bias. In Kenya, tourism proper has seized on the opportunities presented by the interest in poverty through organized visits to Kibera in Nairobi, one of Africa's largest slums. The general manager of the Kenya-based Victoria Safaris was reported to have said: 'People are getting tired of the Maasai Mara and wildlife. No one is enlightening us about other issues. So I've come up with a new thing – slum tours.' A proportion of tourists' fees go to a local project. But it is by no means only tourists who visit Kibera. It has become 'the de rigueur stop off for caring foreign dignitaries...' including the Secretary General of the UN, Ban Ki-Moon. Reported comments have been that 'any journalist wanting a quick African poverty story can find it there in half an hour...', '...there's the plethora of self-help, art, dance, drama, and sports projects going on in Kibera but people just want to talk about poverty, poverty, poverty all the time'. Reactions of Kenyans have been mixed.[16]

Professional bias

This remains powerful, but the multidimensionality of poverty is better recognized. The vocabulary of development common to disciplines has expanded to more often include words like vulnerability, marginalization, exclusion, discrimination, gender, powerlessness, rights and social justice. The widely adopted sustainable livelihoods framework has provided common neutral ground on which professions and disciplines can meet, and has broadened professional perspectives, including as it does the five capitals – natural, physical, human, social and financial, and also processes and institutions.

To these original six, security bias can now be added, and it can be asked whether there is a new urban bias.

Security bias

As pointed out by David Hirschmann (2003, p488), this is probably becoming more important in development work. Considerations of security discourage or exclude visits to areas where the visitor might not be safe. The cumulative effect of this exclusion is that visitors lack experience of being personally insecure, and may fail to appreciate what physical insecurity means to many poor people and the priority many accord to peace and civil order.

Security can be a legitimate concern of hosts. It can also be a convenient excuse for denying access to an area or a group of people. I believe this has been used to prevent me staying in villages overnight, when the real reasons have been the trouble involved and other concerns, however considerate, about food and toilet.

A subset of security bias concerns sickness. When in the 1970s, it was suggested that every donor official should be exposed to and learn about rural life and especially rural poverty by spending two weeks in every year actually living in a village, a senior UN official objected on the grounds of the health risks to his staff (Chambers, 1978). In 2003, when a serious form of malaria broke out in part of Gujarat where SEWA International was organizing immersions for World Bank staff and others, the visitors were diverted to another area unaffected by the outbreak. This cannot have been an easy decision. The issues here are not simple, but they need to be recognized, confronted and the trade-offs seriously assessed.

Urban bias?

Whether there is a new urban bias is open to question. Soweto in South Africa has for many years attracted outsider visitors. Urban slums like Kibera in Nairobi, as we have seen, are increasingly visited. It can be asked whether with less time for visits of any sort those who make them now go to urban more than rural areas. Urban slums and squatter settlements are more accessible, especially during rains. Urban visits may be more convenient, easier to arrange, easier to cancel, and above all take less time. On the other hand, what is close by can be more threatening, and more habitually shut out. Of donor agency staff a well-informed observer has written:

> *I know very few who have ventured into urban slums – fear of something on their own back doorstep seems even greater – perhaps I'll be recognised and pestered? It is less easy to put out of mind...* (pers. comm. Dee Jupp)

Concluding

There is nothing final about this listing. Biases are many, and they change. And crucially they can be tackled in many ways (Chapter 8, pp156–158). At least as important as offsetting those named, is the practice of being critically aware and reflecting on what is happening on a visit, of what is being seen, shown and said, of what is not being seen, shown or said, and how this limits or distorts the reality perceived. Each actor can examine their own experience and identify and enjoy the mistakes made, the traps fallen into, and the successes in avoiding them. This too can generate stories to be told against oneself, help us to take ourselves less seriously than we take our work, and contribute to the folklore of shared understanding and the repertoire of how to do better.

Notes

1   This section is from my book (1983) *Rural Development: Putting the Last First*, pp7–25, Longman now Harlow, Pearson Scientific, London
2   Changes in gender relations and an organization's policies mean that women's careers are perhaps on the whole less disrupted by pregnancy and parenthood than they were, but it still happens on a wide scale.
3   The term 'rural development tourism' was adapted from John P. Lewis, who in 1974 described himself as a 'rural area development tourist' in India.

4   The male biased syntax is deliberate and descriptive. Most rural develop-
    ment tourists are men.
5   Another problem is the cavalcade. The more the layers of hierarchy – inter-
    national, national, regional, district, sub-district – and the more the depart-
    ments and institutions involved, so the number of vehicles increases. This
    adds to dust and mud if the tarmac is left, and to delay even if it is not. The
    record is held by a visit in Indonesia to inspect a road being financed by
    United States Agency for International Development (USAID). Douglas
    Tinsley reports that there were 47 vehicles involved. Ferries had to be used
    where bridges were not complete. At one ferry, it took three hours to get the
    whole procession across. But there was a positive side, one supposes. The
    christening of the road was substantial, and the visitors cannot have been
    too rushed in their inspection of the quality of the roadwork, at least near the
    ferries.
6   'They do not know that there are living people here.'
7   This does not necessarily reflect adversely on the choice of villages, since
    peri-urban villages, like any others, are a legitimate subject of study.
8   An early example is provided by Zambia's fuel shortage which led to fuel
    rationing, following Rhodesia's unilateral declaration of independence in
    1965. One effect was that the Universities of Nottingham and Zambia joint
    research project concerned with the productivity of agricultural labour was
    restricted to work in two areas instead of three, and these were areas which
    were relatively well developed agriculturally, having had large inputs of
    education, extension and communication (Elliott 1970, p648).
9   Or close to the famous tourist site for the VIP, such as the Taj Mahal at
    Agra in India. J. K. Galbraith has written that as hopes and enthusiasm for
    rural community development in India waned, 'a number of show villages
    continued to impress the more susceptible foreign visitors'. He records this
    incident:

> *In the spring of 1961, Lyndon Johnson, then vice-president, was taken
> to see one of these villages in the neighbourhood of Agra. It was, of the
> several hundred thousand villages of India, the same one that Dwight D.
> Eisenhower had been shown a year or two before. It was impressive in its
> cleanliness, simple cultural life, handicrafts, and evidence of progressive
> agricultural techniques. Johnson, an old hand in problems of agricultural
> uplift and difficult to deceive, then demanded to see the adjacent village a
> mile or two away. After strong protesting words about its lack of preparation
> to receive him, he was taken there. This village, one judged, had undergone
> no major technical, cultural, or hygienic change in the previous thousand
> years.* (1979, pp106–107)

10 Mea culpa. In the 1960s, so many of us students and other researchers were
    attracted to work on the (well-documented, well-organized and well-known)
    Mwea Irrigation Settlement in Kenya that farmers complained about
    interview saturation.

11 In February 1979, two British Members of Parliament visited the Anand Cooperatives in India. They saw and were impressed by the delivery of milk from small producers to one centre. Inside, hung a photograph of James Callaghan, the British Prime Minister, taken during his visit to the same centre. Asked if they would like to see a second centre they readily assented. Once inside they found another photograph, this time of the visit to that centre of Judith Hart, the British Minister of Overseas Development.

12 For the statements in this paragraph see Longhurst and Payne (1979) and Chambers et al (1981).

13 Any reader with anecdotes and advice to add, please write to me: r.chambers@ids.ac.uk and indicate whether you wish to be acknowledged as the source or prefer to be anonymous. Who knows, we might in due course be able to put together an anthology.

14 In May 2006 in three days of visits to rural areas outside Kabul, I was only able to have a conversation with two females. I was told that I was exceptionally privileged. I have never experienced such a spectacular male bias, or such meagre scope to offset it.

15 The IRDP was subject to innumerable questionnaire evaluations which were shown by Jean Dreze (1990) in a devastating, detailed and entirely credible article to have built-in positive biases while participant observers in villages often found the programme did more harm than good. Subsequently, attempts were made to rectify some of the worst defects of the programme, but I doubt whether these went far to offset the deep flaws of concept and implementation.

16 I am grateful to Tobias Denskus for drawing my attention to the report by Andrew Cawthorne and Wangui Kanina on which this paragraph is based. See www.alertnet.org/thenews/newsdesk/L06818999.htm Since writing this Kibera has become tragically notorious for violence following the flawed election of late 2007.

3

Microenvironments:
Observing the Unobserved

...you see, but you do not observe. Sherlock Holmes to Dr Watson
(Arthur Conan Doyle, 1891)

Abstract

Professionals underperceive the complexity and diversity of farming and livelihood systems for several interlocking reasons. These include the sites chosen for research and trials, the biases of field visits, short time-horizons, and sheer lack of observation. One consequence is that microenvironments like home gardens and silt trap gully fields are often unobserved and their significance not recognized. They are found in many forms and in almost all conditions. Their properties point to their importance: they are often specialized in their use, with concentrations of nutrients, protected, and diverse and complex in their content. They can provide reserves and fallbacks for bad times, and restrain migration. As sites for innovation and experiment, their complexity and diversity give farmers, with their flexibility, a comparative advantage over scientists. To further exploit the potential of microenvironments requires secure rights and tenure for farmers, and on the part of agricultural and social scientists more acute observation and awareness and a participatory farmer-first approach. Ability to observe and notice things, and then to retain visual images are skills neglected in many 'developed' societies.

Microenvironments unobserved (1990)[1]

As we enter the 1990s, the dominant paradigm of development expressed by normal professionals and implemented through normal bureaucracy is still top-down and centre-outwards. Power is concentrated in hands of the old men in high offices and central places. Knowledge is generated in universities, laboratories, engineering workshops and research stations, and then transferred packaged for adoption. The approach is centralised, standardised, and simple. Non-adoption by farmers is still attributed to their ignorance and to imperfect communication. When farmers do not adopt, it is not the technology that is to blame but a failure of communication, top-down and one-way, from scientist through to farmer.

In recent years this Transfer of Technology (TOT) paradigm has been increasingly questioned, even in the citadels of normal professionalism. Reductionist research, high input packages, and top-down extension have had their successes: in the uniform and controlled conditions of industrial and Green Revolution agriculture they have raised output per unit of land. But the sustainability of that increase is open to question, and TOT does not work well with the more complex, diverse and risk-prone rain-fed agriculture of much of the poorer South. Explanations of non-adoption are now increasingly sought not in the ignorance of farmers, not in the methods of communication, not even so much the lack of access to inputs, but in the technology itself, the concept of package, and the processes whereby the technology is generated.

With this shift of understanding, a new family of complementary approaches to agricultural research and extension have evolved. These are variously described as farmer-back-to-farmer (Rhoades and Booth, 1982), farmer participatory research (Farrington and Martin, 1988), and farmer first (Lightfoot et al, 1987). These seek to reverse centralist tendencies, emphasising farmers' participation in most or all stages of research, and farmers' own analysis, choice and experimentation. The package of practices is replaced by a basket of choices. Searching for what farmers need becomes an important activity for scientists and extensionists. While TOT simplifies and standardises, farmer first enables farmers to do better by complicating and diversifying their farming systems.

Complexity and diversity underperceived

In both agricultural and social sciences, however, complexity and diversity are underperceived, and consequently undervalued.

Sites for research and trials

Sites chosen for research and trials tend to screen out topographical and soil variability. One of the first measures undertaken when the International Crops Research Institute for the Semi-arid Tropics (ICRISAT) was founded was to bulldoze and smooth out some of the surface irregularities of the land, making it more amenable to normal experimental procedures. Sites for on-farm trials may similarly be selected for being flat or having an even inclined slope. According to textbooks, soil variation is a problem in selecting land for trials: the patch of land chosen as a block must be as uniform as possible. For research purposes then, uniform conditions are actively created or sought out.

Field visits

Field visits by scientists are vulnerable to the biases of rural development tourism – spatial, project, person, seasonal, professional and diplomatic [Chapter 2].

They then see field trials, not indigenous experiments; earth bunds covered in good grass near the main road, not the breached bunds which have contributed to erosion further away. Sometimes roads follow flat ridges, as in parts of Kenya, running through fields of arable crops which are then observed and walked through, to the neglect of the steeper slopes and intensively cultivated valley bottoms (Dewees, 1989). Professionals notice and ask about what concerns their specialisation. Since so many are commodity specialists, this focuses attention on field crops. Prudent officials who are hosts and guides follow the same route and the same rigmarole with a succession of visitors, and themselves have their selective perceptions reinforced through repetition of what they see and say.

Short time horizons

In the on-farm situation, it is less farmers and much more non-farming professionals who have short time horizons. Agronomists tend to be concerned with field trials over one or at most a few seasons. Agricultural engineers and soil conservation staff usually work at one-off conservation, carrying out physical works and then moving on to another area. They miss the farmers' experience of what happens to their works over the subsequent years.

Sheer blindness

Observation that is needed and 'natural' to cultivators and pastoralists has often been trained out of professionals. Book and classroom learning de-skill and dampen curiosity, deterring enquiry beyond narrow physical and disciplinary domains. It is also astonishing how easy it is to fail to notice and ask about something of significance. On a recent village Rapid Rural Appraisal (RRA), when trying to observe points of interest, I nearly walked right past a superbly constructed and exploited silt deposition field. And that was while walking a transect and consciously trying to observe. Ken Wilson reports (1989, p374) from Zimbabwe:

> *During one trip with senior agricultural extension officers, in which I was drawing attention to the positive effects that trees were having on early season crop growth, one of them pondered: why is it that I have been telling farmers to remove them all my life, without ever bothering to look at the effects?*

Combined, these biases in perception screen out much of the diversity and complexity of farming systems. To be sure there have been significant shifts among agricultural scientists, recognising the value of the complications of intercropping and of agroforestry. But even with these concerns, scientists and extensionists are still inclined to imprint linear and large-scale patterns, which may or may not make sense. Line sowing is preferred to broadcast sowing; intercropping is in tidy lines; and agroforestry is often taken to mean alley cropping, with trees and crops in straight lines. Trials on farmers' fields are placed on flat or evenly sloping land.

However 'good' the reasons are, the result has been that much has been missed, including farmers' own technology, their experiments, interlinkages within their farming systems, changes over the seasons, and farmers' long-term strategies for soil, water and nutrient concentration.

Livelihoods

In the social sciences, reductionism and professional convenience have also generated a simplified view of rural people's livelihoods. Livelihood can here be defined as means to gain adequate stocks and flows of food and cash to meet basic needs, together with reserves and assets to offset risk, ease shocks, and meet contingencies (WCED, 1987, p3).

In practice, the livelihood strategies of poor people, including resource-poor farmers, are often complex and diverse. Different household members undertake different activities in different places at different times of the year. Besides farming themselves, these can include labouring for other farmers, share-rearing of livestock, work on or for non-farm enterprises, migration, craft work, petty trading, and the gathering, consuming and selling of a large range of common property resources. The livelihoods of poor people can be both complex and different even in the same village (Beck, 1989; Heyer, 1989).

These complexities and differences are underperceived for many reasons:

- The stereotype of poor people is as a simple, uniform, unskilled and inert mass.
- The lack of direct exposure of urban-based professionals to the realities of poor people's livelihood strategies.
- Survey questionnaires for social surveys which are drawn up in offices and omit categories of which urban-based professionals are unaware, thereby excluding many livelihood activities.
- Survey investigators and respondents whose interest lies in short and simple answers which finish the interview faster.
- The tendency of poor people to give prudent replies to questions and to understate their sources of food and income.
- Incomplete accounts in surveys of activities which take place at times of the year other than that of the interview.
- Neglect of the economic activities of women and children.

In consequence, survey data and professional opinion sustain an oversimple view of how poor people gain their livelihoods.

Microenvironments unobserved

These general biases in both agricultural and social sciences combine to hide microenvironments (MEs) from sight, to understate or exclude them in statistics, and to undervalue their importance for livelihoods. In addition, there are other factors specific to the nature of MEs which conceal them from view or insulate them from attention. These can be understood by considering examples of MEs and reflecting on some of their characteristics.

Most agriculture creates or alters microenvironments, through ploughing, irrigation, the micro-climatic effects of crop canopies, effects of grazing and browsing, and so on. The MEs with which we are concerned are more separate and distinct. A microenvironment is a distinct small-scale environment which differs from its surroundings, presenting sharp gradients or contrasts in physical conditions internally and/or externally. Microenvironments can be isolated, or contiguous and repetitive, and natural or made by people or domestic animals. Microenvironments include:

- home gardens (also known as homestead, or household, kitchen, backyard or dooryard gardens)
- vegetable and horticultural patches (protected, with wells etc.)
- river banks and riverine strips
- levees and natural terraces
- valley bottoms (fadama, wadi, mbuga, vlei etc.)
- wet and dry watercourses
- rainstreams (dividing and braiding, etc.)
- dry river beds (nallahs, wadis, luggas etc.)
- drainage lines
- alluvial pans
- artificial terraces
- silt trap fields (depositional fields, gully fields etc.)
- raised fields and ditches or ponds (especially in wetlands)
- water harvesting in its many forms
- hedges and windbreaks
- clumps, groves or lines of trees or bushes
- pockets of fertile soil (termitaria, former livestock pens etc.)[2]
- sheltered corners or strips, by aspect of slope, configuration etc.
- plots protected from livestock
- flood recession zones
- small flood plains
- springs and patches of high groundwater and seepage strips and pockets of impeded drainage
- lake basins
- ponds, including fishponds
- animal wallows (e.g. for buffalos).

Apart from personal observation, the main sources for this listing are Richards, 1985; Pacey and Cullis, 1986; Altieri, 1989; Harrison, 1987; Wilken, 1987; and IIED, 1989.

There are many reasons why professionals have neglected MEs such as these. They include:

1 Smallness and dispersal

MEs are often half-hidden. They are usually small and dispersed, and many are low-lying. The small or intermediate scale of MEs combines with topography and with the way in which water and soil collect in low places to hide many of them in dips, depressions, valleys, gullies and watercourses where they are easily overlooked by a casual visitor. Professional attention focuses on other scales. Gene Wilken has noted (1987, p240) that 'most research has been limited at the technical level to horizontal plant spacing and at the aggregate level to optimum farm size and economies of scale.' Normal soils' maps also miss much. In India their scale is 1:500,000. In both Kenya and Zambia, it is said that soils' maps, because of their scale, have omitted the crucial MEs of riverine strips and areas of seasonal standing water and moisture (known as dambos in Zambia and Zimbabwe).

2 Research station conditions

Most research is conducted on research stations where undulations and irregularities tend to be eliminated and their ME potential ignored. Some ME types created by farmers may not be feasible or found at all on research stations – for example silt deposition fields. And where MEs are created on research stations, as with the watershed work at ICRISAT, it is difficult to avoid creating special conditions quite different from those of farmers.

3 Sequential creation

Most professionals have shorter time horizons than most farmers. Soil and water conservation staff with targets seek to complete works within the financial year. But many farmers' MEs take years to develop. Some silt deposition fields in gullies are built up sequentially over years, with rock walls raised annually. Home gardens, and areas near homesteads, where farmyard manure and household organic wastes are used, gain in fertility over time. Runoff watercourse training may be developed gradually over many years, as may many forms of water harvesting which require physical works. Making raised fields and ditch ponds in wetlands in Indonesia leads to sequential cropping in which tree crops gradually come to dominate after 10 to 15 years (Watson, 1988).

4 Gender

Some MEs, especially home gardens, are mainly the concern of women, and women's concerns are normally neglected by male professionals who are still in the overwhelming majority.

5 'Unimportant' crops

MEs often grow crops (vegetables, multipurpose trees, less common root crops etc.) other than the staple foodgrains, root crops and non-food cash crops which are the priorities of research and extension, which are marketed in bulk, and which are estimated and enumerated in official statistics. In Indonesia, the products of home gardens are mostly consumed locally and rarely appear in the statistical record (Soemarwoto and Conway, 1989, p5).

6 Misfit with normal research

Normal research simplifies in order to measure. But the complexity, diversity and 'untidiness' of many MEs, their non-linear shapes and irregular surfaces, do not lend themselves to standard agronomic trials or measurement, or to mechanisation or high capital inputs. Many MEs use organic, not the preferred inorganic, manures. Many are based on subsoil conditions and rooting patterns which would be costly and tedious to examine and observe. And many develop and exploit diverse complications such as linkages between earth shaping with soil and rocks, the channelling, harvesting and retention of water, a variety of crops and vegetables, livestock including fish, multiple canopies including bushes and trees, and mulches and manures.

Many illustrations of the above could be given. Paul Richards comments on the significance of the niche of run-off (seep-zone) agriculture, in parts of West Africa, on fields which trap moisture and silt from higher up a valley profile, and notes its neglect by 'formal sector' researchers (Richards, 1985, pp81–84). In an RRA in Ethiopia, only by walking a systematic transect was it revealed to outsiders that in a semi-arid environment farmers had, over the years, developed an intensive system for trapping and concentrating silt, water and nutrients in gullies, and growing high value crops including coffee, papaya and chat (a narcotic) in the MEs protected by the gully walls (ERCS, 1988). In India, RRAs undertaken in 1989 by MYRADA in Gulbarga District in Karnataka, by Youth for Action in Mahbubnagar District in Andhra Pradesh, and by the Aga Khan Rural Support Programme in Bharuch District in Gujarat have variously identified the creation of MEs to harvest water and soil as prevalent local technology significant economically but in no case recognized or supported by the official soil conservation programmes.

Home gardens are frequently overlooked or misinterpreted. In Bangladesh, Anil Gupta found (1989, pp28–30) that scientists believed that households used homestead space and other resources inefficiently, and that they planted most trees, bushes and vegetables randomly or just let them grow where they came up. But a survey by women scientists, and maps made of home gardens, revealed great complexity and what appeared to be some order in what had been assumed to be disorder.

MEs are thus largely unobserved. Spatially they are hidden by their dispersal. Professionally they are hidden by their irregular untidiness and their misfit with the mainstream priorities of the major disciplines. And temporally, they are hidden by their use in only certain seasons.

Yet in aggregate, they are at present of major significance to sustainable livelihoods. Because of their generally better moisture and fertility conditions than their surroundings, they provide the more reliable component of a farming household's food supply. Moreover, in many environments, MEs have been developed as a form of intensification linked with increasing population density. In future, as rural populations in many places increase yet further, MEs will be developed even more, and will become even more significant for the livelihoods of poor farming households.

Properties of microenvironments

There are a number of important properties and functions of MEs.

Specialisation

Because MEs differ from their more uniform surroundings, their use also usually differs. An example is paddy grown in silt deposition fields in nallahs in semi-arid India. But specialisation, though general, is not universal. Some gully fields in Ethiopia are used to grow the same crop – sorghum – as in neighbouring, more extensive fields, though it can be expected with higher yields and lower risk.

Concentration

Farmers' own soil and water 'conservation' is often soil, water and nutrient 'concentration'. Soil concentration occurs when soil or silt is dug from common land and carted to build up fields and fertility. Or erosion is exploited for the low cost transport it provides for silt which is then trapped by rocks, brushwood, trash lines, vegetative barriers or earth builds. Water concentration occurs when it is channelled, captured and retained in water harvesting. Nutrient concentration occurs through silt deposition, farmyard manure in and near homesteads and in livestock pens, leaf litter under bushes and trees, and organic manures carted to the ME site. And these forms of soil, water and nutrient concentration interact synergistically (see e.g. Kolarkar et al, 1983).

Protection

For domestic and wild animals, many MEs present attractive islands of green in dry expanses, and they are therefore vulnerable to grazing and browsing. Protection is essential except where, as with some eucalypts, plants are unpalatable. Fences, hedges and barriers are necessary and common. Difficulties in protection against animals can deter the creation or exploitation of MEs, or determine what is grown in them. As for climate, many MEs are protected to create their own microclimates, often sheltered from excessive sun, wind and/or water.

Diversity and complexity

Diversity in species of plant and animal, and complexity in biological relationships between them, are common. Multiple canopies, agroforestry combinations, vining plants, variety of species, and plants at various stages of growth are common characteristics. The movement and arrangement of soil and stones often make the land surface less even and more varied. The untidiness of some MEs incorporates a large number of interactions.

Nutrition and health

Apart from the quantity and relative stability of the flows of food and income to households from MEs, some, especially home gardens, provide two other benefits: medicinal plants, and vegetables, fruits and other foods for diversified diets which also include more vitamins. Recent findings of dramatic drops in child (aged 6 months to 5 years) mortality with vitamin A supplementation (a 60 per cent reduction in a study near Madurai in South India, and a 45 per cent reduction in a study in Indonesia (pers. comm. Saroj Pachauri)) point to the key potential of home gardens as a source of literally life-saving vitamins.

Reserves and fallbacks

MEs frequently provide reserves to meet contingencies, and for lean seasons and bad years. Trees to which people have clear rights increasingly serve as savings banks which can be cashed to meet seasonal or sudden needs (Chambers and Leach, 1989). A very poor family in Kakamega District in Kenya had, in 1988, a line of Eucalyptus at the bottom of their half acre plot, which they cut and sold, they said, in the lean times of February and March 'to buy food and soap'. In Sudan, wadi cultivation is especially significant in bad years (pers. comm. Ian Scoones). In Zimbabwe, key resource habitat patches are important for cattle in bad years (Scoones, 1988a). Leaf fodder from trees on private land was used by some farmers in Gujarat as their last fallback for feeding their livestock during the great drought of 1987–88. By accumulating reserves of value, and by providing output which lasts longer, MEs thus contribute to the sustainability of livelihoods.

Restraining migration

Following the analysis of Ester Boserup (1965), the technology used in agriculture, in this case for MEs, is related to population pressure and labour availability. MEs will then be more and more developed and exploited as population pressure increases. In some environments there may be a critical phase when more labour is needed to develop, protect, maintain and exploit them, and when paths diverge: either people migrate, seasonally or permanently, and leave an unsustainable and risky farming system; or they stay and invest in more sustainable intensification. One illustration is water harvesting near Yatenga on the Mossi Plateau in Burkina Faso, where investment of labour in laying out rock bunds and digging pockets for crops has led to higher and more stable production, and reportedly less out-migration. MEs' greater productivity, stability and spread of production period can thus locally support more livelihoods.

Innovation, experiment and adaptability

MEs play a vital part in innovations, experimentation and adaptation. Some wild plants which are candidates for domestication are tried first in home gardens. Anil Gupta reports that a survey by women scientists in Bangladesh identified a large number of innovations in home gardens (Gupta, 1989, p29). Calestous Juma notes that farmers place such plants first in environments similar to those where they were found, for example in moist ground near a stream (Juma, 1987, p33), and gradually move them out into harsher environments. Paul Richards observes for West Africa that when farmers carry out experiments, they typically begin in the neglected run-off zone (Richards, 1985, pp83–84). Indeed, the past failure to observe farmers' experiments may partly stem from the failure to notice the MEs in which they are to be found. MEs thus contribute to the sustainability of livelihoods by providing locations for experiment, enhancing the adaptability of farmers and their ability to respond to changes and to exploit opportunities.

Whose knowledge and creativity counts?

MEs are a domain where villagers' knowledge, creativity and Research and Development (R & D) have advantages compared with the knowledge and R & D of scientists.

In terms of knowledge, scientists have an advantage in their knowledge of and access to information and genetic material from elsewhere; but their capacity for precise measurement is less useful faced with the complexity and diversity of ME conditions than with the simplicities and uniformities of industrial and Green Revolution agriculture. Villagers, on the other hand, know more about the complex and diverse detail of their livelihoods and of local ecology, and of how these mesh and are managed. Villagers also have advantages in local observations over time.

In terms of creativity and R & D, many MEs have been made and exploited by farmers over the ages without any formal scientific input. Home gardens, silt deposition fields, and terraces are examples. MEs provide support for the view that '…the farmers' role in technology development becomes more critical and increasingly cost-effective as the proposed technology becomes more multi-faceted and complex' (Sumberg and Okali, 1989, p112). With most MEs scientists have serious disadvantages. Research station conditions are likely to be radically different from those of most MEs: wetland patches in dry areas, for example, cannot be replicated on research stations (IIED, 1989). With the possible exception of some basic research, on-station research concerning MEs is likely to mislead and generate recommendations that misfit rather than help.

In contrast, farmers have several comparative advantages. They are constrained neither by an inflexible experimental design nor by the simplifications demanded by reductionist statistical methods. They do not suffer from scientists' relatively short time horizons, but like the settlers in the wetlands of Java, can embark on processes which will take 10 to 15 years to mature. They can manage the complexities of simultaneous land shaping, concentration of soil, water and nutrients, and sequential changes as trees and other plants grow. They can adapt what they do to diverse and irregular topography, and climatic and social conditions. They can plant complicated mixtures of plants, and can place plants individually to exploit tiny pockets of fertility or protection. They can develop MEs sequentially, maintaining and modifying them as they observe and learn.

Not surprisingly, then, there is much evidence of farmers doing better than non-farming officials or scientists in developing MEs. In Singhbhum District in Bihar, it has been found that soil conservation staff are not as good at selecting water harvesting sites as villagers: those selected by the villagers capture more water (Sinha, 1989, p6). In various parts of the world, government soil conservation programmes using contour earth bunds have actually contributed to erosion. As in Ethiopia, Mexico, and India silt deposition fields appear to be entirely a farmer's technology. In India, at least, they are far superior to the standard gully checks of official soil programmes. It is only reasonable to conclude that programmes for the creation, improvement and exploitation of MEs should be largely determined and implemented by farmers

Action for the 1990s

The comparative advantage of farmers and disadvantage of scientists in the creation and use of MEs means that less has been lost from past neglect of MEs by non-farming professionals than might at first appear. All the same, the potential of MEs appears large, especially in the semi-arid tropics. And as populations in many countries continue to increase, the need to develop and exploit MEs will become greater. Already in water harvesting, soil conservation and agroforestry, considerable programmes have been mounted by governments and also Non Governmental Organisations (NGOs), but with only mixed results. The question is what non-farming professionals can do to enable the potential of MEs to be realised more rapidly, effectively and efficiently.

First, clear and **secure rights and tenure** are preconditions. Farmers who sense their tenure is insecure are deterred from taking a long view and from investing labour in land shaping or planting trees. This has been the tragic situation in much of Ethiopia where the 1970s land reform perversely made farmers insecure. In parts of India, too, tree planting and protection by farmers is discouraged by restrictions on rights of harvest and transit (Chambers et al, 1989b). In contrast, land consolidation and the provision of secure land titles to farmers in Kenya has had the opposite effect, supporting a soil conservation programme and also resulting in much tree planting and protection, with research showing the densities of planted trees to be higher the denser the population and the smaller the holdings (Bradley et al, 1985; Peter Dewees, pers. comm.).

Second, **observation and awareness** by professionals are imperative. These can be achieved in many ways. The techniques of rapid and participatory rural appraisal (Khon Kaen University, 1987; *RRA Notes*, 1988 [and Chapter 4]) and especially of agroecosystem analysis (Conway, 1985; McCracken et al, 1988) have much to offer. These include walking transects, mapping village resources, mapping MEs, and the participatory use of aerial photographs to identify MEs and soil patches and zones. The simple act of mapping a home garden or diagramming a transect can have a dramatic effect on personal awareness, sometimes provoking a 'flip' – a professionally and intellectually exciting deeper change in what is seen and how it is seen.

Third, the appropriate paradigm is farmer first rather than Transfer of Technology (TOT). For non-farming agricultural professionals, farmer first entails changes and reversals:

- of location – from on-station to on-farm
- of learning – from learning from literature and from other non-farmers to learning from and with farmers
- of role – from teacher who transfers technology to consultant who searches for technology and supports farmers' trials and experiments
- of content – from the single simple package to the basket spread of diverse choices
- of direction of transfer – from vertical to lateral with farmers' workshops and visits to each others' MEs
- of process – from simplifying and standardising to complicating and diversifying.

Farmers' participation throughout is of paramount importance.

To observe and learn about microenvironments, and to help farm families create and exploit them and improve and intensify their use, presents a challenge to the agricultural and social sciences. Microenvironments demand quiet professional revolutions. These will start not with the lecturer but with the farm family, not just in the classroom but in the field too, not on the research station but in the microenvironments themselves. They will entail not simplifying and standardising but enabling farm families to complicate and diversify. The 1990s will show whether non-farming professionals can make that revolution and usefully meet that challenge, or whether it will be largely unassisted that farmers continue to experiment, innovate, develop and manage on their own.

More observations (2008)

I am uneasy that I do not disagree now with what I wrote in 1990. However, additions can be made, changes have occurred and points have been reinforced. Microenvironments have become more visible and more seen.

In 1990 I did not consider the destruction or decay of microenvironments. Destruction is widespread especially with agriculture which industrializes, simplifies and goes to scale: destruction of forests as in the Amazon, the enlargements of fields and removal of hedges in much Northern agriculture, and the adverse effects of these on biological diversity and quality of life and experience are too well known to deserve elaboration.[3] Dilapidation and decay of MEs occur especially when for whatever reasons labour becomes scarce, and labour-intensive maintenance and management lose their logic.

Agricultural research and extension have evolved significantly. Farmer participation has become more widespread. Gender dimensions and the roles and importance of women in agriculture have become much better recognized. It is no longer unusual to talk of 'The African farmer, she...'. Participation and gender analysis have been promoted and explored within the Consultative Group for International Agricultural Research (CGIAR) by the active and extensive inter-centre initiative Participatory Research and Gender Analysis launched in 1997.

The points about intensive and complex small-scale niches have been reinforced. On Zimbabwean farms in Ngundu, Chivi 'small patches – often around the homestead, but also capitalising on relatively favourable soil and water conditions in small niches (such as former cattle kraals or settlement sites) – may be cultivated highly intensively ... following the model of the mixed farm (intensive tillage and cultivation, manuring etc.) contrasting with adjacent extensive cultivation' (Scoones and Wolmer, 2002, p25). As for home gardens, their significance in both rural and urban contexts, with intensive and complex cultivation near homesteads, using household wastes and animal manures, has now been quite extensively researched and documented. They are now better recognized as 'high-intensity production niches' (Goldman 1992; p260) important for food and income. Six studies in Indonesia reported the proportions of household income deriving from home gardens as variously 10–30, 20–30, over 20, 22–33, 41–51 and 42–51 per cent. Another Indonesia study found the proportion higher among the poor, providing 24 per cent of their income compared with 9 per cent for the well-off (cited in Hoogerbrugge and Fresco, 1993, p12). A study in Ethiopia found a vegetable garden focus was common for poorer groups (Ramisch et al, 2002, p206). The tendency not to notice poor people and what matters to them is then likely to reinforce the other biases against seeing and recognizing the significance of MEs.[4]

Despite this increased attention, the bias of observation away from compound and home gardens is reinforced by gender, crop and spatial factors. Women not only tend to cultivate home gardens and land close to the home, but they also often manage domestic animals and their manure. Men tend to be more involved with more distant field crops and extensive farming cultivation. As Ian Scoones and his colleagues have shown from the research on soil fertility in Ethiopia, Mali and Zimbabwe, organic materials are applied nearer the homestead, and inorganic fertilizer on fields further away (Scoones and Wolmer, 2002). The interests of agricultural scientists in inorganic fertilizers and field crops then draw them away from home gardens, women and the household. There is too a spatial bias in some areas with ridges and valleys. While much varies by local topography, in undulating and dissected landscapes, roads tend to run along ridges, with field crops cultivated on the adjacent relatively flat upland which is visible and accessible from the road. Niche or garden farming on riverine strips, valley bottoms or extended home gardens remains less visible. At the same time, growing vegetables for sale from such microenvironments becomes more significant in household economies where urban markets grow with a shift from extensive outfield cultivation to intensive gardening and niche farming, as noted in a case in Zimbabwe (Wolmer et al, 2002, p180), which may then become more visible for reasons of scale and economic significance, marketing rather than subsistence, and men becoming more involved. The development and intensification of home gardens with a market orientation has also been 'a backdoor into the gender discussion'. In Brazil, partners of ActionAid Brazil have worked with women on developing their 'invisible' home gardens with a size of the order of 15×15 metres, changing the term from 'quintal' to 'quintal productivo'. As the women generated incomes, men's views of women changed.[5]

Permaculture is a celebration of microenvironments. Bill Mollison's *Permaculture:A Designers' Manual* (1990) is a fabulous work of practical vision and love, a treasury of ideas, insights, patterns and relationships. It presents innumerable examples of deliberately created microenvironments. These are more than just complex and diverse. They are expressions of a philosophy, ethics and values.

Urban agriculture is another example.[6] The claim that it is responsible for 15–20 per cent of the world's food production seems high, but that may simply reflect the extent to which it is not seen or recognized. It is not seen, in part because it is often tucked away in corners and in the poorer quarters of an urban area; and the expanding practice of rooftop vegetable gardening is invisible from street level. Yet so widespread has rooftop gardening become that in Germany in 2001 alone 13.5 million square metres (13.5 square km) of roof garden were reported installed. Alec Thornton (pers. comm.), researching urban agriculture in Grahamstown, South Africa, was told by a professional colleague that there was none in densely settled areas, and even those living there said 'There is no farming here in town.' In part this was because it was not a modern thing to do, and in part because the cultivation which took place was not considered farming or agriculture. Yet it was there.

Minilivestock too have been better recognized. Livestock scientists work more on larger animals – cattle especially, and if not cattle, then sheep and goats. But the range of minilivestock used for food is impressive. In a labour of love, Maurizio Paoletti of the University of Padua has edited a book *Ecological Implications of Minilivestock: Role of Insects, Rodents, Frogs and Snails for Sustainable Development* (2005) which to this reader at least is an eye-opener. Twenty-nine contributions from at least 14 countries in all continents except Antarctica show that human diets include not only all six orders of insects, but also spiders and earthworms. Minilivestock that are 'farmed' include house crickets as well as the better known guinea pigs and rabbits. A common sight in Nairobi in season, and easily passed by without really 'seeing' it for what it is, has been women under street lights collecting fallen insects for food. The current contribution and future potential of minilivestock for meeting food needs have been little appraised. They are low status, small, 'looked down on', 'out of sight' and more important to poorer people than to others.

There are also environments which we prefer to avoid, not mention, or only visit with disgust and shame. Areas of open defecation around Asian villages are a case where participatory mapping can identify their location, and transect walks confront residents with unhygienic nastiness as part of a process leading to action to achieve community-led total sanitation (Kar, 2005; Kar and Pasteur, 2005). Observation, and for that matter smelling, are here a key element in triggering changes in behaviour.

Strict, narrow, conventional and convenient professionalism can also blind. We notice what we are taught to notice and what fits our frames of disciplinary relevance and ease of analysis. Soil science provides examples. In a district in Gujarat, farmers were digging up soil on common land on a huge scale and transporting it to their fields. The scars of bare soil were there for everyone to see. Yet the Head of Soil Science at the Agricultural University was unaware of the practice, even though challenged three times. Nor could this, one imagined, be of any interest to him, being no part of his professional paradigm of pedology and his laboratory-centred life of analysing soil samples. But then, none of us are without blinkers: selective perception saves us from the sensory flooding that afflicts some schizophrenics.

Soil science is dominated by soil physics and soil chemistry, both controllable and amenable to standardized reductionist measurements. Soil biology in contrast is a poor cousin. It is out of sight, ever changing, extremely complex, and involves innumerable micro-organisms. Soil physics and soil chemistry overcome these problems by eliminating the biota and studying soil which behaves well, for their purposes, because it is dead. The microenvironments are not just unperceived; they are eliminated to make subject convenient for study.[7]

More generally, transect walks remain a key tool in rapid appraisal, not only systematically exploring an environment and identifying microenvironments, but also training participants in observation. A transect is normally a walk, but can also be a horse or camel[8] ride, or drive in a vehicle. Patterns vary. Walks are often downhill, through agroecological zones. An effort is made to combine representativeness, diversity and outliers and exceptions. Members of a team take responsibility for different aspects – soils, crops, livestock and so on. A transect diagram is then drawn showing the zones and their characteristics. Abilities to notice, ask about and remember are vital.

Anil Gupta in India twice a year spends a week or so on a *shodhyatra* or walk to find knowledge.[9] This actively seeks out innovators and sources of local wisdom. Like a good transect, this is driven by curiosity and much more than just observing. People bring things to the notice of those on the walk and they study and learn from them.

A final microenvironment to be observed is that of the single plant, as two examples illustrate.

First, rice cultivation presents an astonishing case of past failure to observe and follow up on the implications. In this case farmers are involved as well as scientists. Farmers must have seen that though rice can grow in low flooded conditions it can do better on more aerated higher ground, but they have been locked into flooding not least because it saves labour by inhibiting weeds. In

Norman Uphoff's words: 'Millions of people must have walked past fields like that for thousands ... of years and not put two and two together' (pers. comm. 2007). For their part, scientists know about 'edge effects', that plants on the very edge of densely planted fields grow better than those in the centre; but for purposes of measuring yield, and working to increase yields, they avoid the edges precisely because of their higher yields, and concentrate on the lower-yielding more representative inner areas of fields. Yet these edge effects, had they been investigated, could have provided clues that might have led to the System of Rice Intensification (SRI),[10] in which the very young rice plant is transplanted wide apart to give it space and air allowed into its roots. The microenvironment here is that of the individual plant. SRI, evolved in Madagascar by Father Henri de Laulanié, a French priest, sharply raises yields per unit land, water and even labour, and has by the end of 2007 spread to at least BBB countries, especially China and India, and may now cover several million hectares. But some in the scientific establishment, notably in the International Rice Research Institute in the Philippines, have been in a state of denial, unwilling to observe or accept a phenomenon outside their dominant paradigm and professional priorities and belief system. As too in other contexts, believing is not seeing.

The second example comes from the experiential learning of being, living and working with people and noticing and understanding the microdetail of what they do. Koy Thompson (2007), during an immersion with a family in a village in Ghana, took part in his host's farming:

> *Uhuru's farm was about one hour's cycle ride into the forest. Without cattle for ploughing, his fields have literally been cut by hand from the bush. We spent the day weeding – although for Uhuru it was a minute by minute risk assessment and management: what plant is not doing well (pull up and replace), what bit of ground might be too wet or dry (interplant either corn or rice – if one fails because the moisture is wrong the other will do well), how much are the partridges going to take (dig new furrows), which mounds are doing well (shove beans or okra in).*

The intensity of this micro-management of microenvironments was to minimize risks in a tight three-month growing season where so much was as stake, for on this farm there was 'a very real possibility that the damage caused by the partridges could set off a chain of events that results in the death of a child'(Thompson, 2007).

Alert observation is a key. Scientists missed the significance of edge effects. Koy Thompson noticed critical details. I have been struck by how acutely bird-watchers and naturalists notice and remember what they see, sometimes only for a fleeting second, retaining and able to recall the visual image without first translating it into words. Perhaps for many of us, habits of watching and half watching television have weakened our powers of observation, retention and reflection. To the San of Botswana, and many others who have to observe, remember and analyse in order to survive, many of us would appear disabled. In their past environment the disability would probably have been fatal.

Questions and challenges remain. How seriously do we, development professionals, fall short in our skills of observation and retention of visual images? Do our bookish education and our casual attention to the transient trivia of television diminish our ability to observe and remember what we have seen? Do we lack visual curiosity? Do we still fail adequately to notice microenvironments and appreciate their significance, especially to women and poorer farmers? Could those whose livelihoods and food security are marginal be better served if microenvironments were better recognized and supported? What would need to change in professional values, priorities, skills and practices for this to happen? Is it time for educational systems to do more to teach and train students to be curious about what they see, to notice and to remember? Is participatory experiential learning one way forward?

Notes

1   The paper 'Microenvironments Unobserved' which is the core of this chapter appeared as 'Gatekeeper Series No 22', IIED, and was edited by Jules Pretty. It is a shorter version of a paper of the same title that appeared in R. P. Singh (ed) *Proceedings of the International Symposium on Natural Resources Management in a Sustainable Agriculture*, 6–10 February 1990, New Delhi, vol 2, Indian Society of Agronomy, New Delhi.
2   And sometimes where people have lived. The Sands River archeological trail near Gairloch in Wester Ross in Scotland visits scattered sites of prehistoric human settlements on a hillside. The round dwelling sites are conspicuous islands of rich green grass in the heather and bracken. For millennia, it would seem, these must have been maintained by sheep sheltering, manuring and grazing.
3   In the UK a contrary tendency occurs with the return of wild plants and animals to the fringes of main roads and motorways. Even here, though, mindless destruction of microenvironments can occur. For 20 years cycling home from work in the autumn I used to harvest beautiful, big, succulent wild blackberries, the best I have ever found, from a large patch on the edge of the main A27 road. Then every year some authority had them cut down. Readers may likewise have lost special places and common properties like this. It hurts. And how much more for those who depend on them for livelihoods.
4   It is a pleasant indulgence of place dropping, and posing as an observant person, to note another microenvironment. In April 2006, enjoying what must be one of the finest walks in the world, down the Wadi Dana in Jordan, we could see on the opposite side of the valley a cave walled up for keeping animals at night. Immediately below this a rock cleft had been blocked with stones, and was capturing and storing dung, presumably to be carried by donkey to fertilize fields lower down the valley. So dung trap can be added to the list.
5   Pers. comm. Marta and Alberto, staff of ActionAid Brazil, Rio de Janeiro, August 2005.

6   For this paragraph, see www.cityfarmer.org Another source for urban agriculture is www.urbanagriculture-news.com

7   For the background on which this paragraph is based I am grateful to Norman Uphoff.

8   Including camel ride is a bit naughty. I know of no case, and camels are quite limited in the range of conditions they can walk through, especially stones.

9   The source is Peter Day http://news.bbc.co.uk/1/hi/programmes/from_our_own_correspondent/6279929.stm

10   The System of Rice Intensification has spread internationally largely through the efforts of Norman Uphoff of Cornell University and nationally through those of many scientists. See www.ciifad.cornell.edu/sri/

4

Rapid Rural Appraisal: Origins, Rationale and Repertoire

Revolution... 3 a far-reaching and drastic change, esp in ideas, methods etc.
4 a movement in or as if in a circle. (Collins English Dictionary, 2005)

Abstract

In the early 1970s, through errors and opportunism, I stumbled into unconventional approaches to rural research. It then gradually emerged that practical researchers were innovating and using methods which worked for them but which, since they were not respectable in the mainstreams of their disciplines, they rarely wrote about. An IDS workshop (1978) and conference (1979) on rapid rural appraisal (RRA) brought some of them together. The rationale for RRA was that decision-makers needed the right information at the right time but in rural development much information generated was inappropriate or misleading and was slow to become available. Methods of gathering information were often inefficient. RRA at the time was revolutionary. It sought to avoid the traps of large questionnaire surveys (Chapter 1) and rural development tourism (Chapter 2). The need was for information that was relevant, timely, accurate and usable. RRA flowered especially in Thailand. A wide range of experience and methods, including agroecosystem analysis, was brought together in the 1985 international conference at the University of Khon Kaen.

The methods of RRA seek a rigour of cost-effectiveness through exploratory iteration and trade-offs between relevance, accuracy, and timeliness, ignoring inappropriate professional standards. They apply the principles of optimal ignorance and proportionate accuracy (or appropriate imprecision). A repertoire of ten methods illustrates experience and scope. They are cost-effective through their relatively sparing demands on time and resources. Methods of RRA such as transects and semi-structured interviewing are of enduring value and have their own rigour. RRA survived and spread relabelled as Rapid Assessment Process (RAP). Whatever label is used, the principles and practices of RRA remain underused and undervalued, and deserve another revolution, a turning of the wheel, a renaissance.

Errors and opportunism:
One person's stumbling (2008)

Rapid rural appraisal (RRA) was a methodological frontier for inquiry in the latter 1970s and the 1980s. Then it faded away. But its contributions remain valid and vital. It is time for a renaissance, for a revolution of the wheel.

RRA came out of a convergence of many personal journeys, of which mine was only one. In the research in India and Sri Lanka in 1973–74 I was spared survey slavery. As a free-rider on the efforts of colleagues, I had opportunities rare in field research. There I was, in Sri Lanka first, and later in Tamil Nadu, with months and months for fieldwork and no fixed agenda. Far from having a straitjacket of formal hypotheses and a research design, or being tramlined by a logframe, I was free to be flexible, to wander, to explore, to choose what leads to follow. No one breathed down my neck. Benny Farmer, our benign project director, was busy thousands of miles away in Cambridge. My colleagues were far more competent than me in their own fields and got on with what they wanted and needed to do. I was in no way a supervisor. All I could do was try and fail to persuade Barbara and John Harriss to take the holiday I thought they needed. My freedom was an extraordinary privilege.

Later I reflected on what I had done and learnt,[1] trying

> *...to make some sense out of and see some pattern in my own activities during the field stage of the project. For I have been doing **something** during this period, yet it has certainly been neither case study nor extensive survey... I have, it seems, been a research opportunist, if not exploiter, taking advantage of the survey and of my colleagues to try to conduct research quickly and perhaps somewhat unconventionally...*
>
> *There was a sense in which research opportunism was forced on me. A social anthropological approach was out of the question for reasons of training, inclination, family and language. The extensive survey was already (mercifully) being competently handled by the Madras and Colombo teams. With not much more than a year for fieldwork, divided between two countries with neither of which I was familiar, I had to work out the best way to use my time. Being a rather mediocre linguist, it made no sense to try to learn either Sinhala or Tamil well enough to be able to carry out interviews; and I decided it was better to know very little of either language than to spend time learning enough to be able to misunderstand and be misunderstood. An obvious decision would have been to concentrate on work which could be conducted entirely in English. This did apply to seed-breeding and agricultural research... More interesting from the methodological point of view are three other areas of concern requiring field work in rural areas which we tried to explore. These were agricultural extension, water management and inter-village comparisons.* (Chambers, 1974b)

My worst errors were in the work on agricultural extension. I had had to decide about a year in advance what I would work on. Agricultural extension was one of the aspects of the green revolution which we intended to examine and it became primarily my responsibility. But it turned out to be both less interesting and harder to research than I had expected. In tune with the preoccupations of the time, the main questions were to what extent differences in agricultural extension could account for differences in adoption of high-yielding varieties. The method had two main components: questions in the main questionnaire survey, and interviews with extension staff.

Now, in 2008, I am shocked by the arrogance and ignorance of my 'research'. I composed the survey questions in Cambridge and without prior knowledge of the extension programmes in the research areas. At the time of pilot testing of the questionnaire I was still in Africa. Responses to some questions were polluted by others asked earlier in the interview. The precoding of responses was inadequate. In the event about half the results were rejected as unusable, and some doubt remained about the value of the remainder. The lessons are obvious, and I should not have had to learn them.

Interviews with extension staff were also unsatisfactory. While outwardly co-operative, they were suspicious, especially when I wanted to see their (no doubt falsified) diaries. Only after repeated efforts was it possible to discover some details of the extension programme for paddy. The obvious lesson, which again I should not have had to learn, was that research by a foreigner on the lives and work of junior government field staff requires time, patience and rapport, and may have to be carried out by others. So it was that my colleague 'Wicks' was more successful and in spite of my errors we managed to write a joint paper (Chambers and Wickremanayake, 1977).

Water management was so different. At the start of the project we did not see it as a major interest. It coalesced as a focus, as topics do, from many sources, in this case observations in the field, discussions with farmers and among ourselves, an international Food and Agriculture Organization (FAO) seminar, and the guidance of officials in Sri Lanka for whom it was a priority. Unlike agricultural extension, it did not have a large literature or a school of research which had at all adequately examined it. (This was over a decade before the International Irrigation Management Institute was set up.) Consequently, what was required was not so much the research-intensive work needed to push understanding of agricultural extension any further, but less exacting and far more exciting reconnaissance research to open up a new subject. Madduma Bandara as a geographer-hydrologist, John Harriss as a social anthropologist, B. W. E. Wickremanayake in his capacity as fieldworker in charge of the survey, and I all engaged in the exploration. It was thrilling, with happy days paddling through paddy fields and stumbling on ahhas! like the multiple re-use of water 'wasted' in drains. We kept on learning new things, and uncovering new puzzles. It was indeed a 'new' subject, with low-hanging fruit which we eagerly spotted and picked.

Village comparisons were another subject that intrigued and enticed John Harriss and myself. In India we had a stratified sample of 12 villages, astonishingly different from each other, presenting a wonderful research and intellectual challenge, raising questions about dimensions that might be significant in accounting for differences, and inviting a taxonomy. We both visited all the villages. John's insights were deeper and broader than mine. We brainstormed and shared ideas. It was a great stimulation. Significant dimensions emerged of seasonality, livelihoods and irrigation systems, among others. It is to my discredit that we were only co-authors (and of course there is ambiguity because my initial comes earlier than John's in the alphabet) of the resulting Chambers and Harriss 1977 paper, when he should have been the senior author.

Reviewing these experiences it seemed that

> *The ways we have tackled these three topics ... differ in detail but they have in common:*
>
> - *a research-sparing character: in general they have not been research-intensive, but have required relatively low research inputs*
> - *ad hoc collaboration: collaboration has developed as we have gone along, and has not been pre-planned*
> - *eclectic pluralism in the choice of methods.*

and

> *The main lessons here are, first, the value of having sufficient spare capacity in a research team to be able to respond to an unforeseen priority or opportunity, and second, the usefulness of an eclectic use of several low-input research techniques, combined with free discussion and exchanges between researchers, as a system for opening up and exploring a subject.* (Chambers, 1974b)

I might have added the stimulation and even competitiveness of working in a team of ambitious young researchers!

The emergence of RRA

Now, in the latter 2000s, with an exploding variety of participatory approaches and methods, it is difficult to remember and realize again the pervasive tyranny of methodological rigidities and resistances in the 1970s. Social anthropologists believed that only their approach could yield in-depth understandings. Economists and statisticians believed that only questionnaires could generate the numbers needed in rigorous research. The researchers and practitioners who improvised and innovated outside these traditions were a heretical fringe and their methods disparagingly dismissed as 'quick-and-dirty'. They were trying to avoid the long-drawn-out, costly, and often irrelevant, misleading or confusing findings of anthropology or surveys. Their approach and methods came to be known as RRA (rapid rural appraisal).

However cost-effective, relevant and useful the methods of these heretics were, and however reliable their findings, they could feel impelled to make their obeisances to orthodoxy. In the evolution and acceptance of a methodology there is often an experience that is seminal and iconic, and spreads as a trans-formative and legitimizing story. With RRA, this was Michael Collinson's fieldwork in East Africa. In a week he would find out enough about the farming systems of an area to identify priorities for agricultural research. But for the sake of credibility he felt obliged to conduct a conventional questionnaire survey, taking some three months to carry out and even longer to analyse. The findings from the survey never contradicted his earlier conclusions but were necessary in order to convince the establishment (Collinson, 1979, 1981).

In the latter 1970s it became clear that other practically oriented researchers had like Collinson innovated and were using methods which they found good but which were not respectable in the mainstreams of their disciplines. Through networking, more and more were identified. A workshop in 1978 and a larger conference in 1979 were convened at the Institute of Development Studies (IDS) to bring such people together. There was a buzz of mutual recognition and support. The papers were widely distributed but never formally published.[2] The paper that follows, 'Rapid Rural Appraisal: Rationale and repertoire' (Chambers, 1981), was written and published as a poor substitute:

Rapid Rural Appraisal: Rationale and repertoire (1980)

The problem

Decision makers need information that is relevant, timely, accurate and usable. In rural development, a great deal of the information that is generated is, in various combinations, irrelevant, late, wrong and/or unusable anyway. It also often costs a lot to obtain, process, analyse and digest. Although many professionals have given thought to improving information gathering it remains a remarkably inefficient activity. Criteria of cost-effectiveness do not appear often to have been applied, and manifest inefficiency is sometimes met by demanding not better information, or less, but simply more.

The challenge is to find ways for outsiders to learn about rural conditions which are more cost-effective – which lead to information and understanding, which are closer to the optimal in trade-offs between cost of collection and learning, and relevance, timeliness, accuracy and actual beneficial use. A recent workshop and conference on Rapid Rural Appraisal (RRA)[3] have set out to examine this problem, paying particular attention to timeliness and economizing in data demands (Belshaw, 1981a, 1981b). This paper draws on the papers and discussions of those two occasions.

In the context of rural development projects, RRA appears especially relevant for identification and appraisal. Information is needed quickly; decisions are pre-empted by the passage of time. Commitment to projects and to details of projects sometimes becomes irreversible early on, setting a premium on timely information. But RRA is also relevant to implementation, monitoring and evaluation. Its relevance is enhanced by the view that rural development projects are not like construction works, with engineering blueprints which precisely predetermine what will be done, but rather like voyages into uncharted seas where direction and steering will change with new soundings and sightings. Techniques of RRA are hardly a new radar to prevent shipwreck; but they may at least reduce the dangers by showing more clearly and more quickly what is happening.

In practice, however, we seem to be trapped by two sets of inappropriate methods. These can be described as the 'quick-and-dirty' and the 'long-and-dirty', where 'dirty' means not cost-effective.

Quick-and-dirty

The most common form of quick-and-dirty appraisal is rural development tourism – the brief rural visit by the urban-based professional. This can be very cost-effective with the outstanding individual; one example is Wolf Ladejinsky (1969a and b) who in two remarkable short field trips in India saw what was happening in the green revolution and reported it years before plodding social scientists came to the same conclusion to two (spurious) points of decimals. But more commonly, rural tourism exerts biases [see Chapter 2] against perceiving rural poverty, reinforcing, in my view, underestimates of its prevalence and failures to understand its nature.

Many of the other defects of quick-and-dirty investigations are well known, but a list can serve as a warning:

- misleading replies (deferential, prudent, hoping to avoid penalties or to gain benefits)
- failure to listen (thinking the mouth is an organ of hearing)
- reinforced misperception and prejudice (those old hands who 'know-it-all' but who are projecting and selecting their own meanings)
- visible as against invisible: things and activities are seen, but not relationships – indebtedness, interest rates, low wages, patron–client relations, intra-family relations, etc.
- snapshot, not trend: a moment in time is seen, and trends, which may be much more significant for rural development purposes, are not seen.

The list could be lengthened, but the point is made: quick appraisal can be seriously misleading, especially when there is a concern with the poorer people. Rapid is often wrong.

Long-and-dirty

The solutions preferred by many well-trained professionals are longer and more costly. Social anthropologists perpetuate their ritual immersions in alien cultures; sociologists and agricultural economists plan and perpetrate huge questionnaire surveys; and scientists map soils, vegetation, land use and rainfall. All have their uses but most of them do not generate much information in their early stages.[4]

Some are academically excellent but useless: the social anthropologist's field-work published ten years later; the detailed soils map which sits on the shelf; the social survey which asked questions which were 'interesting' but of no use to a planner. ... Rural surveys must be one of the most inefficient industries in the world. Benchmark surveys are often criticised (Chambers, 1974b; Clay, 1978; Conlin, 1979), and yet these huge operations persist, often in the name of the science of evaluation, pre-empting scarce national research resources, and gen-erating mounds of data and papers which are likely to be an embarrassment to all until white ants or paper-shredders clean things up.

Some investigations are long and clean. The point here, though, is that long, however respectable professionally, is often inefficient. Moreover, the longer research takes, the longer and less usable the report tends to be and the greater the time available for sweeping the dirt under the carpet. Often the useful informa-tion from social anthropologists and from extensive questionnaire surveys comes coincidentally and informally during fieldwork, and not through the formal process at all.

Fairly-quick-and-fairly-clean

The question is, then, whether there is a middle zone between quick-and-dirty and long-and-dirty, a zone of greater cost-effectiveness. People in many discip-lines and professions have been converging on this question, but may have been deterred from writing it up because the activities are not quite proper. They have a sense of responsibility to their professional training or more crudely they have been brainwashed by their professional conditioning and reward systems. And yet in natural resources and environmental appraisal (Abel and Stocking, 1979; Richards, 1978; Stocking and Abel, 1979), health and nutrition (Chen et al, 1978; Gordon, 1979; Pacey, 1979; Payne, 1979; Walker, 1979), appraisal for agricultural research (Biggs, 1979; Byerlee et al, 1979; Carruthers, 1979a; Collinson, 1979; Hildebrand, 1979a, 1979b) and the field of socio-economic stratification (Honadle, 1979; Howes, 1979b; Longhurst, 1979) – in these fields and others there is an active search for shortcuts with trade-offs between timeliness, accuracy, relevance and actual use of information.

Formidable obstacles impede this process and this convergence. In the words of one participant at the RRA conference: 'By the time people leave university the damage has been done.' Inappropriate professional standards have been imparted and internalized. Perhaps the biggest single blockage is the hegemony of statisticians (Carruthers, 1979b; Fallon, 1979; Ellman, 1979; Moore, 1979b) and the failure to treat statistics as servant rather than master. In addition, professional values and reward systems deter improvisation in learning about rural conditions which though cost-effective may not seem pure. Better, it is thought, to be long and legitimate than short and suspect.

But cost-effective has its own rigour and should generate its own values. Two linked principles can be suggested:

1   **Optimal ignorance.** This refers to the importance of knowing what it is not worth knowing. It requires great courage to implement. It is far, far easier to demand more and more information than it is to abstain from demanding it. Yet in information gathering there is often a monstrous overkill.

2   **Proportionate accuracy.** Especially in surveys, much of the data collected has a degree of accuracy which is unnecessary. Orders of magnitude, and directions of change, are often all that is needed or that will be used.

With these two principles in mind, it is easier to see that less rigid, less exhaustive, and more rapid methods of rural appraisal may often be more rigorous in relation to cost and use. The following emerging repertoire of approaches and techniques is only part of a beginning. If much of this is common sense or common practice, I hope the reader will not feel insulted but rather will be provoked into criticism, comment and constructive suggestions for additions and improvement.

A start with a repertoire for RRA

What methods are best depends on purpose and circumstances. Some general principles can, however, be suggested:

- Taking time. RRA will avoid the tyranny of strict sampling, of the formal questionnaire, of the massive survey – in vain if time saved is dissipated in rushing. Many of rural tourism's defects come from haste.
- Offsetting biases. Taking thought about biases (urban, tarmac, roadside, project, elite, male, user, dry season, etc.), and deliberately offsetting them.
- Being unimportant. Avoiding the limousine-best-village-garlands-speeches syndrome.
- Listening and learning. Treating rural people as teachers and being their pupil. Assuming that they have much valid knowledge that outsiders do not have. Trying to get inside their skins and see the world as they do. Being open to unexpected information.
- Multiple approaches. Investigating the same questions with different methods, both to cross-check and to fill out the picture.

From the papers and discussions so far, ten disparate techniques for RRA stand out. This list is far from complete, but it illustrates some of the range and possibilities.

I   Existing information

There is often a wealth of information in archives, annual reports, reports of surveys, academic papers, government statistics, and the like. There is also a recurrent tendency to ignore them and to start *de novo*. Time spent searching for such information, even when it is not known to exist, is often well repaid; and it may save unnecessary demands for much new data collection.

2 Learning ITK (indigenous technical knowledge)[5]

Development disasters often follow from failing to learn from rural people. The Groundnut Scheme might have been prevented by more time on the ground (instead of in the air) asking local inhabitants why they did not cultivate in the proposed project area. More radically, rural people often have a wealth of knowledge, and a validity of insight, which the outsider lacks. The Hanunoo in the Philippines are said to have had, on average, a knowledge of 1600 names for plants, 430 more than those in a botanical survey (Howes, 1979a, citing Conklin, 1957). The !Kung San of Botswana have a knowledge of animal behaviour often superior to that of scientists (Blurton Jones and Konner, 1976). Examples could be multiplied. Knowledge of soils, seasons, plants, domestic and wild animals, farming practices, diet, cooking practices, and child care, not to mention social customs and relations, are often rich and likely often to be superior in some or all respects to those of the outsider. The scope for soils mapping using ITK appears largely unexplored. The scope, on the social side, for asking rural people themselves to identify who are the poorer people, has been far from adequately used. Heavy survey expenditures could sometimes be reduced dramatically through using ITK instead of inappropriate 'sophisticated' approaches.

3 Using key indicators

Some indicators integrate several variables. Investigating, calibrating, observing and counting such indicators may then provide a shortcut avoiding more expensive, direct and time-consuming investigations.

Some examples are:

- **Soil colour** as a predictor of particle size distribution, fertility, some important engineering properties such as plasticity and volumetric activity (Stocking and Abel, 1979), and vegetation associations.
- **Plant indicators**, subject to local knowledge, can be 'an extremely reliable, efficient and rapid indicator of natural resources information' (Stocking and Abel, 1979).
- **Birth weight** of children reflects the health and nutritional status of mothers especially in the last trimester of pregnancy and is a predictor of chances of survival and (though less well established) of the future growth trajectory (Philip Payne, personal communication).
- **Housing** as an indicator of poverty or prosperity. There are no doubt qualifications and exceptions, yet this is found again and again (see e.g. Richards, 1978; Honadle, 1979; Longhurst, 1979; Howes, 1979b; Moore, 1979a) and may be useful (not least because so visible and easy to count) as a proxy for relative poverty or prosperity between villages and for the same village over time.
- **Transfers and turnover** in organizations may be a proxy for organizational capability.

While these and other indicators require local validation, they may provide shortcuts to insights; some may also provide simple measures for baselines if before–after evaluation is required, avoiding massive data collection.

4 Adaptations of Hildebrand's 'sondeo'

Peter Hildebrand, working with ICTA,[6] has developed an ingenious method for multi-disciplinary work in preparation for on-farm agricultural research (Hildebrand, 1978; 1979a and 1979b). A homogeneous cropping system among many farmers in an area has first been identified. Hildebrand then takes a team of five agricultural scientists and five social scientists to the area for a week. The team works in pairs, one agricultural scientist and one social scientist. They go out each day and learn what they can from farmers and others, returning in the evening to share experiences, take stock, and decide on further priorities. Each day the pairs change so that each agricultural scientist works for one day with each social scientist and vice versa. A report is written over the weekend. This is 'not a benchmark study with quantifiable data that can be used in the future for project evaluation; rather it is a working document to orient the research program...' (Hildebrand, 1979a).

Hildebrand's method has been used to familiarize staff with an area in which they are to work, and to identify innovations which might be tried out directly with farmers. It is easy to see that it might be adapted for other purposes. For project identification and appraisal, visiting teams might pair with themselves or with local officials. For monitoring and evaluation, it might be used to identify what changes have taken place and their causality. In principle, it might be applied in many fields, including natural resources appraisal (including rural people as sondeo team members), health and nutrition, and social and economic dimensions. It provides a structure for mutual learning between disciplines, and its time-bound form and the mutual checking in the evening sessions provide a stimulus for speed and accuracy.

5 Local researchers

Information can be gathered by rural residents. The use of cultivators and pastoralists (Swift, 1978) for investigating and recording is underdeveloped. School teachers, traders and the rural staff of government departments are a major, but often underused, source for information, including time series data and ad hoc enquiries. The value of research carried out by national university students also deserves to be emphasized. In a matter of a few weeks, a Murundi refugee student in Zaire investigated fishing among Barundi refugees and produced an excellent and practical report. A student who has links with a rural area can be not only key informant but can also very quickly and efficiently find out what needs to be known.

6 Direct observation

A major danger with RRA is being misled by myth. Rural people (like others) often have beliefs about their values and activities which do not correspond with the reality. It is common to be told about a custom, but probing for the last occasion when it was practised reveals that it has either lapsed or perhaps was never practised at all. Conlin records (1979) how he worked as a social anthropologist in an area in Peru where a sociologist carried out a survey. According to the sociologist's results, people invariably worked together on each others' individually held plots of land. This is what people told him. The belief was important to their understanding of themselves as a certain sort of people. Yet in one year's residence in the village, Conlin only observed this practice once. With RRA, direct observation may often not be possible; in that case, multiple checks on information about customs and practices are desirable. The importance of walking, seeing and asking questions is a commonplace. One of the most effective, though time-consuming, ways of learning is by doing. John Hatch hired himself out as a labourer to farmers and found the labour requirement of maize cultivation to be 50 per cent higher than that recorded in surveys (Hatch, 1976) besides learning much else from his farmer teachers.

7 Key informants

While there are well-known dangers, and cross-checking is necessary, key informants are a major tool for RRA. Some of the most useful are social anthropologists who are in the field. They often do not know what they know; they often give precious insights and raise unexpected questions. Key local informants tend to be the better off, the better educated, and the more powerful. The biases this introduces can be consciously offset; and school teachers, in particular, can be a source of somewhat independent-minded views. In organizational appraisal, Honadle (1979) asked staff a question on the lines: 'In all organizations there is at least one pain-in-the-neck, there is always someone who disagrees with all decisions and promotes trouble. Can you tell the names of those people in your association?' Answers were immediate and enthusiastic; individual interviews with those named provided valuable cross-checks and revealed useful additional information. More generally, for any subject of interest, it is worthwhile spending time asking who, or which group of people, are most knowledgeable, and then working with them.

8 Group interviews

Group interviews have several advantages, including access to a larger body of knowledge, and mutual checking. They can also be seriously misleading when the questioner is believed to have power to control benefits or sanctions. They are especially useful for natural resources information, when a wider geographical area and subject matter can be covered than with one respondent. I have used this method for very rapid mapping of soil/vegetation associations in the North-East Province of Kenya. Group interviews may also be good for certain sensitive types of information. To ask, for example, about land quality may arouse suspicion in an individual that his land may be subject to some penalty if he replies truthfully, whereas a group gathered together as people knowledgeable about farming will not feel so threatened (Jackson et al, 1978). Ladejinsky (1969b) records of a landlord in Bihar: 'He first informed us that he owned 16 acres of land but corrected himself under the good humoured prodding of a crowd of farmers that he had failed to mention another 484 acres.' The lapse of memory might have had something to do with the ceiling on land-holdings.

Group interviews have also been used to gather information rapidly on changes in infant feeding practices. Small clusters of 5–6 women of 2–3 generations were assembled, and past, present and expected future patterns of infant feeding discussed. 'There was a self-correcting mechanism within the group because if one person put across an over-favourable picture of her own or her group's behaviour, a peer would give a more realistic observation. In cross-checking with other groups a high degree of uniformity of information was found' (Gordon, 1979).

9 The guided interview[7]

The guided interview is probably a quite widespread but largely unreported activity. There is no formal questionnaire but a checklist of questions which the interviewer uses as a flexible guide. Ellman's (1979) two-page checklist devised for appraisal of a rural refugee situation in Africa, and Carruthers' (1979a) critical review procedure for on-farm interviews are examples of procedures for interviews without pre-set questionnaires, but with an agenda to be covered. Collinson (1979) has developed this approach with guidelines for discussion with farmers, in which not all points are raised with all farmers, but in which a composite picture is built up so that a scenario can be written. This is evidently an effective tool for diagnosing farming problems and opportunities in a matter of weeks, and can be used by investigators with a professional training but who lack extensive field experience.

10 Aerial inspection and surveys

Jokes about experts in aeroplanes should not detract from the selective value of aerial inspection and surveys. Animals are most rapidly counted from the air (Swift, 1978). For certain types of natural resource surveys, there are advantages (Abel and Stocking, 1979), including offsetting urban and dry season biases. The danger is that aerial surveys become substitutes for other approaches, especially understanding and using indigenous technical knowledge. Ground control should usually, if not always, include learning from rural people.

Other points could be added to the repertoire: the use of informal transects (such as walking away from the road at right angles); rural innovators' surveys in which new practices are sought out; methods of establishing rapport, in which liquor so frequently figures[8] in non-Muslim societies; one-day censuses of users of services (Walker, 1979); and linking RRA in with on-going 'long-and-clean' investigations or research, making use of what is already known. But, hopefully enough has been said to show that RRA has a battery of techniques, and to suggest that using combinations with care may be much more cost-effective for some purposes than either quicker or longer alternatives.

Conclusions

This illustrative list of techniques shows that RRA is no panacea. Much of it is merely organized common sense, freed from the chains of inappropriate professionalism. But because it is often cost-effective compared with more conventional alternatives, it deserves to be accorded more attention, more prestige, and more coverage in professional writing.

For project preparation it may provide a battery of methods for improving the chances of being right, and of having information when it is needed. For monitoring and evaluation, it may provide ways into the difficult questions about impacts, trends and causality which are, or should be, the core of evaluation.

That there are dangers of superficiality and error needs no emphasis. The key to successful RRA is not avoiding superficiality and error, but controlling them, trying to achieve cost-effectiveness through optimal ignorance and proportionate accuracy.

Finally, the most critical factor remains time. RRA, by its sparing demands for information, should release time which can be used for checking, for identifying unasked questions, and for noting and pursuing serendipity. Above all, it should release time for more contact with, and learning from, the poorer rural people. In most investigations, whether quick or long, they are the residual category, the last in line, those who are not consulted, those whose problems are not articulated. Shortage of time compounds the interlocking biases which shut them out. More time can be used to let them in. If RRA, whatever its defects, were to enable rural appraisers to spend more time learning about and understanding rural poverty, then the choice, design and implementation of rural projects might shift over time so that the poor gained more. That may be the naive hope of an optimist; but at least it seems worth pursuing.

Postscript (2008)

RRA came of age in the 1980s. The landmark event was the international conference on RRA convened in 1985 at the University of Khon Kaen in Thailand, at that time the leading pioneering institution in the world for RRA. The volume of proceedings (Khan Kaen University, 1987) is an authoritative and inspiring source on RRA, and much of it remains as relevant today as it was in the 1980s.

The conference brought together many practitioners, and many methods and approaches. Among the most significant were agroecosystem analysis (Gypmantasiri et al, 1980; Conway, 1985), evolved by Gordon Conway and his colleagues at the University of Chiang Mai and spread throughout South-east Asia, and semi-structured interviewing which had come to be regarded as at the core of good RRA (Grandstaff and Grandstaff, 1987a, b). Elucidating the paradigmatic significance of RRA, Neil Jamieson (1987) provided theory to support and interpret practice, drawing on cybernetics and emphasizing interaction, relationships, feedback, local knowledge and context, and the need for 'greater epistemological humility and flexibility' (Khan Kaen University, 1987, p100).

After the conference, the core principles of RRA were summarized (Khan Kaen University, 1987, pp9–13):

- Triangulation: approaching information from several intentionally different points of view, informants, sources, methods, places ... 'normally involving conscious non-random sampling in a number of different dimensions' usually at least for team composition, units of observation, and research methods (p10).
- Exploratory and highly iterative research: 'The sooner inappropriate hypotheses can be abandoned or reformulated on the basis of new information, the faster one learns ... semi-structured interviewing is normally one of the principal methods because it enables researchers to rapidly change questions, interviews and directions as new information appears ... RRA researchers must particularly be on the lookout for the unexpected' (p10).
- Rapid and progressive learning: 'RRA's emphasis on rapid and progressive learning is one of the most distinguishing traits of the methodology. This contrasts sharply with survey research and its predesigned and fixed questionnaires where there is a general absence of progressive learning during the majority of field activities' (p11).
- Substantial use of indigenous knowledge: '...an understanding of indigenous knowledge and practices is extremely valuable for viable and appropriate rural development, and many of the methods, tools and techniques of RRA have been selected for their abilities to elicit, evaluate, understand, and avoid misunderstanding indigenous knowledge' (p11).
- Interdisciplinary approach and teamwork: 'A small team of researchers representing different disciplines is normally used in RRA to obtain the range of expertise needed to better understand rural situations... Team members acquire valuable additional learning from each other when they interact closely in the field... Methods and techniques are employed that facilitate this...' (pp11–12).
- Flexibility and use of conscious judgement: '...an important principle of RRA is not just to "plan the work", but also to "work the plan" in a flexible manner that allows for creativity and modification ... the RRA team must be prepared to revise their time schedules and travel and interviewing plans in the same manner that they are prepared to revise hypotheses... Two of the most important and basic types of decisions the team has to make, at the start of and during the course of an RRA, are what types of information are needed and what degrees of precision are required or possible" applying the principles of appropriate impression and optimal ignorance' (p12).

These are striking as precursors of participatory rural appraisal (PRA). A major shift in the transition to PRA was that the intense interactions within multidisciplinary teams that characterize classical RRA became intense interactions among local people, often in small groups. Another is who does the appraisal and analysis – outsiders with RRA, local people with PRA. But that said, the commonalities are strong and RRA passed on many of its genes to PRA.

Using this form of words makes RRA sound passé. Tragically, many of the practices and principles of RRA have been forgotten. It is as though their shelf life has expired. It is a sad reflection on the short memories and fickle fashions of development practice that when PRA came along in the early 1990s, many came to regard RRA as old hat and many of its good practices were lost. It became unusual to find the label used.[9] It was easy to denigrate RRA as outsider-driven and extractive, whereas PRA was participatory and empowering. But in practice PRA methods were often used in an extractive RRA mode! And the visual methods of PRA were so attractive, and effective, that the old wonderful practices of just talking, of having a good conversation, and even of a flexible semi-structured interview with an informal checklist, were downgraded, rushed or entirely overlooked. But RRA approaches and methods will always be important and valuable. They complement those of PRA. They deserve a revolution, a turning of the wheel, a renaissance.

Appendix: Some sources, approaches and methods

Sources include three collections of articles on RRA from the 1980s:

1   Longhurst, Richard (ed) (1981) 'Rapid Rural Appraisal: Social structure and rural economy', *IDS Bulletin,* vol 12, no 4, October, with an editorial and articles by Geof D.Wood, Paul Richards, Deryke Belshaw, Richard Longhurst, Ingrid Palmer, Mick Howes, Mick Moore and ODA Food Strategy Team, together with a list of papers to the IDS 1978 workshop and 1979 conference on RRA.
2   Carruthers, Ian and Robert Chambers (eds) (1981) Special Issue on Rapid Rural Appraisal. *Agricultural Administration,* vol 8, no 6, with articles by the editors, Peter Hildebrand, Michael Collinson, C. D. S. Bartlett and J. E. Ikeorgu, Antony Ellman, Michael Stocking and Nick Abel, and Jeremy Swift.
3   Khon Kaen University (1987) *Proceedings of the Conference on Rapid Rural Appraisal,* Khon Kaen University, Thailand, 2–5 September 1985, contains Summary Report; the need for RRA, its evolution and underlying concepts (four papers); the range of methodology: important methods, tools and techniques of RRA (five papers); contexts and types of RRA application (six papers); and an extensive bibliography.

The best documented continuation and development of RRA (apart from PRA, for which see Chapter 5) has been named RAP, standing for Rapid Assessment Procedures (Scrimshaw and Gleason, 1992) or Rapid Assessment Process. James Beebe's (2001) book *Rapid Assessment Process: An Introduction* is the most substantial, authoritative and useful recent source of which I know. It includes practical advice and a good list of sources.

Approaches are many and have many labels (Beebe, 2001, pp152–153, lists 55). They make use of many **methods** including:[10]

- existing information/secondary data
- indigenous technical knowledge
- key indicators
- teamwork, and team contracts and interactions (Hildebrand, 1981; Beebe, 2001)
- local researchers
- direct observation – see for yourself
- key informants – seek out the experts
- group interviews
- semi-structured (or guided) interviews
- aerial inspection and surveys
- offsetting the biases of rural development tourism (see Chapters 2 and 8)
- transect walks (see Chapter 3)
- sketch mapping (see Chapter 7)
- Kipling's Six Servants:

   I keep six honest serving men
   (They taught me all I knew);
   Their names are What and Why and When
   And How and Where and Who
   (from 'The Elephant's Child' in *The Just So Stories*)

- progressive sequences of sources and analysis
- key probes (key exploratory questions to open up topics and areas)
- non-directive probes (Beebe, 2001, p38)
- time lines
- diagramming (seasonal, trend, histograms…).

Practitioners of RRA and RAP have tended not to facilitate participatory mapping and diagramming, but in the spirit of eclectic pluralism (Chapter 9) these can and do strengthen RRA-type practices and processes.

Notes

1   In two papers: 'Practices in Social Science Research: Some heresies' presented in Colombo and 'Opportunism in Rural Research' presented in Cambridge, UK in December 1974 and from which the quotations in this section were taken.

2   The IDS Conference on Rapid Rural Appraisal was funded by the Ford Foundation, but the budget did not include dissemination. Despite having an experienced and enthusiastic editor, Arnold Pacey, able and willing to edit the papers, the needed $10,000 could not be raised. I have often wondered how much faster the evolution of RRA, and perhaps even of PRA, would have

been if that small sum had been found and an authoritative book published. Excellent material was there. But then in those days dissemination had a much lower priority than it (correctly) does now.

3   The Workshop on Rapid Rural Appraisal, 26–27 October 1978 (Barnett, 1979), and the Conference on Rapid Rural Appraisal, 4–7 December 1979, both at the Institute of Development Studies, University of Sussex. Appraisal is used here in its general sense and not just that of project appraisal.

4   There are exceptions, especially in natural resources surveys.

5   For six articles on this, see IDS (1979). In this paper, I am treating ITK simply as a resource to be tapped. This ignores its capacity for development and growth, and its importance as a dynamic entity enabling people to control their environment and enhance their quality of life.

6   Instituto de Ciencia y Tecnologia Agricolas, Guatemala.

It might complement very nicely the Benor Training and Visit System of Agricultural Extension. [I lament the way this footnote shows that at the time I approved of the Training and Visit System, which now I consider to be fundamentally flawed.]

7   The guided interview is better known now as the semi-structured interview (Grandstaff and Grandstaff, 1987a; Beebe, 2001, pp35–40).

8   Thus Paul Richards, on failing to identify unasked questions 'Luck, persistence, a sixth sense and palm wine are potential antidotes, but palm wine is probably the best' (1978), and Marie Therese Feuerstein on rapport 'Good informal rapport can be established by moderate drinking, smoking, singing, and particularly dancing or the playing of a musical instrument' (1979).

9   Notable exceptions were RRAs to inform policies on land tenure in Tanzania (Johansson and Hoben, 1992), and Madagascar and Guinea (Freudenberger, 1998). These led officials who took part to change their views of land tenure quite radically.

10 Sources for this listing are this chapter and 'Notes for Participants in Whose Reality Counts? Very short (1–2 day) PRA/PLA-related Familiarisation Workshops in 2008', available at www.ids.ac.uk/ppsc

5

PRA: Pathways, Practice and Principles

Bliss was it in that dawn to be alive. (Wordsworth, *The Prelude*)

Abstract

RRA, agroecosystem analysis and other approaches and methods converged in the late 1980s. Ahha! experiences, like discovering that local people could map and diagram, and do these better than outsiders, led to the explosion of innovation known as PRA (participatory rural appraisal) which spread into many countries and organizations, with many applications. PRA and the more inclusive PLA (participatory learning and action) are families of participatory methodologies. During the 1990s and 2000s PRA/PLA has spread and been applied in most countries in the world. Among the multifarious domains of application, some of the more common have been natural resource management and agriculture, programmes for equity, empowerment, rights and security, and community-level planning and action. Related participatory methodologies, which have co-evolved and spread widely as movements, include farmer participatory research, integrated pest management, Reflect, Stepping Stones and Participatory Geographic Information Systems (PGIS) (Chapter 7). Ideologically and epistemologically, PRA/PLA seeks and embodies participatory ways to empower local and subordinate people, enabling them to express and enhance their knowledge and take action. It can be understood as having three main components that feed into and reinforce current creative diversity: first, facilitators' behaviours, attitudes and mindsets linked with precepts for action; second, methods which combine visuals, tangibles and groups, and understandings of group-visual synergy and the democracy of the ground; and third, sharing without boundaries. These raise questions around power, roles, realities and whose reality counts? As different methodologies, approaches and methods have multiplied and merged, it has become less clear what PRA/PLA is or should mean. The future lies not in branding and boundaries but in eclectic pluralism, a theme taken up in Chapter 9.

Practice: What has happened?

Participatory rural appraisal

Since the mid-1970s there has been an accelerating evolution of participatory methodologies in development practice. One part of this has been a sequence known by its acronyms – rapid rural appraisal (RRA) (Chapter 4), participatory rural appraisal (PRA), and participatory learning and action (PLA). These can be described as sets of approaches, methods, behaviours and relationships for finding out about local context and life. All three continue to be practised and are in various ways complementary. In the late 1980s and early 1990s PRA evolved out of RRA. In PRA outsiders convene and facilitate. Local people, especially those who are poorer and marginalized, are the main actors. It is they, typically in small groups, who map, diagram, observe, analyse and act. The term 'participatory learning and action', introduced in 1995, is sometimes used to describe PRA but is broader and includes other similar or related approaches and methods. Because of the continuities and overlaps this methodological cluster or family is sometimes referred to as PRA/PLA or even RRA/PRA/PLA. Some, as in Pakistan, have sought to accommodate the shifts in practice by taking PRA to mean participatory reflection and action.[1] But increasingly practitioners in this tradition have moved beyond these labels and created new and specialized adaptations, some of these with other names. While continuing to use and evolve PRA methods and principles, many practitioners have become eclectic methodological pluralists.

In the early 1990s the main features of PRA emerged, with three principal components. These were shown as three connected circles: methods; behaviour and attitudes; and sharing.

PRA methods, as they are often called, are visual and tangible and usually performed by small groups. These are the most visible and obviously distinctive

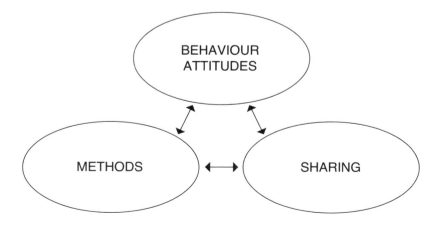

Figure 5.1 *Three principal components of PRA* (Mascarenhas et al, 1991, p35A)

feature of PRA. Maps and diagrams are made by local people, often on the ground using local materials, but sometimes on paper (Chapter 7). Many sorts of map are made – most commonly social or census maps showing people and their characteristics, resource maps showing land, trees, water and so on, and mobility maps showing where people travel for services. Using earth, sand, stones, seeds, twigs, chalk, charcoal, paper, pens and other materials, and objects as symbols, women, men and children make diagrams to represent many aspects of their communities, lives and environments. The methods include time lines, trend and change diagrams, wealth and well-being ranking, seasonal diagramming, Venn diagrams, causal linkage diagrams, and proportional piling. Matrix ranking and scoring are used for complex and detailed comparisons. And there are many variants and combinations of these and other methods or tools.[2]

Behaviour and attitudes, later construed as mindsets, behaviour and attitudes, were from early on regarded by many of the pioneers as more important than the methods. They were the focus of a South–South international workshop which led to the publication of the *ABC of PRA* (Kumar, 1996), where ABC stands for attitude and behaviour change. Some behaviours and attitudes were expressed as precepts (see Box 5.1, p98) like 'Hand over the stick', 'Don't rush', 'Sit down, listen and learn' and 'Use your own best judgement at all times'.

Sharing initially referred to villagers sharing their knowledge, all sharing food, and the sharing of training, ideas, insights, methods and materials between organizations, mainly non-governmental organizations (NGOs) and government. By the mid-2000s the sharing circle had come to include relationships. The key phrase 'sharing without boundaries' (Absalom et al, 1995) came out of an international workshop of PRA practitioners and sought to make doubly clear the principle of openness and sharing between methodologies. It was also a preemptive strike against the claims of branding and exclusive ownership which go with some methodologies.

The evolution of PRA and PLA

In the evolution of PRA there was much intermingling and innovation (Chambers, 1994, 1997). Among other sources were the approaches and methods of action science (Argyris et al, 1985), reflection-in-action (Schön, 1983, 1987), popular education (Freire, 1970) and participatory research and participatory action research (BRAC, 1983; Rahman, 1984; Fals-Borda and Rahman, 1991). From farming systems research came recognition of local diversity and complexity (Norman, 1975), and from social anthropology the richness and detail of indigenous technical knowledge (e.g. Brokensha, et al, 1980; Richards, 1985). The work of the Highlander Research and Education Centre in Rural Appalachia (Gaventa and Horton, 1981; Gaventa and Lewis, 1991; Gaventa, 1993), contributed the seminal insight that local people with little education were much more capable of doing their own appraisal and analysis than professionals believed.

In the origins of PRA, the largest stream, though, was the confluence of agroecosystem analysis (Gypmantasiri et al, 1980; Conway, 1985) with RRA (Khon

Kaen University, 1987 and Chapter 4). RRA had semi-structured interviewing at its core (Grandstaff and Grandstaff, 1987a). Agroecosystem analysis crucially contributed sketch mapping, diagramming, transects and observation. The big breakthroughs were then the discoveries (or rediscoveries, for there are almost always antecedents) that with light and sensitive facilitation local people could themselves make the maps and diagrams, and that, especially when they worked in small groups, what they presented demonstrated a complexity, diversity, accuracy and for many purposes relevance far superior to anything that could be elicited or expressed using earlier extractive or observational methodologies. This led to the practical principle that 'They can do it' applied to activity after activity, recognizing that local people had far greater abilities for analysis, action, experimentation, research and monitoring and evaluation than had been supposed by outside professionals or by themselves.

The stream flowed from RRA to PRA to PLA. PRA was most clearly identifiable in the first half of the 1990s. In 1995 the core publication for PRA experiences, still known as *RRA Notes*, was renamed *Participatory Learning and Action (PLA) Notes*.[3]

For both RRA and the PRA/PLA that grew out of it there was a multiplicity of parallel and simultaneous innovations which co-evolved, spread and inspired. The Sustainable Agriculture Programme at the International Institute for Environment and Development, in London, played a key part in the RRA–PRA–PLA evolutions, transitions and spread. In what was labelled PRA, several traditions developed. An early form in Kenya was evolved by Clark University and the National Environment Secretariat, adopted by Egerton University, and embodied in handbooks (e.g. PID and NES, c.1989) which supported stand-ardized training for a sequence of activities leading to Community Action Plans. This approach was then applied in parts of East and West Africa, for example in The Gambia (Holmes 2001; Brown et al, 2002). In India, a few staff in two NGOs – the Aga Khan Rural Support Programme (AKRSP) (India) in Gujarat and MYRADA in Karnataka and Tamil Nadu – were major contributors to an epicentre of PRA innovation which generated the more open-ended approaches that then spread much more widely in India and the world.[4] These approaches in turn took different forms (Pratt, 2001): some stressed methods more; others were more reflective and more concerned with quality of facilitation, attitudes and behaviours. In the early 1990s a proliferation of acronym labels marked an early stage of enthusiastic innovation and claims of ownership. Like the phyla of the Cambrian explosion or the steam engines of the early industrial revolution, many of these labels soon died out. What persisted were the practices and the acronyms PRA and PLA, the latter adopted, though sometimes used synonymously with PRA, in order to be more inclusive of other participatory methodologies in the spirit of sharing without boundaries.

In the 2000s PRA and PLA have diffused, borrowed and interpenetrated with other approaches. They have evolved and merged into a new creative pluralism (Cornwall and Guijt, 2004) in which earlier traditions survive but in which many methods have been evolved and adapted. Many of the early PRA practitioners have become more reflective and self-critical (Cornwall and Pratt,

2003). Others continue in earlier, sometimes routinized, traditions. In the latter 2000s it is not clear what the term PRA can or should now usefully describe. For many it remains associated with group-visual activities, and with behaviour, attitudes and relationships of facilitation which empower participants. In parallel with the persistence of traditional PRA, and of other established participatory methodologies, more and more practitioner/facilitators have become creative pluralists, borrowing, improvising and inventing for particular contexts, sectors and needs.

Reflecting critically on the evolution of PRA, theory has been implicit in and has co-evolved with practice. As with RRA earlier (Jamieson, 1987), theory was induced from and fed back into practice. Practice itself was driven and drawn not by academic analysis, nor by a reflective analytical book like *Pedagogy of the Oppressed* (Freire, 1970), but by the excitement of innovation, discovery and informal networking. The main pioneers were not academic intellectuals but workers and staff in NGOs in the South, especially India, and a few from research institutes in the North, all of them learning through engagement in the field. And the detail of the methods came from the creativity and inventiveness of local people, once they had the idea of what they could do, as well as from the outside facilitators.

Ahhas! Excitement

This dry history gives no idea of what the experience was like. Since I have had the time and opportunity to write about RRA and PRA, my own part in their development has been exaggerated. All the same, I had the luck and privilege to be part of the process, and especially to have two years in India in 1989–91, funded[5] and free to spend time with the Indian innovators who were so rapidly co-evolving with villagers the main methods and approaches of PRA.

We could hardly believe what was unfolding. We kept on saying to one another – 'This is amazing'. There were so many ahhas! and wows! Jenny McCracken (1989) and Meera Kaul Shah (2003, p189) have written about an early one – the seminal experience at Lathodara in Gujarat in 1988 when in an RRA mode the outsiders drew maps and diagrams and then asked the villagers to present them. The villagers had difficulty: the headman eventually turned the sketch map upside down in order to see it his way. And some others could not understand the seasonality and transect diagrams, and so presented the information in their own manner.

My own pathway had a sequence of ahha!s parallel to that of others. The most striking were:

- In Ethiopia, in 1988 when two Ethiopian interviewers asked three farmers questions comparing labour demand by month and then drew a histogram. When they asked the farmers if they could understand the diagram, they looked and replied: 'Yes, you have drawn what we said.'[6]
- In the Sudan in February 1989, how embarrassed we and the villagers were in an RRA training when we checked out a village map we had spent two days

drawing, and the villagers said: 'You have shown only one bakery, but we have three.'

- In West Bengal, later in 1989, when tribal men and women drew on the ground their own histograms of agricultural labour by month, and then the women capped it by adding a big block for all their other tasks.
- In the first PRAs in late 1989 in India, the discovery that villagers could map and model so much better than we could.
- In Karnataka in August 1990, seeing the first (for me) matrix scoring, different from the ranking we had been doing, of five varieties of millet, facilitated by Vidya Ramachandran.
- In Gujarat, the first (for me) causal linkage diagramming by a farmer, for flows and effects of an irrigation system, facilitated by Anil Shah.

In 1989–91, in India, many began to innovate. To name some and not others risks unfairness, but prominent innovators included Jimmy Mascarenhas, Sam Joseph, Anil Shah, Parmesh Shah, Meera Kaul Shah, Sheelu Francis, John Devavaram, Somesh Kumar, Prem Kumar, Kamal Kar, Ravi Jayakaran and Neela Mukherjee, many of whom went on in the 1990s to introduce and spread PRA around the world. And the wonder and elation did not die away as the pioneers travelled to other countries. Here are extracts from a letter from Jimmy Mascarenhas dated 13 May 1993:

> *I just got back from Zimbabwe/South Africa after a thoroughly rewarding and I think extremely fruitful trip.*
>
> *...Every time, I am amazed at the miracle of transformation that takes place in terms of the 'participant flip'! The other miracle that takes place **every time** is the one of villager participation. You know, we've done so many of these PRA field exercises – and in varied locations and conditions too. Every time I undertake one, there is a small voice in the back of my head asking 'Are the villagers going to participate? Is it going to work this time? Am I going to be able to demonstrate the methods to these guys?' And every time the same miracle takes place. Not only do the villagers participate, but they actually take over. In my last PRA in Zimbabwe, I had the rare spectacle of the interviewers (Forestry Commission Staff) reading newspapers and baby sitting for the interviewees, who were a group of farm women, while the women did resource mapping, matrix ranking and seasonality exercises in connection with a forestry plan! They **knew** what they wanted and told us so. One of the Forestry Commission staff who was with us made a remark saying that in 30 years of extension he had never ever experienced anything like this!*

Spread and applications

From 1990, the spread of PRA was rapid throughout much of the world (Singh, 2001; Holmes, 2002; Cornwall and Pratt, 2003). By 2000 practices described as PRA were probably to be found in well over 100 countries, of the North as well as of the South. They were being used by all or almost all prominent international non-governmental organizations (INGOs) and many of their partners, by many donor and lender supported projects, and by a number of government departments, for example in India, Kenya and Vietnam.

With rapid spread, bad practice became rampant. The methods were so attractive, often photogenic, and so amenable to being taught in a normal didactic manner that they gained priority over behaviour, attitudes and relationships, especially in training institutes. Manuals proliferated and were mechanically taught and applied. Donors and lenders demanded PRA. Behaviour and attitudes were neglected or totally ignored in much training. PRA was routinized, local people's time was taken and their expectations raised without any outcome, methods were used to extract information not to empower, and consultants who had no experience claimed to be trainers. Communities were 'PRA'd'. Some in Malawi were said to have been 'carpet-bombed with PRA'. Just as academics began to wake up to what had been happening, there was much to criticize. The looseness of the one sentence principle 'Use your own best judgement at all times' could be liberating, giving freedom to improvise and invent; and it supported much brilliant performance and innovation. But equally, it could combine with an exclusive fixation on methods to allow sloppy and abusive practice.

Academic critics of PRA were not always able to draw on personal experience, or sometimes drew on their own defective practice. In consequence, some of the criticisms, for example in *Participation: The New Tyranny?* (Cooke and Kothari, 2001), were not well informed. Much was made of the well-known shortcomings of community public meetings, overlooking the value and widespread use of smaller groups. And criticisms that should have been made were overlooked, for example the common bias against women's participation inherent in PRA visual analysis since this tends to require undisturbed blocks of time usually harder for women to find than for men. Many practitioners, keenly aware of this problem, took determined steps to offset it. And from the mid-1990s, articulate practitioners were increasingly self-critical and reflective in a rich range of publications.[7]

In parallel, the applications of PRA approaches and methods, not alone but often combined and adapted with others, have been and continue to be astonishingly varied. They are constantly evolving and being invented. To at least some degree, all entail an element of participatory research. Most have never been recorded or published. The incomplete but illustrative list in Table 5.1, for natural resource management and agriculture, and for programmes for empowerment, equity, rights and security gives some sense of the range.

In addition there have been innumerable applications in other rural and urban domains, not least in community and local planning (Swantz et al, 2001; *PLA Notes* 44, 2002 and 49, 2004; Swantz, 2008), market analysis (*PLA Notes* 33, 1998), health (*RRA Notes* 16, 1992), food security assessment (e.g. Levy, 2003), water, sanitation (Kar references), organizational analysis, and participatory spatial analysis and Geographic Information Systems (Chapter 7). PRA approaches and methods have been used for policy analysis. There have been many applications in participatory monitoring, evaluation and impact assessment (e.g. Guijt, 1998; Estrella et al, 2000; Mayoux and Chambers, 2005). There has been increasing methodological pluralism and inventiveness that

Table 5.1 *Some applications of PRA approaches and methods*

Natural resource management and agriculture	Programmes for empowerment, equity, rights and security
(Pimbert, 2004; Borrini-Feyerabend et al, 2004; Gonsalves et al, 2005) including agriculture, crops and animal husbandry (Catley and Mariner, 2002; PLA Notes 45, 2002; PRGA, c. 2002)	Participatory Poverty Assessments (Norton et al, 2001; Robb, 2002) and understandings of poverty and well-being (White and Pettit, 2004)
Forestry, especially Joint Forest Management, and agroforestry (Forests Trees and People Newsletter)	Consultations with the Poor, in 23 countries (Narayan et al, 2000), as a preliminary for the World Development Report 2000/2001 (World Bank, 2000) on poverty and development
Participatory irrigation management (Gosselink and Strosser, 1995)	Women's empowerment and gender awareness (Guijt and Shah, 1998; Akerkar, 2001; Cornwall, 2003; Kanji, 2004)
Participatory watershed management and soil and water conservation (Kolavalli and Kerr, 2002a and b)	Applications with and by children (PLA Notes 25, 1996; Johnson et al, 1998; Cox and Robinson-Pant, 2003; Chawla and Johnson, 2004) including action research by primary schoolchildren on decision-making in their own classrooms (Cox et al, 2006)
Conservation and use of plant genetic resources (Friis-Hansen and Sthapit, 2000)	Work with those who are powerless and vulnerable, besides children including the homeless (AAA, 2002), the disabled, older people (Heslop, 2002), minorities, refugees, the mentally distressed, prisoners and others who are marginalized
Biodiversity, conservation, and protected area management (Pimbert and Pretty, 1997; Guija et al, 1998; Roe et al, 2000)	Identifying, selecting and deselecting people for poverty-oriented programmes
	Participatory analysis of livelihoods leading to livelihood action plans
Integrated pest management (Dilts and Hate, 1996; Dilts, 2001; Fakih et al, 2003)	Emergency assessment and management, including participation by communities and their members in complex political emergencies
Plant breeding (Stirling and Witcombe, 2004)	Participatory human rights assessments and monitoring (Blackburn et al, 2004)
Animal husbandry and veterinary epidemiology (RRA Notes 20, 1994; Catley, 2007; Abebe et al, 2007)	Violence, abuses and physical insecurity (e.g. Moser and McIlwaine, 2004)
Fishing (PLA Notes 30, 1997)	Sexual and reproductive behaviour and rights (Cornwall and Welbourn, 2002; Gordon and Cornwall, 2004) and HIV/AIDS (International HIV/AIDS Alliance, 2006a and b)

goes far beyond PRA, with an emphasis on surprises, learning and adaptation (Guijt, 2008) and negotiated learning and collaborative monitoring in resource management (Guijt, 2007b).

Co-evolving streams of participatory methodologies

Beyond this bald illustrative listing, more of a sense of what has happened can be given through seven[8] examples of parallel and intermingling participatory research and action which have gone or are going to scale. Approaches, methods, ideas and experiences have over the past two decades flowed freely in all directions between these and RRA, PRA and PLA. The first four – farmer participatory research, integrated pest management (IPM), Reflect and Stepping Stones – are already widespread movements and are practised in many countries. The last three – the Internal Learning System (ILS), Participatory Action Learning System (PALS) and Community-Led Total Sanitation (CLTS) – are promising approaches which are to varying degrees going to scale, and which illustrate the potentials of sensitive and inventive pluralism:

I Farmer participatory research

Farmer participatory research (Farrington and Martin, 1988; Okali et al, 1994) and Participatory Technology Development (PTD) (Haverkort et al, 1991) preceded and paralleled the evolution of PRA. They have been a strong trend that has gained widespread acceptance. Important distinctions were made by Biggs (1988) indicating degrees of farmer participation, from researcher design and control to farmer design and control. From the late 1980s there has been a progressive shift towards the latter, as indicated by the many activities and publications of the system-wide Participatory Research and Gender Analysis (PRGA) programme of the Consultative Group for International Agricultural Research (CGIAR).[9] As with streams of PRA and PLA, the capacities of local people, in this case farmers, were found to exceed by far what professionals had thought they were capable of. One example was the successive involvement of farmers in seed-breeding with scientists, pioneered by D. M. Maurya (Maurya et al, 1988) in the 1980s. Then it was radical to involve them in any part of the breeding and selection process; but later innovating scientists (Witcombe et al, 1996, 2005) went further and found that outcomes were substantially improved by farmers' involvement in the whole process, including selection of the original crosses. Worldwide, farmers' research and participation in research have been spread through the International Agricultural Research Centres, National Agricultural Research Institutes, and INGOs such as World Neighbours.

2 Integrated pest management (IPM)

IPM has been a parallel movement, sharing characteristics with PRA and PLA. IPM in Indonesia started in the late 1980s, with the first training of trainers in 1989. Behaviour and attitudes of facilitators are considered critical (Pontius et al, 2002). IPM enables farmers to control pests in rice with sharply reduced applications of pesticide. By the early 2000s there were some one million farmer participants in Indonesia alone, and several millions worldwide. In IPM farmers are brought together in farmer field schools for in situ learning through their own action research. They observe, map, experiment and analyse, set up and study their own 'zoo' for insects and pests, and come to their own conclusions about how to manage and control them. In the words of Russ Dilts (2001):

> *A people-centred IPM movement has grown in Asia over the last ten years, and is now spreading to parts of Africa, Latin America, and the Middle East. During this period, many variants have evolved and continue to evolve...*

Even in a repressive and authoritarian social order, the farmer-centred approach of the farmer field schools provided 'a safe space for social learning and action' (Fakih et al, 2003, p95). In Indonesia, IPM groups came together and formed the IPM Farmers Association, in effect a national movement. The Association has engaged in advocacy to promote farmers' rights and discuss farmers' problems at local and district levels, and then nationally with a National Congress attended by the responsible minister (Fakih et al, 2003, p111).

3 Reflect

Reflect[10] is a participatory methodology (PM) which combines Paulo Freire's theoretical framework on the politics of literacy with PRA approaches and user-generated materials from PRA visualizations (*Education Action*, 1994 – continuing; *PLA Notes*, 1998; Archer and Newman, 2003; Archer and Goreth, 2004). Piloted through action research projects in El Salvador, Uganda and Bangladesh between 1993 and 1995, it has spread through the work of at least 350 organizations including NGOs, community-based organizations, governments and social movements, in more than 60 countries. A standard manual was soon abandoned as too rigid (Phnuyal, 1999; Archer, 2007, pp20–21). Local differentiation and ownership have become marked features. Reflect has taken many different forms with 'immense diversity' (Archer and Goreth, 2004, p40).

At the core of Reflect are facilitated groups known as Reflect circles. These meet regularly, usually for about two years, and sometimes continuing indefinitely. The balance between literacy and empowerment has varied. Analysis by circles, combined with networking, has confronted power and abuses and asserted human rights. Reflect's core principles include these: starting from existing experience; using participatory tools; power analysis; creating democratic spaces; reflection–action–reflection; self-organization; and recognition that Reflect is a political process for social change and greater social justice. These principles are manifest in *Communication and Power: Reflect Practical Resource Materials* (compilers David Archer and Kate Newman), the outcome of a widespread participatory process. First put together in 2003 in a loose-leaf form, its sections include Written word, Numbers, Spoken word, Images, and Reflect in action, with a strong emphasis on empowerment to enable people to do their own appraisal and analysis, leading to their own awareness and action.

4 Stepping Stones (SS)

Stepping Stones (Welbourn, 1995, 2002, 2007) is an approach and methods to facilitate experiential learning concerned with social awareness, communication and relationships. It was evolved by Alice Welbourn and first tried in Uganda in 1994. Groups of people in communities meet for a sequence of interactions and reflections especially on the inequalities that govern gender and other social relations in the context of HIV/AIDS. A review of evaluations by Tina Wallace (2006, p20) reported that SS had been adapted and used in over 100 countries. Most countries had no estimates of coverage but a World Bank estimate was that in Mozambique alone half a million people had been reached over four years.

Wallace's review found 'almost universal support for, and appreciation of, SS as a change process from those with first hand experience of using it or seeing it used' including 'better inter-generational communication, more openness about discussing sex, less stigma and more care for those with HIV and AIDS, and a willingness of PLWHA [People Living With HIV/AIDS] to be open.' (Wallace, 2006, p10). Another evaluation summarized as follows:

> *The response of communities across the globe has been overwhelmingly positive and the results extremely encouraging. Reductions in gender violence, increased self-esteem and confidence among women and girls, improved sex lives between married couples, radical reconfiguration of gender relations and the gender division of labour in the household, relinquishing harmful cultural practices, such as wife sharing and widow inheritance … are but a few examples of the reported impact.'* (Hadjipateras et al, 2006, p8)

5 The Internal Learning System

The ILS, pioneered in India by Helzi Noponen, was conceived as a participatory impact assessment and planning system. The pictorial diaries and workbooks which are its most conspicuous feature were developed independently of PRA. Poor, often illiterate participants use them to keep their own records of changes over time. The intention is to reverse normal power relationships: poor participants 'are the first to learn about programme impact and performance, and alter plans as a result … [they] are not only data gatherers, but they are also analysts, planners and advocates for change' (Noponen, 2007). The ILS has evolved for different conditions including the work of the NESA (New Entity for Social Action) and its partners in South India for the empowerment of Dalit and Adivasi women and children (Nagasundari, 2007); and of Pradan (Professional Assistance for Development Action) and its partners in North India with self-help groups for the generation of sustainable livelihoods for poor rural people (Narendranath, 2007). Among other outcomes have been action on social and gender issues previously too sensitive for discussion, and many micro-level manifestations of social change especially awareness and empowerment of women and others who are marginalized.

6 Participatory Action Learning System

PALS, pioneered by Linda Mayoux, is 'an eclectic and constantly evolving methodology which enables people to collect and analyse the information they themselves need on an ongoing basis to improve their lives in ways they decide' (Mayoux, 2007). Core features are the inventive use of diagram tools (Mayoux, 2003a), their integration with participatory principles and processes, linking individual and group learning, and the adoption and adaptation of approaches and methods from many traditions. Typically, diagram tools are designed and piloted, and incorporated in a manual for each context (e.g. Mayoux, 2003b). Applications and developments of PALS have included women's empowerment with ANANDI, an NGO in Gujarat (Mayoux and ANANDI, 2005), participatory monitoring and evaluation with the Kabarole Research and Resource Centre in Uganda, and impact assessment of micro-finance in several countries.

7 Community-Led Total Sanitation

CLTS (Kar, 2003, 2005; Kar and Pasteur, 2005; Kar and Bongartz, 2006), pioneered by Kamal Kar in Bangladesh, is a remarkable initiative using PRA approaches and methods in which small communities are facilitated to conduct their own research and analysis into their practices of defecation and their consequences. This is done through mapping, transects, observation, calculations of quantities produced and ingested, and reflections on pathways from faeces to the mouth. This quite often leads to community decisions to dig holes, construct latrines and introduce total sanitation to become open-defecation free. The approach has been introduced and is reported to have been adopted by thousands of communities spread over Bangladesh, Cambodia, India, Indonesia, Pakistan and other countries in South and South-east Asia, and has been introduced into East and Southern Africa, South America, and Yemen in the Middle East.

These seven examples are original and distinct methodologies which to varying degrees draw on, share and have contributed to PRA/PLA approaches, methods, behaviours and mindsets and which have creatively invented and evolved their own diverse and varied practices. All can be seen as forms of, or closely related to, participatory action research. All frame and facilitate sequences of activities which empower participants to undertake their own appraisal or research and analysis, and come to their own conclusions.

Principles: Theory from practice[11]

Practices, principles and theory intertwine and co-evolve. Theory can exist as an intellectual abstraction without practice, but practice cannot exist without implicit theory. When theory and practice co-evolve, one or the other may exercise more influence. If theory and reflective practice have led more in action research (Reason and Bradbury, 2001), practice and experiential learning have led more in the RRA–PRA–PLA sequence. At times, as in the 1989–91 explosion of PRA, not all the implicit theory was immediately made explicit. But critical reflection followed practice, and principles were induced and articulated on the run drawing on experience. And this continues: among practitioners, researchers and activists engaged in the rapid spread of participatory GIS (Chapter 7), for example, it is generally agreed that PGIS practice is more advanced than the theory behind the applications (Rambaldi et al, 2006).

PRA/PLA practical theory appears robust.[12] It can be described at two levels. The first, as expressed by Jethro Pettit (pers. comm.), is more overarching: that most practitioners would share an epistemological or ideological perspective, articulated in the PRA literature, that expert and professional knowledge and ways of knowing need to be humble and to appreciate people's own knowledge and ways of knowing. Professionals, and people who are dominant in contexts and relationships ('uppers'), habitually underestimate the capabilities and the value of the knowledge of those who are subordinate in contexts and relationships ('lowers').[13] A role of the professional is to transform these relations by facilitating, enabling people to express and enhance their own contextual and specific knowledge. PRA behaviours, methods and orientations are a means towards this. The core is that uppers facilitate, support and protect processes through which lowers and local people empower themselves and power relations are transformed.

The second level supports the first. It is more detailed and can be induced from practice, from what has been found to work. Methods, approaches and methodologies have evolved through borrowing, inventing and experiential learning driven by the discipline, pressures and opportunities of engagement in the field. Innovation has taken place through improvisations forced by the challenge of immediate social situations. There will be, and should be, a range of views about this second level of theory. What is presented here is only my interpretation. Focusing on PRA experience and also drawing on the seven examples above, together with PGIS, three clusters of principles can be distinguished. These are evolutions of the original three principal components of PRA (Figure 5.1) becoming: behaviours, attitudes and mindsets – precepts for action; methods – visuals, tangibles and groups; and sharing – pluralism and diversity.

Behaviours, attitudes and mindsets: Precepts for action

Empowering processes require changes of behaviours, attitudes and mindsets, and typically changes of role from teacher to facilitator and from controller to coach. To promote and sustain the spread of good PRA the practical theory has been expressed as short and simple precepts with the idea that these will embed and spread as expressions and behaviours; and that the experiences these bring will transform attitudes, predispositions and mindsets among uppers and transform relationships with lowers.

One basic reversal is through asking 'who?' and 'whose?' and answering with 'theirs', referring commonly to lowers, in practice often local people and most of all to those who are poor, weak and marginalized. These questions vary by context, but a decade ago (Chambers, 1997, p101) were summarized as:

- Whose knowledge counts?[14]
- Whose values?
- Whose criteria and preferences?
- Whose appraisal, analysis and planning?
- Whose action?
- Whose monitoring and evaluation?
- Whose learning?
- Whose empowerment?
- Whose **reality** counts?
- 'Ours' or 'Theirs'?

The overarching question 'Whose reality counts?' forces reflection on how powerful outsiders tend to impose their realities on local people, especially when they are bringing 'superior' knowledge or technology. The wide span of 'who?' and 'whose?' questions can be illustrated by the listing generated by practitioners reflecting critically on the ethics of PGIS.

Some of the main behavioural precepts of PRA[15] are:

Box 5.1 Behavioural precepts of PRA

Precept	indicating
Introduce yourself	be honest, transparent, relate as a person
They can do it	have confidence in people's abilities
Unlearn	critically reflect on how you see things
Ask them	ask people their realities, priorities, advice…
Don't rush	be patient, take time
Sit down, listen and learn	don't dominate
Facilitate	don't lecture, criticize or teach
Embrace error	learn from what goes wrong or does not work
Hand over the stick	or chalk or pen, anything that empowers
Use your own best judgement at all times	take responsibility for what you do
Shut up!	keep quiet. Welcome and tolerate silence

Methods: Visuals, tangibles and groups

Many PRA methods involve visual and tangible expression and analysis, for example mapping, modelling, diagramming, pile sorting, or scoring with seeds, stones or other counters. These are usually but not always small group activities. What is expressed can be seen, touched or moved and stays in place.[16] These visible, tangible, alterable and yet lasting aspects contrast with the invisible, un-alterable and transient nature of verbal communication. Symbols, objects and diagrams can represent realities that are cumbersome or impossible to express verbally.

These visual and tangible approaches and methods reverse power relations and empower lowers in five ways.

The first is group-visual synergy. As in Figure 5.2, group motivation, cross-checking, adding detail, discussing and cumulative representation generate a positive-sum synergy through which all can contribute and learn. A facilitator can observe and assess the process for its rigour of trustworthiness and relevance.[17] The outcomes are then empowering through collective analysis and learning, and because they are at once credible and an output created and owned by the group.

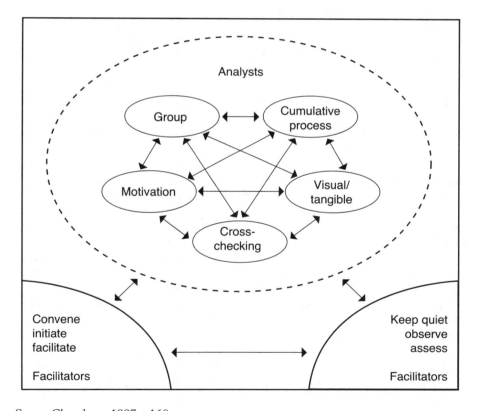

Source: Chambers, 1997, p160

Figure 5.2 *Group-visual synergy*

The second is democracy of the ground (Chambers, 2002, pp94–95, 186–187). Much PRA mapping and diagramming levels or reverses power relations by taking place on the ground. Those taking part have less eye contact, talk less and can dominate less easily, than in normal upright positions face to face. Hands are freer to move tangibles than mouths are to speak words. Those who are more powerful, sometimes older men, may stand on their dignity and not get down on the ground at all, whereas those who are younger and women may.

The third is the representation of complex realities and relationships. Visual and tangible approaches and methods enable local people and lowers generally to express and analyse complex patterns of categories, comparisons, estimates, valuations, relationships and causality, across an astonishing range of topics, from social and census maps of communities to causal and linkage diagrams of causes and effects of poverty, from scored matrices for varieties of crops and domestic animals to different forms of violence, from characteristics of different sorts of sexual partners to seasonal analyses of work, income, debt, expenditures, sickness and other aspects of life, from on-farm nutrient flows to priorities for local development, and much, much else.

The fourth is using visuals as instruments of empowerment. Over the past decade rapid developments have generated a new repertoire for subordinate and marginalized people. The visual diaries of ILS in South India empower low-caste women, arming them with visual representations of their realities and experiences, enabling them to track and discuss changes in their lives over time, and to take action when patterns of marginalization (such as caste or gender discrimination) persist (Nagasundari, 2007). With PGIS, the geo-referenced maps of forest dwellers and other peripheral people give them credible and potent aids for asserting and securing their rights and boundaries. Making three-dimensional PGIS models has enabled local communities to express and display their knowledge and realities, and to plan, whether for land management, conservation, or cropping patterns. Large PGIS models can hardly fail to belong to communities and be retained by them. And they provide a natural and efficient locus for dialogue and decision-making (Rambaldi and Callosa-Tarr, 2000, 2002).

The fifth is participatory numbers. A diverse and versatile family of innovations has been evolved to generate numbers and statistics from participatory appraisal and analysis and are discussed in Chapter 6. To a striking degree, the numbers generated through participatory methods and processes have been found to combine accuracy, authority and utility, and to empower those whose appraisal and analysis have produced them.

These five ways in which visuals, tangibles and numbers empower often combine and reinforce each other. Their force is then more than the sum of their parts. Together they can be potent means for transforming power relations, strengthening the power of lowers and local people not just to understand their realities but to take action, and to negotiate with uppers and outside powers-that-be.

Sharing, pluralism and diversity

Sharing without boundaries was a principle that emerged from a workshop of PRA practitioners in 1994 (Absalom et al, 1995). To be sure, there have been a few practitioners who might be described as PRA fundamentalists, who have sought or claimed some sort of exclusive expertise and ownership. But sharing was one of the three principal components of PRA enunciated in 1990, and a corollary of sharing and of 'use your own best judgement at all times' is to endorse and celebrate pluralism.

It is striking how PRA, PLA, IPM, Reflect, PGIS and most of the other PMs have been open and porous, and how they have diversified creatively as they have spread. Methodological diversity is an enabling condition for creativity (van Mele et al, 2005). Those with standard manuals and detailed instructions have been less successful or have run into problems: Reflect's Mother Manual was quickly abandoned when found to inhibit more than help (Box 9.1, p175). A key to good spread, and to becoming a movement, has often been holding firm to minimum principles, and then allowing and encouraging practices and behaviours which empower, through local creativity and ownership. An indicator of this is in the labels used: Reflect in Nepal, for example, is not known by its English name but has 16 different Nepalese names and identities (pers. comm. Bimal Phnuyal). Creativity, diversity and local ownership and responsibility have been at the core of the successful spread of these participatory methodologies.

This inclusiveness of sharing and borrowing raises questions about how the three components – of behaviours, attitudes and mindsets, of methods using visuals, tangibles and groups, and of sharing, pluralism and diversity – can relate to other theories and theoretical frameworks.[18] In PRA/PLA terms, an answer can be given by 'Use your own best judgement at all times'. For some, who want a bounded and labelled methodology, this will look and feel too loose, both personally and because it can appear to open the door to bad practice. For others it will turn responsibility back from an external authority or a predetermined process to personal reflective judgement, liberating through freedom to decide and choose what to learn from, borrow and adapt. It can then encourage eclectic opportunism and creativity to enhance local relevance and fit to contribute to the empowerment of others, especially lowers.

Beyond PRA, brands and boundaries

The PRA label has been a problem, spreading often without PRA principles and practices. In the 1990s, by claiming some sort of ownership of PRA, a few consultants negated its spirit of sharing but in the 2000s this has become less evident. Another problem has been how some have misunderstood PRA.[19] Sadly, too, some working in other traditions, have regarded PRA as competitor rather than colleague. This may have contributed to some action research practitioners' surprising lack of interest in the added value of PRA approaches and methods, and to their seeing PRA as extractive research conducted on local and poor people, not research conducted by and with them as in the movements, methodologies and applications described above. In these movements, as amply documented, practice and theory have been oriented towards empowering those who are marginalized and weak, using new approaches and methods to enable them to do their own appraisals and analysis, and to gain voice and take their own action.

Much of the discourse and practice has now moved beyond PRA. At one level, the use of some PRA methods is quite stable and practical: wealth ranking (also known as well-being grouping), for example, is extensively used by INGOs and their partners as a means of enabling people in communities to identify those who are worse off using their own criteria. At another level, good participatory practice is improvised and invented as performance in ever changing conditions, leading to a multiplicity of expressions which are unique and ever new.

The more inclusive usage of the term PLA has helped here, as for example by the International HIV/AIDS Alliance (2006b) for whom PLA is

> *A growing family of approaches, tools, attitudes and behaviours to enable and empower people to present, share, analyse and enhance their knowledge of life and conditions, and to plan, act, monitor, evaluate, reflect and scale up community action.*

and

> *a way to help people to participate together in learning, and then to act on that learning.*

The agenda has, then, moved beyond branding and boundaries. These can inhibit and limit more than help. It has become less clear what PRA is or should usefully mean. The priority is not the spread of PRA but inclusively of participatory approaches, attitudes, behaviours, methods and mindsets. A key element in this is personal, the capacity to adapt, improvise and innovate; and that is something in which practitioners from all traditions can share. Paradigmatically, this is part of the shift from things to people, from top–down to bottom–up, from standard to diverse, from control to empowerment. Brands, boundaries, exclusiveness and claims of ownership dissolve to be replaced by openness, generosity, inclusiveness and sharing. The future lies not in branding and boundaries but in creative and eclectic pluralism, the theme of Chapter 9. And this opens up the potentials of a new world.

Notes

1   'Participatory reflection and action' has the sequence of words wrong. It would be better putting action first, as 'participatory action and reflection', but the acronym PAR was already in use for participatory action research. However, an advantage has been that more practitioners have abandoned

their use of brand labels and become explicit about their pluralism (see e.g. Shah, 2003).

2 For what are known as PRA methods, typically including visuals and/or tangibles, see Jones, 1996a, b; Chambers, 1997; Shah et al, 1999a, b; Kumar, 2002; Mukherjee, 2002; Jayakaran, 2003; International HIV/AIDS Alliance, 2006b. See also www.ids.ac.uk/ppsc for more.

3 *RRA Notes* Issues 1–21 (1988–94) was published by the International Institute for Environment and Development, whose Sustainable Agriculture Programme had much to do with the evolution and spread of PRA and which was documented in the Notes. Issue 22 in 1995 was renamed *PLA Notes* with the explanation: 'Participatory Learning and Action (PLA) has been adopted ... as a collective term to describe the growing body of participatory approaches and methodologies.'

4 The first major accessible publication was *RRA Notes* 13 Participatory Rural Appraisal: Proceedings of the February 1991 Bangalore PRA trainers workshop, which shows how rapid the evolution and spread of PRA had been in India in its first year or two.

5 I was co-funded by the Ford Foundation, the Overseas Development Administration of the British Government, and the Aga Khan Foundation.

6 Photographs of this interview and events from the early years of PRA can be found in Chambers, 2004.

7 For a selection of critical reflections by practitioners of PRA/PLA see *PRA Notes* 24 (1995); the 32 individual contributions to *Pathways to Participation: Reflections on PRA* (Cornwall and Pratt, 2003); *Participation: From Tyranny to Transformation* (Hickey and Mohan, 2004); and the 50th issue of *Participation Learning and Action* (2004), entitled *Critical Reflections, Future Directions*.

8 In an earlier draft, an eighth example was Participatory Geographic Information Systems (PGIS). I have removed it here to avoid duplicating Chapter 7. The PGIS experience reinforces the points made on the basis of comparing the seven methodologies analysed here.

9 See www.prgaprogram.org

10 Reflect originally stood for Regenerated Freirian Literacy with Empowering Community Techniques but this usage has been dropped and it is now referred to simply as Reflect.

11 For an earlier and fuller statement of PRA theory from practice see Chambers, 1997, chapter 7, 'What Works and Why'.

12 The word 'robust' is a response to reactions of colleagues to an earlier more modest draft of this chapter. They have argued against an apologetic stance which might imply that the RRA/PRA/PLA sequence was somehow a theoretical second-best because of the degree to which it was driven by experiential learning. The contrary is the case.

13 For elaboration and qualification of the concepts of upper and lower see Chambers, 1997, pp58–60, 207–10, 221–228.

14 The phrase 'Whose knowledge counts?' originates with Zoe Mars who as editor of *IDS Bulletin* thought of it as the title for vol 10, no 2, in 1979.

15 Fuller listings of PRA-related precepts and behaviours can be found in *Participatory Workshops* (Chambers, 2002, pp7–9).

16 Visuals and tangibles can, though, be vulnerable – on the ground to wind, rain, dust storms, trampling by people or animals or consumption by hungry hens whose alternative view of the value of matrix scoring can dramatically diminish scores. Paper is vulnerable to crumpling, smudging, fire, decay and, most of all, retention or removal by NGO staff who so often take maps away from the communities which have made them.

17 The rigour of trustworthiness and relevance is explored in more detail in Chambers, 1997, pp158–161.

18 This sets down a challenge to theoreticians to show how their theories and categories could enhance the quality of field practice. Some of these theories are expounded in Reason and Bradbury (eds) (2008) *Handbook of Action Research*, 2nd edition. See also Chandler and Torbert, 2003.

19 PRA has for example been taken to stand for Participatory Research Appraisal or Participatory Rapid Appraisal. In *Participation: The New Tyranny?* (Cooke and Kothari, 2001, p88 and index) PLA is misrepresented as participatory learning analysis instead of participatory learning and action, despite the latter having been the meaning of the periodical *PLA Notes*.

6

Who Counts?
Participation and Numbers[1]

Numbers are the masters of the weak, but the slaves of the strong.
(Charles Babbage, *Passages from the Life of a Philosopher*, 1864)

We opted ... for participatory approaches, both because we wanted to give communities a voice and because we wanted to gather information that is too complex to be handled by questionnaires. The challenge for us was to generate reliable statistics from research using participatory methods. (Barahona and Levy, 2003, p1)

Abstract

Participatory approaches and methods can generate quantitative as well as qualitative data. Mainly since the early 1990s, a quiet tide of innovation has developed a rich range of participatory ways, many of them visual and tangible, by which local people themselves produce and can own numbers. The approaches and methods have variously entailed counting, mapping, measuring, estimating, valuing and scoring, together with comparing and combinations of these, and have had many applications.

The methodological pioneers in going to scale in the 1990s rarely recognized the significance of what they had been doing. The pioneers of the 2000s have shown ingenuity, skill, patience and courage, sometimes in the face of opposition driven by conventional reflexes. Participatory numbers have been taken to scale most notably through participatory surveys with visuals and tangibles, through aggregation from focus groups and through wealth and well-being ranking. There have been breakthroughs in producing national statistics, and also on subjects and with insights inaccessible through questionnaires.

Statistical principles can be applied to participatory numbers.[2] Ways have been found of overcoming the vexing problem of commensurability between communities. As with all ways of finding out, there are trade-offs, in this context notably between participatory open-endedness and standardization for comparability.

The question 'Who counts?' raises issues of ownership and power. Participatory monitoring and evaluation (PM and E) has taken many forms, with varied degrees of ownership and empowerment. Whether participatory statistics empower local people is sensitive to official attitudes and acceptance, and whether these lead to changes in policy and practice that make a real difference. Questions are raised of how the quiet revolution of participatory numbers can be win–win, with learning by outsider facilitator/researchers and empowerment of insider analysts, and with the best of both qualitative and quantitative worlds.

Introduction

This chapter is about participatory approaches and methods which generate numbers, participatory numbers for short. It challenges the normal reflex that for numbers we must have questionnaires. It presents evidence which I believe should excite and inspire researchers and those who fund and sponsor research. Participatory numbers with their burgeoning repertoire are part of a quiet revolution, unrecognized in professional mainstreams, which has taken place in the past decade and a half. There is a parallel with rapid rural appraisal (RRA) (Chapter 4) in the 1970s. During that decade more and more professionals were innovating with ways of finding out about rural life and conditions which were quicker, better and more cost-effective than either traditional questionnaire surveys or in-depth social anthropology. Similarly, participatory numbers were marginal in the 1990s but are now increasingly facilitated, used and recognized, as RRA came to be, not as a second best but more and more often as a best. Even so, it is still little recognized how much participatory numbers can substitute for conventional methods like questionnaires.

In writing I have tried to be balanced. Nevertheless, the reader should be warned. My bad experiences with large questionnaires have tended to predispose me against all questionnaires and to support alternatives. I have caught myself being misled by this. So it was that for this I seized gleefully on a diagram comparing proportions by month in 2001/02 and 2002/03 of those who were extremely food insecure in Malawi. Ahha! Here was another case to demonstrate the superiority of participatory numbers over questionnaires. On checking, though, I was chastened. The source was a questionnaire: it was short and simple, not long and complex, but nevertheless a questionnaire (Barahona, 2005, pp80–81). And I was once again driven by the evidence to modify my view and to embrace a more eclectic methodological pluralism, albeit one in which participatory numbers usually remain the first and best option, especially, but by no means only, for topics which are sensitive or complex or both.

The question 'Who counts?' can have two meanings: who is the active agent in generating numbers?; and who matters and whose reality matters? These two threads weave through this chapter. Let me invite the reader when thinking about the examples that follow to imagine the processes and relationships that were central to them, with sequences of activities, and with outsiders ('us') as facilitators not enumerators and local people ('them') as analysts not respondents; and to reflect on how much more often than in common practice the answer to the question 'Who counts?' can and should be 'They do'.

Debates about ways of finding out often concern the contrasts and complementarities between qualitative and quantitative approaches. This was the focus of a conference convened by Ravi Kanbur at Cornell in March 2001 which led to the book *Q-Squared: Qualitative and Quantitative Methods in Poverty Appraisal* (Kanbur, 2003). *A Methodological Framework for Combining Quantitative and Qualitative Survey Methods* (Marsland et al, 2000) is of interest as the work of statisticians. It identifies three types of combination:

1   swapping tools and attitudes: merging (e.g. participatory mapping to provide a sampling frame)
2   sequencing (e.g. informal before formal, or formal before informal)
3   concurrent use of tools (e.g. questionnaire and RRA in parallel, then compared).

Valid and valuable as mixed methods have been and will continue to be, they have not much engaged with or gained from the quiet revolution in which local people themselves generate numbers.

Gains from quantitative approaches

Quantitative approaches usually means research using standard sampling techniques, questionnaires and statistical analysis. They are so widely used because of the many potential benefits from statistics and numbers. It is as well to start by recognizing some of those that are more common and better known:

• time series comparisons to identify trends in whatever dimensions are measured
• cross-section comparisons between different individuals, households, groups and communities, and across regions, countries and continents
• correlations which identify associations which raise questions of causality and covariant changes
• estimates of prevalence and distributions within populations and areas
• triangulations and linkages with qualitative data (Booth et al, 1998; Booth, 2003)
• the credibility of numbers in influencing policy-makers
• the utility to policy-makers and policy-influencers of being able to put numbers on trends and other comparisons.

The case argued from the evidence in this chapter is that frequently these and other gains can come better from participatory numbers than from questionnaires.

Beyond conventional qual–quant complementarities

Qualitative research too has its well-recognized advantages, not least of depth of insight and of being open to the unexpected. The value of qualitative 'precision in meaning' tends to be contrasted with the value of quantitative 'accuracy in measurement'.[3] In recent years increasing attention has been paid to mixed methods that combine qualitative and quantitative methods in research (e.g. Booth et al, 1998; Marsland et al, 2000; Kanbur, c. 2003; Kanbur and Shaffer, 2006) to gain the best of both worlds.

Complementarities have been recognized between depth and detail from qualitative research and representativeness and statistical robustness from quantitative research. The two also inform, correct and augment each other. Qualitative studies can contribute to the content of questionnaires, their interpretation and correction. Questionnaires can raise issues for probing and explanation. To give just one example, in a study of destitution in Ethiopia, qualitative inquiry showed how a questionnaire was likely to underestimate the impacts of death of an able-bodied adult because it would not recognize the break-up of the household itself that commonly resulted (Sharp, 2005, p19). The many benefits of these 'qual–quant' or Q-squared interactions are not now seriously in dispute. They can be seen as combinations of the SW (conventional qualitative) and SE (conventional quantitative) quadrants in Figure 6.1.

However, qualitative and quantitative have in common that whether separately or together their dominant mode is extractive, that is, they are used to gather and take away data for analysis. Valid and valuable as they can be, either separately or as mixed methods, they have not much engaged with or gained from the revolution in which it is local people themselves who conduct their own appraisals, investigations and research. Linda Mayoux (2005) has asked whether quantitative, qualitative and participatory are three different worlds of research and has laid out their contrasts and complementarities, and issues of relevance, reliability and ethics, arguing for optimizing combinations for context and purpose. This now is about that major part of the participatory world where local people generate and to varying degrees are empowered by their own numbers. A minimalist view could be that participatory numbers can be complements or checks to conventional and established methods. The evidence below shows that in many contexts participatory numbers are often much more than checks; they are often better alternatives, with their own rigour and range.

Who counts? questions and experiences take us, then, beyond conventional complementarities. Two common linked assumptions are shown to be false: first, that participatory approaches only generate qualitative insights – the NW quadrant in Figure 6.1; and second, that quantitative data can only be produced by questionnaire surveys or scientific measurement – the SE quadrant.

Numerous experiences now confound and contradict these two assumptions. Largely unrecognized in academic and official government and aid agency mainstreams, a whole new field has opened up. This is represented by the NE quadrant. This takes us beyond conventional complementarities. Especially since the early 1990s, a tide of innovation has developed a rich range of participatory ways by which local people can themselves produce numbers. The methodological pioneers have rarely recognized the full significance of what they have been doing. For brevity, the generation of numbers using participatory approaches and methods will be referred to here as participatory numbers.

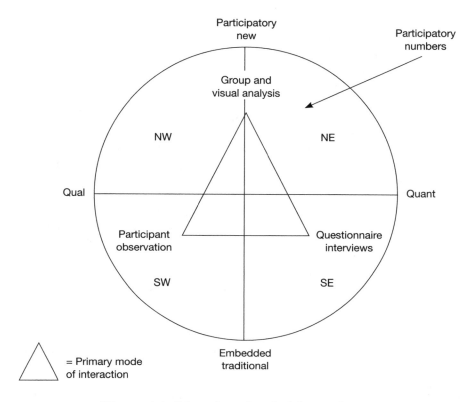

Figure 6.1 *Dimensions of methodology and outcome*

Modes of participatory number-generating[4]

Participatory activities can generate numbers in different ways and for different purposes. Four categories of activities and ownership of the numbers can be described.

First, groups of people can be facilitated to put numbers on their characteristics as individuals. This can occur in both local and community contexts, and often through public raising of hands. It can also be private and confidential with voting behind a screen or marking on anonymous slips. As ever, the validity of the numbers depends on context and sensitivity, with public and visible cross-checking in some cases, and anonymity in others. These methods are common in school classes and in participatory workshops (Chambers, 2002, p23). In the latter, standing in groups or clusters is often effective, and can quickly identify (and celebrate) characteristics, for example the number of mother tongues in an international group.[5]

In this mode the numbers are either publicly visible to all, or can be shared by whoever counts the numbers which are individually confidential.

Second, there are numbers generated by local people which they retain and use or do not need or bother to keep. These may or may not be shared or needed by others. Examples can be found in participatory monitoring and evaluation (M and E) (pp120–122).

In this mode, the numbers are more 'theirs', that is, they belong to and are used by local people.

Third, in a comparative research mode, there is the analysis of secondary data which have been generated in a participatory manner without pre-standardization. Deciding categories and allocating to them can be difficult but the results can be significant and persuasive. Karen Brock (1999) gathered findings from participatory research on poverty, and analysed what had come from 58 groups and individuals in 12 countries who had been asked to identify key criteria for poverty, ill-being or vulnerability. She then used the NUDIST programme to classify and count these by criteria, separated into urban and rural, and men and women, and presented the results diagrammatically to show frequency of mention as percentages. One striking finding was that water came out as a higher priority for poor people in urban than in rural areas.

In this mode, the numbers are 'ours', that is, they are derived and used by the outside analyst.

Fourth, the main focus here, is the generation of numbers from several or many sources using participatory approaches, methods, and behaviours which are usually to some degree standardized. These practices have evolved and spread quietly, almost unnoticed. Often the methods are visual and tangible (see e.g. Mukherjee, 1995, 2002; Jones, 1996a, b; Shah et al, 1999a, b; Jayakaran, 2002, 2003, 2007; Moser and McIlwaine, 2004; Kagugube et al, 2007). The activities can be by individuals, but most often they take place in groups: different groups of people do similar things which provide numbers which can be added, averaged, compared, or used as a basis for various calculations. Local people can do calculations themselves at their own level, but in practice it is usually the outside researchers or facilitators who aggregate and calculate beyond the level of the group.

In this mode, ownership and use depend on context and facilitation. Many modes, combinations and processes are possible. Kay Sharp (2007, p275), for instance, included proportional piling in the sequence of a household questionnaire survey in Ethiopia. Her account of the participatory visual and tangible part of the interviews gives a sense of process:

> *The exact number of 100 beans (pre-counted by the interviewer)[6] was used to facilitate the checking and recording of numbers in the field, and subsequent data entry ... a few people counted the beans, but most estimated the income proportions first roughly allocating smaller or larger handfuls to each circle, then visually comparing the size of the piles, and moving beans around according to discussion and spontaneous pair-wise comparison (e.g. 'didn't we get more from firewood than from eggs?').* (Sharp, 2007, p275)

Participatory methods, applications and activities

Methods[7] often used to generate numbers include:

*   participatory mapping (ActionAid-Nepal, 1992; Chambers, 1997; Barahona and Levy, 2003)
*   participatory modelling (Rambaldi and Callosa-Tarr, 2000, 2002)
*   proportional piling (Watson, 1994; Jayakaran, 2002, 2003, 2007; Sharp, 2005, pp20–24)
*   card writing, marking, sorting, ordering and positioning (Kagugube et al, 2007)
*   matrix ranking and scoring (Abeyasekera, 2001; Abebe et al, 2007)
*   pair-wise ranking (Mukherjee, 2002)
*   linkage diagramming (Burn, 2000; Galpin et al, 2000)
*   pocket voting (van Wijk-Sijbesma, 2001).

Often in practice there are combinations of visuals and tangibles – maps, models, diagrams and counters of various sorts (stones, seeds etc.).

These have many common **applications** including social and census mapping, household listing and scoring, well-being ranking, trend and change analysis, seasonal diagramming, preference ranking, causal-linkage analysis and problem trees.

The participatory **activities** which generate numbers are counting, calculating, measuring, estimating, ranking, valuing and scoring. In practice, these are not always distinct and may be combined in the same activity. Comparing things is often involved, giving numbers or scores or positioning cards, to indicate relative degrees, sizes or values.

Examples of **counting** are social and census maps. These tend to be very accurate for identifying and listing households, for headcounts and for household characteristics which are common knowledge. Participants can 'see what is being said' and correct and add detail. For community census purposes, the outcomes have proven very accurate indeed, and where there have been discrepancies, community analysts have wanted to check until they reach agreement (Chambers, 1997, pp143–145).

An example of **calculating** comes from the triggering process of Community-Led Total Sanitation. Evolved in Bangladesh, CLTS has been spread to numerous other countries in Asia and Africa. As part of a facilitated appraisal local people calculate the quantities (e.g. cartloads for the whole community) of shit (the crude word is used) produced by their households in a day, multiply out for longer periods, and add up for the whole community, concluding sometimes with community cartloads per annum (Kar, 2005; Kar and Pasteur, 2005).

Examples of participatory **measuring** can be found with timber stocks, water flows, crop yields, arm circumferences, and land-use areas from participatory GIS mapping and modelling (Chapter 7).

Examples of **estimating** are often associated with comparing and relative proportions, as in historical matrices (e.g. Freudenberger, 1995; PRAXIS, 2001) which indicate trends and changes; seasonal food calendars which show seasonal variations in things like amount and type of food consumed (e.g. Mukherjee and Jena, 2001) and health problems (Shah et al, 1999a, 1999b); and as in proportional piling for income and food sources (e.g. Watson, 1994; Eldridge, 2001; and Stephen Devereux and Henry Lucas pers. comms). There are many applications with variants of methods such as the 'ten seed technique' (Jayakaran, 2002) in which ten seeds are allocated between two or more options, or the allocation of 100 seeds, stones or other counters to give percentages (see Box 7.1, pp144–145).

Examples of **valuing and scoring** are preference ranking, matrix ranking and matrix scoring (Jones, 1996b). Things compared range from crop varieties in Zambia (Drinkwater, 1993) and India (Manoharan et al, 1993) to contraceptive methods, from markets in Bangladesh (Kar and Datta, 1998) to political parties, from girls' preferences for sex-partners in Zambia (Shah et al, 1999a, 1999b) to wild plants collected for winter feeding of goats in Afghanistan (Leyland, 1994). The allocation of ten as with the ten seed technique has been used in China with aggregation from household self-monitoring booklets for problems managing a water supply, the ten seeds being allocated between three columns – happy, middle and unhappy respectively (Vernooy et al, 2003). Another example is the Pachod Paise Scale from Maharashtra in India (Kapadia-Kundu and Dyalchand, 2007). Participants are asked to say how many paise (100 paise to the rupee) they would give to something, as with 'How many paise in a rupee do you feel that a woman should be given more food during pregnancy?' It has proved versatile and has been used to measure, for example, attitudes, emotions, intention and client satisfaction. In the UK uses of scoring include comparing health providers in an estate in London and assessing candidates interviewed for a university post.[8]

Comparing is a common feature in these methods and applications. Comparisons are made in many ways, often directly through the numbers. The numbers or scores can also be generated as a second stage of a physical activity of grouping or positioning, often of cards representing households. The best known and most widespread is wealth or well-being ranking, where analysts group household cards according to their judgements of personal or household conditions (see below). Placing on a scale is another. In Uganda small groups have placed household cards on a rope symbolizing climbing out of poverty, with the best condition at one end, and the worst at the other, leading to scores between 0 and 10 (Kagugube et al, 2007) (see pp119).

Analysis by local people can generate numbers in all the above ways. In practice, this is usually with facilitation by one or more outsiders. Those who take part can be individuals but are more usually groups. Local people can also themselves be facilitators, but outsiders' skills have so far usually been needed where participatory activities occur on a scale which requires later aggregation, with or without statistical analysis. In these situations, some degree of standardization of process is common to assure comparability and enhance the validity of aggregation.

Going to scale with participatory numbers

There is a prehistory of social anthropological approaches and methods which generate numbers (Pelto and Pelto, 1978). However, serious innovation in going to scale with such numbers appears to have begun only in the early 1990s. Three parallel and overlapping methodological streams stand out: participatory surveys; aggregation from focus groups; and wealth ranking.

Participatory surveys

The earliest case of a large-scale survey with participatory visual analysis and no questionnaire may[9] have been the 1992 use by ActionAid of participatory rural appraisal (PRA) methods, mainly mapping, in over 130 villages in Nepal (ActionAid-Nepal, 1992). This was a survey of utilization of services and assets. It covered the whole population in the villages and generated 13 tables. These covered, for example, literacy, children going to school, income-generating activities, and health activities (Table 6.1) tabulated variously by area and by ethnic group. The population summed to 35,414.

Table 6.1 *Household use of health activities*

Goan Bikas Samiti	Total households	Drinking water facility	Health care services	Pit latrine	Family planning
Bhotechaur	872	654	785	93	135
Thakani	625	398	273	91	48
Haibung	504	368	109	97	77
Sindhukot	602	331	539	158	74
Bansbari	822	389	NA	185	161
Melamchi	691	472	151	122	80
Ichowk	965	329	389	103	55
Mahankal	860	238	74	89	5
Talamarang	603	419	310	172	34
Total	6544	3598	2630	1110	689
Percentage	100	55	40.1	17	10.2

Source: ActionAid-Nepal, 1992, p29

Another remarkable example was a study conducted by Save the Children Fund (SCF) (UK) in 20 districts in three countries – Malawi, Zambia and Zimbabwe. After pilot testing, it was decided to standardize on 60 rather than 100 for pile sorting. This was then used, together with rankings and other participatory methods for a retrospective study on how individual poor farmers coped with the 1992 drought (Eldridge, 1995, 1998, 2001).

More recently, aggregation from maps has taken place on a wide scale in Rwanda where some 16,000 rural communities have made their own permanent social maps on cloth. These show all households in the communities, their levels of poverty or wealth, and other data (Ubudehe seminar, 2007; Shah, 2008).

Aggregation from focus groups

Aggregation of numbers from focus groups appears to have begun, at least in poverty studies, in the mid-1990s.

Participatory Poverty Assessments (PPAs) (Norton et al, 2001; Robb, 2002) in Kenya and Tanzania led by Deepa Narayan produced statistics by using standardized picture cards in an approach which combined RRA, PRA and SARAR (Srinivasan, 1990; Rietbergen-McCracken and Narayan, 1996).[10] In the Tanzania PPA, a team of 36 Tanzanian researchers covered 85 villages and interacted with 6000 men and women, using participatory mapping as an entry activity. Statistical outcomes were derived not least to influence policy-makers, and expressed as percentages, for example for the preferred attributes of savings institutions (which came out as interest 27.8 per cent, safety 20.4 per cent, and so on) (Narayan, c.1996).

In a Bangladesh PPA (UNDP, 1996) led by Dee Jupp and Neela Mukherjee, focus groups of poor urban and rural women and men were convened and facilitated to analyse their priorities for 'doables', practical measures that would make a difference to their lives. These were aggregated by sex and location to produce cumulative Prioritized Problem Indices of Poor (cPPIPs) which gave them comparative numerical values. These were then presented in histograms. Among the findings were, for example, that the top priority for rural women was work, and for urban women water (UNDP, 1996, p68).

In the later 1990s aggregation from focus groups was applied in remarkable studies of urban violence. Participatory research by Caroline Moser, Cathy McIlwaine and others in Jamaica, Guatemala and Colombia identified different types of violence, their seriousness, and the importance, positive or negative, of different institutions (Moser and Holland, 1997; Moser and McIlwaine, 2000a, 2000b, 2004; Moser, 2003). In the Guatemala study this led, for example, to a table derived from 176 focus group listings which showed the frequency of mention of 22 different strategies for coping with violence (Moser and McIlwaine, 2000b).

Other smaller-scale applications were developed in the course of the research, coordinated by the International Food Policy Research Institute (IFPRI), on the poverty impacts of the Consultative Group for International Agricultural Research (CGIAR) (Adato and Meinzen-Dick, 2007). Various participatory techniques were devised to generate numbers. In Western Kenya, for example, 24 focus groups evaluated agroforestry dissemination practices by pile sorting to score with 100 beans or grains of maize, applying this to seven external providers of information, and ten media used (Adato and Nyasimi, 2002).

In contrast, the study known as Voices of the Poor (Narayan et al, 2000) is probably the largest to have used aggregation from groups to date. This was undertaken to inform and influence the World Development Report 2000/2001,

Attacking Poverty (World Bank, 2000). After field-testing various combinations of methods in Bolivia, India, Sri Lanka and Thailand, a Process Guide of partially standardized, partially open-ended, methods was evolved by Meera K. Shah and others (World Bank, 1999), teams were trained, and focus groups of over 20,000 poor women and men were convened and facilitated in over 200 communities in 23 countries. Classification of outcomes and their aggregation generated proportions and percentages for directions of change in violence against women, differentiated by region. These were presented in pie diagrams. For perceived importance and effectiveness of institutions in poor urban and rural people's lives they were presented in histograms (Narayan et al, 2000, pp125, 201–202).

As is well known, the representativeness of focus groups can be an issue. With groups that convene casually, this can be a problem. How serious this is depends on context and purpose. Some common characteristics in a focus group like gender or age are easy to know and often relatively easy to assure. For social or census mapping of a village on the ground, what is shown may be common knowledge: what matters then may be diversity and breadth of participation to assure coverage and cross-checking. For other topics, purposive selection may be appropriate.[11]

Participatory wealth ranking and well-being grouping

An early form of wealth ranking (Grandin, 1988) involved separate individuals or groups sorting cards of households into piles according to their wealth. When this was done by several individuals or groups, an averaged score was calculated for each household, leading to a scored rank order by attributed wealth. This method was used initially with pastoralists for whom wealth and livestock were close to synonymous.[12]

A pioneering effort in Kenya went to scale using wealth ranking to enable Borana pastoralists to separate out three groups – rich, middle and poor; 24 rich, 17 middle and 27 poor groups were convened separately and facilitated to play a ranking game for the relative importance of problems. The results were then averaged and revealed sharp differences. As problems, livestock management scored 87 for the rich, for example, but only 7 for the poor (Swift and Umar, 1991).

Early in the 1990s wealth was more and more often replaced by well-being (*RRA Notes*, 1992), which better expressed the criteria used especially by non-pastoralist people, and grouping replaced ranking. However, the term wealth ranking continued to be used, as it will be here, for what would more accurately be described as well-being grouping. In its most common form this starts with social mapping on the ground to identify households. These are then written on individual cards. Small groups sort the cards into piles according to whatever categories of well-being or in most cases of a related concept represented by a local term, they decide upon.

In the early 1990s, ActionAid in Pakistan went to scale, and used wealth ranking for over 12,000 households. Since then other INGOs such as Plan

International have used it on a very large scale indeed as a standard practice for programme purposes in many countries, serving as an entry and exploratory activity to identify those who are considered to be worse off in communities.

Poverty: The challenge of comparisons and commensurability

Comparisons of poverty levels between communities surfaced as a problem in the Kenya PPA in the mid-1990s. There was no equivalent of a poverty line based on a questionnaire survey which notionally at least would have the same cut-off point wherever it was applied. Classical wealth ranking as articulated by Barbara Grandin (1988) produced intra-community scores for each household but these were not valid between communities. With well-being grouping, the numbers of groupings (often three, four or five) were liable to differ, and the cut-off points between the groupings were most unlikely to be identical. But now (2007) ingenious participatory solutions have been found. There may well be others besides those that follow.

Poverty lines from participatory wealth ranking in South Africa

Participatory wealth ranking (Simanowitz and Nkuna, 1998) has been evolved and applied to almost 10,000 households to assess the number of poor households and their level of poverty (Hargreaves et al, 2007). This combines qualitative and quantitative data to increase comparability across contexts, with local perceptions of poverty used to generate a wealth index of asset indicators. The information generated from a large number of rankings was used to determine indicators that were consistent between rankings. These were then used to classify households into socio-economic welfare rankings. Because many of the indicators were economic or assets, it was possible to benchmark to national poverty statistics and to assign poverty lines.

Food security in Malawi

Identifying the food insecure with conventional surveys is slow, expensive and inefficient. The Directors-General of IFPRI and the International Crops Research Institute for the Semi-arid Tropics (ICRISAT) wrote in 1997 that 'Most indicators traditionally used to identify food-insecure and undernourished households and individuals are based on the time-consuming process of assessing household consumption (by measuring total expenditures, for example) or the nutritional status of individuals' and pointed to the need of project managers for new more cost-effective indicators, which mixed qualitative and quantitative research had sought to identify (Chung et al, 1997). As with the evolution of RRA, inventiveness has been driven by practical need.

   In Malawi, the Targeted Inputs Programme (TIP) sought to provide agricultural inputs to those who were poorer. To answer the question 'Did the intervention succeed in targeting the poor?' three categories of households were

identified by participatory processes in communities: those who were food secure
– having enough to eat throughout the year from harvest to harvest; those who
were food insecure – having enough food to last from harvest to Christmas but
not between Christmas and the next harvest (in April/May); and those who were
extremely food insecure – having a longer period of not having enough to eat.
Each household in the villages visited by the study was classified into one of these
categories. The study also recorded whether or not households had received the
input package. The comparison between food security category and receipt or
non-receipt of inputs is shown in Table 6.2

Table 6.2 *Correlation between receipt of TIP and food security status*

Food security status	TIP recipients	Non-recipients	Total
Food secure	21.2	33.5	28.9
Food insecure	38.5	39.7	39.3
Extremely food insecure	40.3	26.8	31.8
Totals	100.0	100.0	100.0

Source: Levy, 2003, p22

Besides generating these numbers, the study was able to shed light on the criteria
used by communities to select beneficiaries, inclusion errors related to village
power structures, perceived unfairness, and inter-regional and local variations
(Barahona and Levy, 2007, p336).

Destitution in Ethiopia

A study of destitution in Wollo in Ethiopia used self-assessment of household livelihood viability (Sharp, 2005, p10).[13] Destitution was defined in terms of ability to
meet subsistence needs, access to livelihood resources and dependency. Qualitative
village studies contributed to the content and analysis of a questionnaire designed
for household members in a group situation. This concluded with discussion of
a carefully phrased self-assessment question. Other data from the questionnaire
were combined using weights derived from principal components analysis to
derive a 15-indicator 'objective destitution index'. The correlation in identifying
destitute households was close between the self-assessment and the objective
destitution index.

The Participatory Poverty Index in China[14]

In China, a clever participatory system was devised in 2000/01 for commensurable comparisons within and between communities. The Participatory Poverty
Index (PPI) relies on self-assessment. After preparatory investigations and
iterative pilot testing, a team identified eight common indicators representing
people's perceptions of how poverty is manifest, in priority order, in their

community. In the methodology, each household ranks its priorities and its degree of deprivation. Discussions lead to a consensus relevant to the community as a whole and weights are assigned to each indicator. To ensure comparability across communities, the weights are summed to unity. A composite PPI is calculated for each community, allowing a comparison of relative perceived deprivation between communities (Li et al, 2003; Remenyi, 2007; Li and Remenyi, forthcoming). The higher the PPI the greater is the incidence of poverty in the village and the deeper the experience of poverty. The methodology was tested and proved robust. Local poverty alleviation offices in China were quick to see the value of the eight poverty indicators, which were widely used as a basis for village poverty reduction planning. However, the PPI has not been adopted on a similar national scale, reflecting institutional commitments and political implications that would follow from the generation of a 'participatory' map of the incidence of poverty across rural China that would be in open competition with extant income-based measures (Remenyi, 2007).

The stages of progress method

The 'stages of progress' method evolved by Anirudh Krishna (2004, 2005, 2006) stands out as a remarkable achievement. To develop the method took Krishna six months of field research 'including four months experiencing nothing but failure, before a potentially workable methodology started taking shape' (Krishna, 2006, p2). Evolved and invented in Rajasthan, it has now been applied in five contexts – in Gujarat and Andhra Pradesh in India, and in Kenya, Uganda and Peru. Representative groups in communities are asked to define stages of progress that poor households typically follow on their pathways out of poverty. These are defined in terms of the sequence of what they spend on, food always coming first. Participatory classification of households according to the stages they are at, and where they were 25 years earlier, combined with household histories, give insights into why some progress and others fall back. Numbers are generated for those that have risen and fallen, and unlike conventional panel data, the reasons for rising or falling are identified. '…because Stages is easy to apply, enjoyable in practice, and its logic is intuitively clear, it can help community groups undertake analyses by themselves' (Krishna, 2006, p9). The findings have policy implications. The most striking has been that in all but one context, poor health and health-related expenses have been the most common reason associated with falling into poverty, having been identified as a factor in from 60 to 88 per cent of cases in the five contexts (Krishna, 2006, p16).

Inventiveness has been manifest in the evolution of all these methods. Typically, they have not been taken off the shelf but developed iteratively with piloting and trial and error, puzzling with problems of finding out, experimenting with processes, and taking weeks or months to evolve. Because they are new, there is much to be learnt from critical evaluation. At the same time, their lack of any methodological fundamentalism, instead relying on eclectic pluralism and an ingenious use of sequences, suggests a huge potential for future innovation.

Producing national statistics

The most remarkable breakthrough in recent years has perhaps been the use for the first time of participatory (PRA) approaches and methods to produce national statistics (Levy, 2007; Barahona and Levy, 2007). Much of this has been the work of researchers and consultants at, or associated with, the Statistical Services Centre at Reading University (www.ssc.rdg.ac.uk) and their collaborating colleagues in Malawi and Uganda. They have applied statistical principles with participatory (PRA) methods. Following the study of food security in Malawi, described above, two further developments have been with the Malawi National Census and the Uganda National Household Survey (UNHS).

In Malawi, the national census 1998 gave a total rural population of 8.5 million people, in 1.95 million households, while a national programme for supplying starter packs for agriculture was working on the basis of 2.89 million households. To attempt to resolve this discrepancy, statistical principles and PRA methods were combined. Participatory community censuses were facilitated in 54 villages selected using probability methods. Participatory mapping was used to identify households (Barahona and Levy, 2003, pp4–9). The findings indicated a rural population of the order of 11.5 million, some 35 per cent higher than the official census figure.

More recently, a further breakthrough has been achieved in Uganda, applying a participatory module to a subsample of the UNHS (Kagugube et al, 2007). The Ugandan team included government staff with years of experience of participatory approaches and methods in the Uganda Participatory Poverty Assessment Process (UPPAP). They spent much time and effort devising a 'qualitative module' known as the Rope Technique. In this module, community participants placed household cards on a rope. The top and bottom of the rope represented extreme conditions for seven dimensions – having assets for production, food security, sending children to school, access to medical services, having enough money, having many dependents with few resources, and powerlessness. The top and bottom extremes were described verbally. The rope was then divided equally into ten, and scores from one to ten allocated. The rope scores for each dimension could then be integrated across sites. Questions have been raised, for example concerning major differences between income findings from the UNHS questionnaire and 'having enough money' in the qualitative module. The discrepancies are little short of spectacular and cry out for investigation. This method, and possible future variants of it, open up scope for calibrating and cross-checking national questionnaire surveys, and for time series trend data on dimensions like powerlessness previously considered purely qualitative and not comparable between communities.

In sum, the potential is not just producing national statistics; it is producing national statistics that are more accurate, that illuminate domains hitherto inaccessible, and that measure dimensions that have previously been seen as only qualitative. A whole new professional field has been opened up for exploration, innovation and application.

Who counts?

Participatory Impact Assessment (PIA) to inform policy

PIA to inform policy has been successfully pioneered in Ethiopia in two livestock-related studies (Abebe et al, 2007). Participatory methods were standardized. The first study, repeated with ten groups, assessed the impact of Community-based Animal Health Workers (CAHWs) on animal diseases. Standard statistical methods found significant reductions for camels, cattle and sheep and goats for a range of diseases. The second study, with 114 households, assessed the impact of a commercial destocking intervention in drought and compared its benefits with other interventions. These studies included locally defined impact indicators, local community priorities, the use of a wide range of PRA tools, testing of tools for measurement, choice of sample size, triangulation, assessment of multiple causality, and feedback to communities. The findings were used to influence policy, contributing for example to the official recognition of CAHWs in national legislation and guidelines (Catley, 2007).

Participatory M and E and empowerment

The processes of participation in these examples have tended to be more ex-tractive than empowering, in the sense of outsiders obtaining information rather than local people gaining and using it. Extractive–empowering is not, however, a simple dichotomy but a continuum with nuances, mixes and sequences. Spread out across the range of this continuum are the processes labelled participatory monitoring and evaluation (PM and E), and only quite rarely treated separately as participatory monitoring on its own, or participatory evaluation on its own.

Practices of PM and E have proliferated, a thousand flowers in a thousand places, and much has been written about them[15] (e.g. Estrella and Gaventa, 1997; MacGillivray et al, 1998; Guijt, 1998, 2000; Estrella et al, 2000). In PM and E processes, the usual questions about power and ownership are raised:

- Whose monitoring and evaluation?
- Whose indicators and numbers, for whose purpose?
- Analysed and used by whom?
- Who learns, and who is empowered?
- Who gains?

Numbers could be expected to be a common part of PM and E. A drive for participatory numbers often comes from outside the local context. Even so, participants can still gain: insights and numbers can often be of interest and use to community members. To an extent easily overlooked, people enjoy and learn from the processes of analysis and sharing of knowledge, values and priorities, and feel good at discovering what they can show and express, and having their views heard. A typical observation has been that, 'People participating in the groups seemed to enjoy the discussions and exercises and most stayed for the entire duration' (Adato and Nyasimi, 2002).

In principle, the more participatory a process, the more local people will identify their own indicators and then monitor them. The Nepal Utilization study (ActionAid-Nepal, 1992) stated that 'the monitoring should be a participatory process which involves the community in deciding information to be collected, in collecting and in analysing ... and finally using the information for programme improvements'. The indicators can be numbers that are counted, qualities that are scored, quantities that are measured or estimated, and so on.

However, the literature I have reviewed that is directly on PM and E is striking for how rarely it records cases of local people actually using numbers for monitoring of change over any length of time. This is excepting practices of keeping financial accounts in self-help and savings groups, and other local organizations, all of which entail numerical monitoring but which are not considered part of PM and E. One reason for the few cases may be that some of the literature is describing ideas that seem good but have not been implemented. Another may be that periods of observation that get written up in accessible papers tend to be short. Yet another, and perhaps more common, may be low relevance and utility to the people concerned given the time and cost of collection and assessment. There are anecdotes of local people keeping numerical records for a time simply to please or pacify a visitor or official but stopping as soon as they feel they can.[16] Overall, the paucity of examples may reflect rational assessments of the costs and benefits of counting or measuring compared with less formal assessments. Numbers may be sought and needed much more by outside agencies and by professionals with trained mathematical backgrounds than by local people who have many other modes of assessment, monitoring and evaluating. Indeed, the more numbers are stressed by outsiders in PM and E, the less participatory the processes may often become.

The most common cases of PM and E with numbers that I have been able to trace are of four types:

1   **Retrospective assessments** indicating how present conditions differ from those of the past. These are one-off activities often of high interest to participants. They may be evaluative, but they are not ongoing and so not strictly monitoring. For example, in Somaliland, herders most impressively evaluated wells by scoring them before and after improvement according to their own 45 criteria (Sanaag CBO, 1999; Joseph et al, 1994).
2   **Short-term intense monitoring** for a short period of acute relevance, as by a farmer or a farmer field school during a crop season, or by a community during a campaign like CLTS (see pp96–97).
3   **Gathering empowering data**, especially statistics that a group or community can use as part of their armoury to gain or improve a service, assert their rights, or obtain a better deal.
4   **Monitoring natural resource management**, for example fisheries (CBCRM, 2003a, 2003b) where the indicators may be catches, sizes of fish and so on. In a river in Laos, the number and size of bubbles were taken as indicators of the number and size of fish stocks (pers. comm. Mark Dubois)

An increasingly widespread use of numbers in PM and E is with CLTS (Kar, 2005; Kar and Pasteur, 2005; Kar and Bongartz, 2006; Kar with Chambers, 2008). Communities that engage with the process of making themselves totally open-defecation free often make and display maps showing all households, those that have access to latrines, and those that do not, and use these to monitor their own progress, sometimes with symbols or colours to represent different weeks of completion or gaining access. During CLTS campaigns in some sub-districts of North-west Bangladesh, these figures were regularly reported upwards from hamlet to ward to union to sub-district headquarters, and aggregated for monitoring at those higher levels. In Hatibandha sub-district, figures were reported for the numbers of latrines of three categories so that improving standards could also be monitored.

Three-way tensions can arise between the desire of agencies for numbers, the objectives of empowerment and the time of facilitating staff. One example from India is the ILS (Internal Learning System) developed by Helzi Noponen (Noponen, 2007) and with her involvement adopted and adapted by two large NGOs – NESA (the New Entity for Social Action) and Pradan (Professional Assistance for Development Action), and their partners. Its most striking element is visual diaries which poor people keep and use for their own analysis and for recording change. NESA with its partners has introduced these diaries into some 2000 villages in South India: women enter scores from one to five, every six months, for aspects of life like degree of satisfaction with equal treatment of their girl and boy children, physical violence against them, how much their husbands share in domestic tasks, and so on (Nagasundari, 2007). Pradan has evolved an application with self-help groups and for livelihood planning (Narendranath, 2007). With both NESA and Pradan, there have been issues of optimizing combinations and trade-offs between complexity or simplicity, the time of facilitating staff, standardization, and the remarkable learning and empowerment that can be achieved.

Similar issues have arisen with another family of PM and E approaches, PALS (Participatory Action Learning System) pioneered and propagated by Linda Mayoux (2004, 2007). This is an eclectic and constantly evolving methodology using a set of diagram tools and participatory processes which enable people, including very poor non-literate women, men and children, to collect and analyse the information which they themselves need on an ongoing basis to improve their lives in ways they decide. Though the diagrams are simple and quickly learnt, there are balances to be struck between people gaining confidence and learning on the one hand, and standardization and making a difference with higher-level decision-makers on the other.

Participatory statistics, empowerment and policy influence

Participatory statistics can reverse the quotation at the head of this chapter. Their numbers can be servants of the weak to master the strong. How they can empower local people and groups is an emergent field. CIRAC, the International

Reflect Circle, has included an excellent short guide 'Alternative Statistics' – how PRA techniques can be used to produce local statistics – as part of its practical resource materials (Archer and Newman, 2003). These are designed for use by Reflect facilitators and groups. The authors point out that 'Because many of the graphics [produced by Reflect groups] are about recording local reality they are the perfect starting point to produce statistics', and cite maps, calendars and matrices as examples. The resulting numbers can be used for policy influence. A group in Mozambique used various graphics to collect a diverse range of statistics, including some concerning schooling. In Bangladesh, a Reflect circle used a matrix to track daily wages for different jobs, and different people (men, women and children). They used this as evidence that the national minimum wage was not being met.

Participatory statistics have also supported decentralized and democratic governance. In the Philippines (Nierras, 2002) grass-roots health workers made their own classifications and disease maps, conducted their own analyses, and produced village figures at variance with official statistics, but which officials came to accept. Remarkably, they identified priority actions which led in a matter of months to a sharp decrease in mortality. Or again, participatory investigation of land holdings in the Philippines led to revisions of figures which doubled local government takings from the land tax, the principal source of revenue. These compelling examples open one's eyes to what appears to be a widespread potential.

Participatory statistics can be persuasive and more credible than those from questionnaire investigations. But they may be discounted when they challenge official statistics and threaten professional reputations. Malawi has one of the poorest and most vulnerable rural populations in the world, demanding special interventions. The professional and statistically rigorous participatory mixed – methods study of 54 carefully selected villages reported by Barahona and Levy (2003) indicated a rural population of 11.5 million, 35 per cent higher than the 1998 census figure of 8.5 million![17] The implications were not trivial. But the study findings:

> *...have not been taken seriously by the NSO [National Statistical Office of Malawi], Malawi government policy-makers or donors, who continue to uphold the 1998 census. When questions are raised about official population figures, stakeholders should demand further exploration of the data and, if necessary, commission further ground truth studies. If the 1998 census did seriously underestimate the rural population, as our work suggests, this has important consequences for government and donor-funded interventions as well as official figures such as GDP per capita.'* (Barahona and Levy, 2003, p8)

And they conclude that 'We should not ask communities (or groups within them) to spend time on research if we do not believe the policy-makers will take the findings seriously' (Barahona and Levy, 2003, p43).

These experiences are both sobering and inspiring: sobering in the Malawi case, because even though rigorously professional, the participatory statistics were in some quarters not taken seriously; inspiring in the Philippines because they were accepted as superior and made significant differences. For the future, there is much to be learnt: about why responses such as these can be so different; and about the how, what, when, where and in what form to generate and present participatory statistics so that they empower poor and local people, credibly present truth to power, and make a real difference for the better.

Enough is already known, though, to move forward. Sarah Levy (2007) has presented 'a vision for the 21st century' with locally owned information systems. She writes of:

> *...the need to rebuild the information systems that exist in developing countries, incorporating new indicators and new methods of data collection and management which better respond to the needs of development in the 21st century. The current system and approaches are based on methods that were seen as modern 60 years ago, but are no longer in tune with our information requirements...'* (Levy, 2007, p145)

She argues that for decentralization, empowerment at the local level, policy influence, and achievement of the Millennium Development Goals (MDGs), information should be collected and analysed at the level of a village, a set of villages and their urban and semi-urban equivalents. To inform and influence both local and higher-level action the information would include, for example, indicators of poverty and hunger; enrolments in primary and secondary education (by gender); data on child mortality and maternal and other aspects of health. She concludes that locally owned and managed information systems, feeding into higher level statistics:

> *...gives us an opportunity to reform out-of-date over-centralized information collection systems. The development challenges of the 21st century – among them meeting the MDGs – require new approaches to the production and ownership of information. If we want to empower poor people to take part in reducing poverty and promoting development, we must end the monopoly of information by central governments. The development of participatory methods capable of producing local as well as national statistics means that the potential now exists, even in remote and marginalized communities, for people to produce their own information. The results have the potential to be more reliable than those produced by outsiders. To governments and donors I would say: this is an opportunity that should not be missed...* (Levy, 2007, p149)

The best of all worlds?

Apart from vested interests tied to professional conservatism and inertia, the potentials from participatory numbers appear to be win–win, with promise of the best of all worlds. They can combine qualitative contextual relevance (with local knowledge, categories etc.) with quantitative significance. Beyond this, in assessing potentials, even erring on the side of caution, other strengths of participatory numbers are striking. Not only are there dimensions of empowerment, but four other overlapping strengths stand out: validity and reliability; insights into sensitive subjects; unexpected findings with policy implications; and power and learning.

Validity and reliability

Dimensions of validity and reliability have been repeatedly illustrated and confirmed. Group-visual synergy (see p99) has proved a powerful source of cross-checking, successive approximation, and bringing out additional information and insights. Its trustworthiness and rigour are confirmable by observation of the group process and by the relevance to participants of the analysis which assures their commitment and engagement. The extreme accuracy of most social mapping in a census mode has been repeatedly confirmed (Chambers, 1997, p144–147; Barahona and Levy, 2003, p6), especially when there is triangulation between groups from the same community. In an Indian village four groups met separately and came up with populations of 239, 239, 242 and 247. When villagers checked, they found that 242 had three cases of double-counting, and 247, made by a small group on the edge of the village, included a family of eight who were in dispute with the rest of the village (pers. comm. Jules Pretty). So there was highly credible cross-checked consensus: a population of 239 without the family of eight, or 247 with it.

Where there is standardization with participatory methods there are issues of validity and sample size. Using a minimalist approach to sample size, the Participatory Approaches to Veterinary Epidemiology project in East Africa determined the minimum number of repetitions to shift results from qualitative to quantitative using conventional statistical principles: for some methods such as matrix scoring and seasonal calendars as few as eight repetitions allowed quantitative estimates of reliability to be calculated (Catley, 2007).

Insights into sensitive subjects

Well thought out and facilitated participatory processes have shown a remarkable capacity for opening up and giving numbers and proportions to subjects so sensitive that they are usually hidden. The limitations of verbal responses to sensitive subjects are well known. We now know that, contrary to some professional belief, approaches which involve groups as well as individuals, and elements which are visual and tangible, can encourage and enable people to express and analyse aspects of life and conditions which they most likely would not otherwise reveal. Here are some illustrations:

- In China, the balance of power between male and female in whether to use a condom (Jayakaran, 2003, p132) using the ten seed technique. The outcome was nine male, one female.[18]

- In Tamil Nadu, the identification and location within a village of abusive and drunken husbands (pers. comm. John Devavaram and Sheelu Francis, 1991).
- In Orissa, a participatory study gave the caste-wise breakdown of the number of families with addiction to alcohol, and a matrix by caste showing who consumed alcohol, frequency, variety, expenditure, and domestic violence (PRAXIS, 2001, p33).
- In Malawi (see pp116–117) the major divergences between those meant to receive starter packs and those who did were revealed (Levy, 2003).
- In Zambia, an astonishing range of information was brought out about pre-pubertal and adolescent sexual behaviour, including ranking and scoring matrices for girls' typologies of sex partners and preferences, and using an anonymous slips method, for both girls and boys (in separate groups) the age of first sex and number of sexual partners they had had (Shah et al, 1999a, pp45–46, 63–64).

Unexpected and striking insights for policy

Participatory numbers throw up striking insights with policy implications, and do this in a statistical form (for detailed reports of which the reader is referred to the sources cited). The credibly established 35 per cent undercount in the Malawi rural population census already mentioned (Barahona and Levy, 2003) is an instance with huge implications for government policy and even for calculations of per capita GDP. Other illustrations are:

- The SCF study of responses to drought, by putting numbers to them, showed how remittances declined for the poor but were slightly up for the better-off, how the poor spent more on food than the rich, and how income reductions were greater among the poor because they were more dependent on natural resources (Eldridge, 1995, 1998).
- Moser and McIlwaine's work in nine urban communities in Colombia elicited numerous types of violence, and produced the unexpected finding that 54 per cent of the types of violence identified were economic (related to drugs, insecurity, robbery, gangs etc.) as against only 14 per cent political (related to police abuse, war, paramilitaries, assassinations etc.) contrary to the common belief that political violence was the bigger problem (Moser and McIlwaine, 2000a, p62).
- The Bangladesh PPA (UNDP, 1996) found that the second and third 'doable' priorities for poor urban women (their first was water) were a private place for washing, and action on dowry.
- The Starter Pack study in Malawi used pair-wise ranking across villages to generate scores for 15 indicators of sustainability that farmers themselves had identified during piloting. These placed crop diversification and access to seeds top, and remarkably (since this conflicted with professional views) put agroforestry and fallow at the bottom, suggesting an over-riding short-term priority given to adequate food (Cromwell et al, 2001, p6).

Power, reversals and learning

Power and learning are bottom lines, with the promise of win–win solutions which combine local learning and local empowerment and at the same time supply numbers useful to outsiders and their organizations, and for policy influence.

All then learn. It is not only, or even mainly, the outsiders who gain useful knowledge. Chung et al, (1997, p60) reported that 'Some villagers were astonished by their own food charts; they had not imagined they ate so many kinds of foods. Some spontaneously asked 'Are we eating OK? What should we eat?' Quantification is one of the channels through which local appraisal and analysis can lead to local learning and action.

Participatory numbers can also reverse power relations. Most obviously this is through the persuasiveness of statistics presented to policy-makers, as noted above. The reversal can also be face to face, where the power relations and feedback are transformed through a participatory process (see Box 7.1).

Alternatives to questionnaires

The cumulative experience and evidence, some of it presented above, builds a case for much more widespread use of participatory numbers in development practice and research. In many contexts and for many purposes, processes generating participatory numbers appear better than traditional questionnaires. This has been becoming evident since the early 1990s. For entities which are visible, known about and can be counted, like people, they can produce highly cross-checked and accurate numbers, as with the Malawi census; they can put numbers on qualitative dimensions; and they can provide 'numerical data on complex issues about which questionnaire surveys are not able to produce reliable statistics, such as community poverty targeting' (Barahona and Levy, 2007, p338). Participatory epidemiology (PE) methods such as proportional piling to assess livestock disease incidence and mortality, and matrix scoring, have been found to be 'more valid than conventional methods such as questionnaires... In many cases, PE methods have proved to be far more useful than questionnaires because many epidemiological questions are well-suited to the visualization and scoring methods of PE, and PE uses local language' (Catley, 2007). Conducted well, participatory methods promise win–wins with more valid numbers, better insights, and gains for local people in their own knowledge and understanding.

For special studies, participatory numbers can now be considered such a strong option that they should be considered first. Again and again the verdict of the 1991 Nepal survey conducted through participatory village mapping has been confirmed: 'The participatory method for information collection, compared to the conventional one is proved to be more effective and convenient' (ActionAid-Nepal, 1992, p23).

Comparisons of costs and accuracy of questionnaires and participatory numbers have been decisively in favour of the latter (Chambers, 1997, pp122–125). A reasonable rule of thumb is that conventional questionnaires should be used only if no participatory alternative can be devised, or should be used only in a light and quick manner for confirmation and triangulation with other methods. There is a reversal here of mental set and reflex. When numbers are needed, participatory approaches, methods and behaviours replace questionnaires as the standard approach that first comes to mind.

The case for continuing long-term time series, like the National Sample Survey in India and some Living Standards Measurement Surveys may appear strong, at least in the short and medium term. Flawed though they may be, they do provide materials for comparisons over time and between contexts. All the same, the recent innovations by professional statisticians using PRA methods to generate national statistics in Malawi (Barahona and Levy, 2007), together with the participatory module in the UNHS (Kagugube et al, 2007), reinforce the already strong case for exploring and piloting not just complements but alternatives. At the very least, these innovations make further methodological research a priority.

Because this field is so largely unexplored, its potential is difficult to assess. The normal professional reflex from many economists, statisticians and others, will be to reject this suggestion out of hand. But enough has now been learnt, as evidenced above, to make the case for innovation and piloting to learn more about what can be done. The unknown potential may be big. If so, it could be professionally transformative and lead to better understanding of realities, better numbers, and better policies and practices.

There will always remain issues for innovation and research. These include, for different contexts and purposes, updating and analysing evidence and experience, comparing different participatory and other approaches for their relative costs and relative benefits. But enough has been known for over ten years to justify decisive innovation and change. Many who are mentally and physically cocooned in citadels of professional power may not want to know, but the evidence and the signposts are clear. Much more of the future lies with the inventiveness, relevance and creativity associated with participatory numbers than they may be able or willing to recognize.

Methodological challenges

The methodological challenges are, however, not trivial. The pioneers of participatory numbers and statistics have had to show ingenuity, skill, patience and courage in the face of conventional reflexes. Some of the issues concern applying statistical principles. Others entail optimizing trade-offs; for example:

*   **Standardized, closed and commensurable versus open, diverse and empowering**: trade-offs between the rigidity of preset categories and the diversity of categories likely to result from open-ended participatory processes. David Booth has expressed concern that the exploratory, responsive, and reflexive nature of inquiries will be sacrificed through standardization to permit aggregation upwards (Booth, 2003). It is important to

confront this issue. The more standardized the process, the more extractive and less empowering and accommodating of local priorities and realities it is likely to be. The less standardized it is, the harder the outcomes are to analyse. A partial solution can be found in progressive participatory piloting and evolution towards degrees of standardization as in the first Malawi starter pack study (Cromwell et al, 2001). This can lead to standardizing some categories, for example entities and criteria in matrix scoring, and leaving others open, limiting statistical analysis to those which are standardized.

- **Scale, quality, time, resources and ethics**: the issues here are far from simple. Smaller scale, more time, and more resources can allow for higher quality and better ethics but loss of representativeness; and vice versa. And if there are gains to local people through awareness and empowerment, wider scale with lower gains may mean greater gains overall.

- **Quality of facilitation versus speed, scale and cost of implementation**: in these approaches, the quality of facilitation is critical (Nandago, 2007). To achieve good facilitation requires time and resources devoted to careful selection of facilitators, their training and then their supervision in the field. This may add to costs and slow implementation and limit its scale, even if the outcomes are still highly cost-effective compared with alternatives. An adequate number and availability of skilled facilitators may be the most serious constraint on the widespread adoption of participatory numbers.

- **Ease and spontaneity of convening groups versus representativeness**: where groups are involved, and as is well known with focus groups generally, those who are most easily convened may be unrepresentative or dominated by one or a few people, or by one sort of person (for example, men in a mixed group of men and women). Care in selection, in judging size of group, and observation and facilitation of process can offset these dangers but take time and effort and can entail a loss of spontaneity. That said, for many purposes, for example appraisal of animal diseases, it is not representativeness as much as relevant knowledge that matters in a group.

The future

The evidence presented is only the tip of an iceberg. More and more cases and examples of participatory numbers are coming to light. We have come a long way from the time when rapid and participatory approaches were seen in discord with statistics. The potentials of the NE quadrant – participatory numbers – in Figure 6.1 are gradually being recognized but with nothing like the attention or intensity they deserve. The question now is how to establish spread and practices which are good both methodologically and ethically.

Conditions can be compared with the early days of RRA in the late 1970s (Chapter 4), and PRA in the late 1980s and early 1990s (Chapter 5), when it was becoming clear that something was about to happen on a wide scale. Both RRA and PRA challenged and presented alternatives to professionally embedded methodologies. With both there was some excellent and inspiring good practice as they spread. But there are dire warnings. Both RRA and PRA became fashionable labels, demanded by donors and promised by consultants. With rapid spread and heavy demand, many who claimed to be RRA or PRA trainers and practitioners had top–down attitudes and behaviour, and lacked practical experience. Much practice was abusive – imposed, routinized, insensitive, unimaginative, exploitative and unethical. People were alienated, data were unusable and unused, and the approaches misleadingly discredited.

Three differences from those early experiences with RRA and PRA give grounds for hope.

The first is the serious professional and academic interest in qualitative–quantitative issues and going to scale, including the application of group-visual methods. This is evident in publications such as *Participation and Combined Methods in African Poverty Assessment: Renewing the Agenda* (Booth et al, 1998), publications of the Statistical Services Centre at Reading University, the Cornell March 2001 Qualitative–Quantitative Workshop (Kanbur, 2003), and the Swansea July 2002 Conference on Qualitative and Quantitative Methods in Development Research. Since 2002, the International and Rural Development Department and the Statistical Services Centre at the University of Reading have convened workshops for participatory practitioners on 'Dealing with data from participatory studies: Bridging the gap between qualitative and quantitative methods', combining statistical professionalism with participatory practice and ethics.

The second difference is that the application of participatory numbers approaches requires more serious preparation than PRA. Almost anyone can do almost anything participatory and call it PRA. To generate numbers, however, requires more thought, preparation, pilot testing and discipline. It has been the repeated experience of pioneers like Carlos Barahona, Sarah Levy and their colleagues at Reading, and Anirudh Krishna, who after four months of field experimentation was on the verge of despair, that evolving a methodology can take time, patience and creativity. This characteristic should to some degree exercise a built-in discipline.

The third ground for hope is that much has been learnt from the RRA and PRA experiences. We have been here before. RRA and more so PRA taught us above all the crucial importance of the personal dimension, often summarized as behaviour and attitudes, to which now can be added mindsets. What we are able to learn, and its quality, depends not just on what methods we use, but on what sort of people we are, how creative and inventive we are, how we relate to others, and how open we are to learning.

The examples, experiences and evidence presented in this chapter point to important potentials: for those in power to be better and more realistically informed and more persuasively influenced; and for those who are marginalized and misunderstood to express their realities in ways which are convincing: through their counting to count more.

For these potentials to be realized, professionals, especially bureaucrats and researchers, have to examine and challenge their conditioning, habits and mindsets, and rethink. This should often lead to the adoption of participatory processes in place of others of current convention, especially questionnaires. The implications are radical: for university and college curricula, for textbooks, for teachers, for statistical organizations, for research institutes, for professional training, and for development professionals generally. The challenge is greatest in those organizations – universities, funding agencies and governments – trapped by inertia, repetition and tradition, and where power lies with senior people who are out of touch and out of date. So far, progress has been scattered and sporadic, at times ephemeral. An inspiring exception is veterinary epidemiology (Catley, 2007). In that discipline, statistics generated through participatory approaches have been accepted as participatory epidemiology has been institutionalized, at first in East Africa: in university teaching and research, peer-reviewed international journals, a standard textbook (Thrusfield, 2005), and national and international research organizations. Momentum is building in other disciplines too but participatory numbers are not yet in the mainstreams of their professional practice. Least of all, perhaps, are they recognized by the powerful economists in the citadels of Washington DC. Why do so few recognize and enter this new world, or make space for others to do so? Will future generations of development professionals look back and wonder why we were so slow to see what had opened up, and to change?

Notes

1   This chapter is a slightly shortened version of IDS Working Paper 296 *Who Counts? The quiet revolution of participation and numbers*, December 2007. Predecessors were presented to the March 2001 Cornell University workshop on Qualitative and Quantitative Poverty Appraisal: Complementarities, Tensions and the Way Forward; the July 2002 University of Swansea conference on Combining Qualitative and Quantitative Methods in Development Research; and the November 2003 University of Manchester conference on New Directions in Impact Assessment. For comments and information I thank participants at those conferences. Others who have contributed with criticism, advice and information are too many to name. I am grateful to them all, and especially to those who took part during 2001–04 in the informal 'Party Numbers' group which met in the UK at the Centre for Development Studies, Swansea, the Centre for Statistical Services, Reading, the Institute of Development Studies, Sussex, the International HIV/AIDS Alliance, Brighton, the Overseas Development Institute, London, and the International Institute for Environment and Development, London.

2   For a clear and authoritative statement of the application of statistical principles to these processes see Barahona and Levy, 2003, pp23–41, and 2007. Staff at the Statistical Services Centre at the University of Reading have been outstanding in piloting, pioneering and disseminating statistical rigour and ethical concerns in the generation of participatory numbers. Much can be found on their website www.ssc.rdg.ac.uk

3   I have taken these terms from van der Riet n.d.

4   An increasing number of handbooks include participatory methods that generate numbers, for example Mikkelsen, 1995, 2005.

5   The largest number of mother tongues in my experience to date has been 36, in a workshop with 70 graduate students at Reading University, UK, equalled, but by a larger number of students, at IDS Sussex and the University of Sussex in October 2007.

6   If analysts themselves count out the number of beans, they tend to have a greater sense of ownership of the process.

7   There are many methods and combinations and sequences of methods. The multiplicity is illustrated by the title of Neela Mukherjee's (2002) book *Participatory Learning and Action with 100 Field Methods*.

8   I was a participant in an appointments board which considered five candidates for a post. After interviewing them, we reviewed our criteria, drew a matrix, and scored each box with beans out of five. The scores were easy to debate and change. The process was fun and free of the tensions and conflict which are so common. I think it was much more focused, fast and consensual than it would otherwise have been. The candidate appointed went on to an outstanding career.

9   I shall be grateful to anyone who can tell me of any earlier case.

10 SARAR stands for Self esteem, Associative strength, Resourcefulness, Action planning and Responsibility.

11 For further discussion of these issues see Mayoux and Chambers, 2005, pp282–285.

12 The same word *mali* in Swahili is used by Kenya pastoralists to mean both wealth and livestock.

13 Sharp cites Bevan and Joireman (1997) for an earlier example, the insertion of a personal wealth-ranking question in a questionnaire survey.

14 For reasons of space and balance, the account of the methodology given here is compressed and cryptic. For fuller exposition and explanation the reader is referred to the references.

15 For selected abstracts see www.ids.ac.uk/ids/particip

16 Polite and prudent maintenance of records for authority is so widespread that it can be regarded as an embedded feature of the modern human condition.

17 Reportedly the undercounts were most marked in those areas supporting opposition parties.

18 For other applications to sensitive topics with similar methods see Jayakaran, 2007.

Whose Space? Mapping, Power and Ethics[1]

Mapping as an activity brings with it the power to name, to define, to locate and to situate... Maps can be made through presence, practice, words, paper, or code, but always depend upon and facilitate the exercise and recognition of power. (Rocheleau, 2005)

Abstract

Local people's abilities to make maps only became widely known and facilitated in the early 1990s. In recent years, changes have been rapid in both participatory methodologies and spatial information technologies (SITs). The phenomenal spread of participatory mapping has manifested in many variants and applications in natural resource management and other domains. The medium and means of mapping, whether ground, paper or Participatory Geographic Information Systems (PGIS), and the style and mode of facilitation affect who takes part, the nature of outcomes and power relationships. Cartographic maps and SITs can tend to serve the state and outside interests, disempowering and dispossessing local people. PRA/PLA and spatial information technologies have combined as a form of counter mapping to reverse and prevent this, empowering minority groups and those traditionally excluded from spatial decision-making. Much depends on the behaviour, attitudes and commitment of the facilitators who are technology intermediaries, and on who controls the process. Ethical issues present dilemmas with questions of empowerment, ownership and use of maps. Questions to be asked, again and again, are: 'Who is empowered and who is disempowered?' and 'Who gains and who loses?'

Of all the visual activities, often referred to as participatory rural appraisal (PRA) methods, that have taken off and been widely adopted, participatory mapping has been the most widespread. Participatory modelling has also made a breakthrough through the work of Giacomo Rambaldi and his colleagues in the Philippines and elsewhere (Rambaldi and Callosa-Tarr, 2000, 2002). Other methods, like matrix scoring, seasonal diagramming, Venn diagramming, causal-linkage and flow diagramming, and wealth or well-being ranking, have been adopted and used, one can almost say 'all over the world'. But the versatility and power of participatory mapping, the relative ease with which it can be facilitated, the fun, fulfilment and pride which people derive from it, and its multiple uses by so many stakeholders, have helped it to spread more than the others. It has been a meme:[2] an idea and behaviour that have been taken up on a wide scale as people have heard about it or seen examples. Spread has been explosive and exponential, like wildfire, with innumerable adaptations and variations. By 2008 well over a million participatory maps must have been made.

The origins and history of participatory mapping

It is astonishing and sobering to see how far we have come and how fast, and how ignorant we were just a few years ago. It is also striking how easy it is to overlook early innovations.

Before the late 1980s and early 1990s when some of us were so excited at what we were finding local people could do, indigenous, local and participatory mapping had already taken place in different regions, countries and continents. Indigenous cartographies[3] – mapping and various forms of spatial representation by local people – have a long history, and very likely a prehistory. Some remarkable examples are shown in the delightful book *Maps are Territories* by David Turnbull (1989). The earliest is a wall painting dating to 6200 BC, from Catal Huyuk. There are coastal charts carved in wood and carried in their kayaks by the Greenland Inuit. There is a manuscript map of the Mississippi by Non Chi Ning Ga, an Iowa Indian Chief, presented in 1837 in Washington as part of a land claim. And most remarkable of all are stick charts from the Marshall Islands in which shells represent islands, and sticks show currents and lines of swell. Yet other examples in the book express cultural knowledge and senses of place of Australian Aborigines and the San of the Kalahari.

Mapping facilitated by outsiders is more recent. More remarkable than what local people had already done in mapping and other forms of spatial representation was 'our' educated professional ignorance of their mapping abilities. Not even social anthropologists appear to have facilitated mapping as part of their normal repertoire. We simply did not know what people could do. There were initiatives which hindsight can see as precursors of what was to come. In Kingston, Jamaica, in the 1970s, Frances Madden (pers. comm.) asked youths to draw a map to show where waste bins should be located; but when she showed the map to her supervisor he told her to go away and do a proper one. Around the same time Robert Rhoades (pers. comm.) facilitated 3D modelling by farmers in the Andes. A little later, Jeremy Swift[4] and his research team asked Wodaabe Fulani pastoralists in Niger to draw maps, which they did without difficulty: their maps showed ecological zones and special areas, including one where their cattle developed night blindness in the dry season forcing them to leave otherwise good pastures. Reportedly, World Vision facilitated mapping in Tamil Nadu in the early 1980s. Participatory soil maps were reported in the latter 1980s (Behrens, 1989).[5] The value of mapping was discussed at the 'Farmer First' conference at the Institute of Development Studies (IDS) in 1987. We were on the edge of the breakthrough, but it is fascinating to read what was written and understood at the time, and to see that the cutting edge of the discussion was still more in terms of mapping **with** farmers than mapping **by** them (Gupta and IDS workshop, 1989; Conway, 1989). And doubtless there were other examples. There was a flood tide of recognition of the richness, detail, validity and value of indigenous technical knowledge but not yet full appreciation of farmers' capabilities in mapping, diagramming and analysis. We (agricultural extensionists and 'educated' professionals in general) were still so conditioned by our own cartography and ideas of what were proper maps, and by the belief that only we could make them, that we did not realize how well and how usefully local 'uneducated' people did, and could, make their own. So these earlier initiatives remained isolated and did not spread.

Even if personal journeys give distorted views of events, they may throw some light on process, timing and sequence. I was lucky to be a participant-observer through the enthralling revolution which took place. First, before it began, in the early 1970s, for work on social and organizational aspects of pastoral development, I needed a map of soil–vegetation associations of the north-east of Kenya. An oil-prospecting map covered the eastern half. The western half was largely blank, with only a few widely spaced place names. I spent much time being, as I thought, rather clever, filling in the blanks by asking pastoralists how many hours it would take them to walk to places they could name but which were not on the map from places which were on the map, and then triangulating and entering the location. They then shouted out the dominant soil type of the area. It never occurred to me to ask them to draw the map themselves! Agroecosystem analysis (Conway, 1985; Gypmantasiri et al, 1980) was then a methodological breakthrough of the 1980s, and contributed the practice of sketch mapping to rapid rural appraisal (RRA). But the maps were still made by 'us' and often had serious inaccuracies and omissions.

A seminal incident took place in 1988 in an RRA training at Lathodara in Gujarat with the Aga Khan Rural Support Programme (AKRSP) (India) (McCracken, 1989, p20; Shah, 2003, p189). A headman found it difficult to understand the map the outsiders had drawn until he turned it 'upside down' to see it his way. This story went around.

Then during another RRA training in February 1989, in a village in the Sudan, we asked a teacher to draw a map on the ground. A participant objected that this was demeaning. He was educated and should do it on paper. The result was small and not useful. So over two days we made our own sketch map. When we checked it out with villagers, we, and they, were embarrassed: 'You have shown only one bakery, but we have three'.

We were teetering on the brink of learning that 'They can do it'.

Ground and paper mapping

The breakthrough came later in 1989 during the early evolution of PRA in India. Villagers showed that they could themselves make their own often brilliant maps on the ground and on paper. It came with moments of ahha! and wow!

These were astonishing at the time. The first PRA event, in Kalmandargi village in Gulbarga District, was led by Jimmy Mascarenhas of MYRADA. While two artists made useless pretty drawings of the view from the top of a hill, five farmers nearby, facilitated by Prem Kumar and others of the MYRADA team, dug up a grassy patch, and in a few hours fashioned a spectacular 3D model of their village and watershed, using coloured rangoli powders to show land types and uses. At the end one villager said with satisfaction and pride: 'This is something I have been wanting to do all my life.'

In the second PRA, in Kistagiri village in Mahbubnagar District, the first social and resource maps were made. For me, the contrast could hardly have been starker or more dramatic between what happened there and an earlier experience. In 1974, I spent two hot days in a village in Tamil Nadu trying, and failing, to make a map to show all the wells in the fields. In Kistagiri, when Sam Joseph invited farmers to make their own map they plotted all their wells with much animated cross-checking and correction, and then indicated which were in good condition, and which were not. And they did this in 25 minutes!

In this dawn, as with hindsight it was, we kept wondering whether these were near-miraculous one-off anomalies. We hardly dared to hope that they could be repeated. But they were, again and again, and they sparked an explosion of participatory mapping in India which quickly spread to other countries.[6] Colourful illustrations of maps with slides were one reason why PRA spread so fast and so easily and overwhelmed educated scepticism.[7] I look back now on the 1980s, before participatory mapping took off, with something close to disbelief and shame that we could have been so ignorant for so long before discovering what local people could do.

There are several reasons for estimating that the participatory maps that have been made now number over a million: PRA methods have spread to over 100 countries; other participatory methodologies also use mapping; it has proved quite straightforward to facilitate; people usually enjoy it, see their spatial realities in a new way, and learn from what others show; it is a common and good entry activity for other participatory processes; mapping is versatile for different themes and purposes; and often several maps have been made in the same community by different groups. In 2002 when a project facilitated community soil mapping in Bangladesh, it was found that most of the communities had made simple maps before, in other meetings with outsiders (Saleque et al, 2005, p91). And in Nepal a forester was intercepted before he even entered a village by a man who produced a piece of paper and started drawing a map. 'Have you done this before?' 'At least a hundred times' (pers. comm. Yam Malla).

Applications and uses

Participatory ground and paper mapping has been used for many purposes.[8] Some of these are:

- Social mapping, identifying households, people, livestock, children who do and do not go to school, people in different livelihood and other social categories, wealth and well-being groups. Census mapping is one form of this (see Chapter 6 p119 and Barahona and Levy, 2003).
- Mapping to provide sampling frames (Marsland et al, 2000).
- Mapping for planning – where to locate services, land uses, cropping sequences or a route for a transect walk.
- Health mapping, for people with health problems, disabilities, special health skills and knowledge and so on in communities. In the UK participatory mapping by women has shown the location and concentrations of breast cancer (Lynn et al, n.d.).
- Mobility mapping, showing who goes where for what, how often, taking how long and at what cost (Theis and Grady, 1991).
- Education, in schools, by school children, with varying degrees of creative or didactic style (e.g. Govinda, 1999).
- Mapping in Reflect circles for empowerment, awareness and literacy (Archer and Nandago, 2004).
- Water and sanitation, for example in rural villages in India (Joseph, 1994), and in Dar es Salaam (Glöckner et al, 2004). Mapping areas of open defecation is a key element in the Community-Led Total Sanitation movement in numerous countries (Kar, 2003, 2005; Kar with Chambers, 2008).
- Farm mapping. This has been combined with mapping of nutrient flows within the farm and over the farm boundaries (as undertaken by many organic farmers in Karatina, Nyeri District, Kenya in 1996).
- Forage and animal illness maps (Conroy, 2005, pp216–217).
- Locations of danger and crime: in South Africa (Liebermann and Coulson, 2004); in Tanzania with the identification of locations of molestation, assault and rape and their degrees of risk by women in villages in Mwanza Region in Tanzania; and in Cali, Colombia to show dangerous urban places associated with gangs and drugs (McIlwaine and Moser, 2004, pp57–58).
- Resource thematic mapping, for example of water resources, local land-use classifications, cropping patterns and aquifers in India (Shah, 1994, p119), and soil fertility mapping in Bangladesh (Saleque et al, 2005).
- Natural resource management, covering forestry, watersheds, irrigation, coastal management, fishing, pastoralism, traditional territories, parks and conservation, biodiversity, distribution of species, cultural sites and so on. Such maps range from comprehensive resource mapping to mapping of just one resource, for example livestock forage (Conroy, 2005, pp51, 55), or the distribution of one species. The uses of these maps include resource and land-use planning, co-management, wildlife conservation, identifying tenure and rights, negotiating boundaries and resource uses, and resolving conflicts.

- Participatory monitoring and evaluation (PM and E) deserves special note. Maps were used for impact monitoring of soil and water conservation and changes in farming practices at least as early as 1990 by AKRSP (India) in Gujarat (Shah et al, 1991b): farmers made baseline and impact maps which could be compared, analysed and presented to other farmers. Participatory monitoring of progress towards total community sanitation in hamlets in Bangladesh has been recorded and updated on social maps in public places where all can see them (Kar, 2003, 2005). Experience to date with the use of participatory and other maps for monitoring and evaluation deserves its own review study.[9]

Ground and paper maps can have multiple applications and uses. The same map can be a frame for and agenda for discussions of a wide range of issues. 'Interviewing the map' has advantages over purely verbal discussion: a map is a visual agenda; local detail and spatial relationships can be seen all at once instead of referred to sequentially in disappearing words; discussion can be focused by pointing to features; and rich insights can result.

Spatial information technologies and participatory GIS

In the late 1980s it became more widely recognized that local people, not necessarily literate, could readily interpret black and white aerial photographs, 1:5000 being a good scale (Dewees, 1989; Mearns, 1989; Sandford, 1989). Then in the 1990s, in parallel with the explosive spread of ground and paper mapping, spatial information technologies (SITs) were evolving rapidly and became widely available – satellite imagery, Geographic Information Systems (GIS), Global Positioning Systems (GPS) and open access software. These gave rise to the concern that being high-tech, precisely proportional, capable of extreme exactitude, and controlled and understood by outsiders, SITs would be used to disempower and dispossess local people and to exploit them and their natural resources. As with cartographic maps, these would empower the state, corporations and others who could command them. Differential access could lead to gains to powerful outside interests to the disadvantage of communities and poorer local people, further marginalizing those already marginalized.

A workshop was convened at the University of Durham in the UK in January 1998 (Abbott et al, 1998) to discuss dangers and potentials. As a counter movement, participatory GIS (PGIS) had already begun. The range of experience that could be brought together then was quite limited but the stakes were clearly high. Since 1998 PGIS – used as a generic term for combinations of participatory learning and action (PLA) and SITs has spread and evolved fast and much has been learnt. PGIS has sought to empower minority groups and those traditionally excluded from spatial decision-making processes (Mbile, 2006; PLA, 2006; Fox et al, 2006; Rambaldi et al, 2006). In the words of Giacomo Rambaldi, a major pioneer, advocate and disseminator of PGIS:

> *PGIS is a practice resulting from a spontaneous merger of participatory learning and action (PLA) methods with GIT & S [Geographic Information and Technology and Systems]. It builds on the integrated use of tools, methods, technologies and systems ranging from simple sketch mapping, to participatory 3D modelling, collaborative aerial photo-interpretation, and the use of GPS and GIS applications. With PGIS applications, indigenous spatial knowledge is composed in the form of virtual or physical 2 or 3-dimensional maps that are used as interactive vehicles for spatial learning, information exchange, support in decision making, resource use planning and advocacy actions.* (Rambaldi, 2005)

In PGIS, local people have been trained to use the technologies to construct their own maps and 3-D models (see Rambaldi and Callosa-Tarr, 2002 for modelling, and Corbett et al, 2006 and Rambaldi et al, 2006 for overviews) and use these for their own research. These maps and models differ from the ground and paper maps of PRA in their greater spatial accuracy, permanence, authority and credibility with officialdom.

Applications have been many. They have included (Rambaldi et al, 2005, p3): protecting ancestral lands and resource rights; management and resolution of conflicts over natural resources; collaborative resource-use planning and management; intangible cultural heritage preservation and identity building among indigenous peoples and rural communities; equity promotion with reference to ethnicity, culture, gender and environmental justice; and hazard mitigation, for example through community safety audits and peri-urban planning and research. PGIS applications have been documented (Mbile, 2006; PLA, 2006) for countries as diverse as Brazil (Amazon), Cameroon, Canada, Ethiopia, Fiji, Ghana, Indonesia, Kenya, Nepal, Namibia, Nicaragua, South Africa, Tanzania and Uganda. In addition, there are '...hundreds of non-documented cases where technology-intermediaries (mainly NGOs) support Community-based Organisations or Indigenous Peoples in using [Geographic Information Technology and Systems] to meet their spatial planning needs and/or achieve some leverage in their dealings with state bureaucracy' (Rambaldi et al, 2005, p4).

Medium and process

Different media, processes and power relations fit different applications and lead to different outcomes. The question arose in the early days of PRA-type mapping as to whether maps should be on the ground, with which many people were more comfortable, or on paper. It came to be realized that the advantages of one were disadvantages of the other. The same categories can be used for PGIS.

Process and sequence have proved important. For ground and paper, the obvious conclusion from this comparison is for mapping on the ground to precede drawing on paper. Mapping, especially on the ground, is a cumulative process with detail added and corrected. With forage mapping, Conroy (2005, p51) observes that 'It is quite likely that people will forget to show certain forage

Table 7.1 *Pros and cons of modes of mapping: Ground, paper and participatory GIS*

Ground	Paper	Participatory GIS
More temporary, cannot keep, vulnerable to animals and people, trampling, rain, wind…	More permanent, can store but is vulnerable to water, mould, tearing, fire	Most permanent. Can be stored electronically as well as on paper
Familiar and comfortable for many	Unfamiliar and inhibiting for some, especially non-literates	Unfamiliar to many and may require special efforts to make accessible and usable by most
Easy to alter, add to, build up, extend	Committing, harder to alter, build up or extend	Alterable by those with access
More democratic, less eye contact and verbal dominance than usual, many can hold the stick and modify	More exclusive, men and the educated may hold the pen, presenting more their own than a group view	Limited to those able to spare time for training and for taking part over a longer period
Freely creative with local materials	More restrained, with materials from outside	Disciplined, requiring training and supervision
Locally owned, outsiders cannot remove (except as photographs)	Vulnerable to removal by outsiders	Variable. Large 3-D models not vulnerable to removal
Cannot be used for monitoring	Can be used for monitoring, with updating	Can be used for monitoring, with updating
Not convincing or usable with officials (unless presented as a digital photograph)	Can empower when presented to officials	Very empowering vis-à-vis officials, the state and outside interests
More cross-checking and triangulation	Less cross-checking, fewer may see	Potentially considerable cross-checking but depends on process
Local power and ownership more dispersed	Local power and ownership liable to be more concentrated among a few	Local power and ownership depends on facilitation and process

resources on the map, and that it will need to be revised'. In the mapping of agroecological zones in Eritrea (Box 7.1) five were mentioned, but when farmers mapped they added a sixth. The public nature of ground mapping is a strength. Passers-by offer comments, corrections and additions: in one South Indian village the huts of the harijans were initially omitted until a passer-by pointed it out.

Who maps, and who draws, also matter. Initially there was the idea that outsiders should copy the ground map onto paper, but that meant loss of detail and quality. Soon it was realized that when local people did it, they redrew the map, often improving on paper the sketch made on the ground, and that this usually added detail and quality. A new twist is that ground and paper maps can be now be copied, taken away and reproduced more easily by outsiders as digital photographs.

With PGIS, further questions arise concerning training required, the duration of the mapping or modelling process, the effects of the use of alien or unfamiliar equipment, the need to visit places on the ground, and the balance between the marginalization of some and the mastery, pride and ownership experienced by others.

Maps, realities and power

Maps are instruments of power. They give visual expression to realities which are perceived, desired or considered useful. For the same area, whether rural or urban, land or sea, forest, pasture, farmland, waterway or park, hill or plain, the form given to a map is determined by the motivation, interests, knowledge, materials, instruments, time, care, training and social context of those who make it, by the social process of its creation, and by those who commission or facilitate it. There can be many different maps for the same place. As above, they can differ in theme, in purpose, in what they show, in precision, and in legibility to different people. They can be complementary or they can conflict. They can be used to assert and establish territorial and usufruct claims, for negotiation, for recording information, for planning, implementing, monitoring and evaluation, and for finding one's way around. They can be what Rocheleau (2005) describes as maps-as-usual (property, terrain and administrative maps) or counter maps which express, present and assert other realities, perceptions and claims. They are as richly diverse in form as they are versatile and multiple in uses.

All maps then raise the questions: Whose realities do they express? Whose purposes do they serve? And who stands to gain and who to lose?

Power and realities within communities

In participatory community mapping, there are differences within communities. These were early recognized by pioneers of RRA and PRA. Andrea Cornwall reported in 1991 on the differences between models (ground maps) made by men, women and children in the same community in North Omo in Ethiopia:

the men gave prominence to the farming land, the women to the rivers and watering points, and the children to grazing land which their elders had left out. Men normally dominated group proceedings, but when separate mapping by the women and by the children was facilitated they were able to express the issues and realities that they knew about and that were important to them (IIED and Farm Africa, 1991, pp46–48; Jonfa et al, 1991). Alice Welbourn's seminal 1991 article 'RRA and the analysis of difference' identified four axes of intra-community difference in villages where she had worked – age, gender, poverty–wealth and ethnicity. The axes of difference vary by community and may also include religion, caste, lineage, political allegiance or faction. They also overlap in various ways so that clusters of significance will be different. Any of these clusters could make their own map. In a PRA training she co-facilitated in Zimbabwe four groups from the village worked and mapped separately – children, women, younger men and older men (Redd Barna, 1993).

Differences in participatory maps by the gender of those who make them appear universally significant. In many cultures as they grow older boys are free to move and expected to be adventurous and explore, while girls are progressively restricted and expected to live and work in or close to the home area. This is reflected in the maps they draw: in a village in Kenya, 13-year-old boys drew maps with more roads and environmental detail, while 13-year-old girls' maps had a narrower concept of space and less environmental detail, and gave prominence to home and school (Matthews, 1995). In a village in Sierra Leone where men and women mapped separately men showed interest in roads and junctions, while women were concerned with the well and hospital and wanted them close by. Again and again it has been important to enable women to draw their own maps as a means of expressing and analysing their priorities. Wherever it is women who fetch water, for example, their preferences for the location of a water supply will deserve priority over those of men.

The key for a facilitator in any community is to identify which axes or groupings are most significant, a point repeatedly made now in the literature. In a community in the Brazilian Amazon 'It was found important that different groups (formal and informal, divided by a gender, age, religion and origin) were asked to draw the landscape and the resource uses...' (Viana and Freire, 2001). The key is to ensure that subordinate groups are encouraged and can claim space and not be marginalized, for example that women are not ridiculed by men if their maps show less extensive detail. The practical and ethical principle is to ensure the free and usually separate participation of subordinate groups, whether children, women, those who are poorer, or those considered of socially lower status, and then to enable their realities and priorities to be presented, appreciated and fairly acted upon.

State maps, counter maps and combinations

'Maps-as-usual' represent the surface of the globe as a two-dimensional surface, what Rocheleau (2005) calls the 'Iron Grid of Descartes'. She identifies four types: topographic (terrain) maps, thematic (special topic) maps, cadastral maps denoting property boundaries, and political maps with a focus on administrative units. These simplify by being able to represent with their x and y coordinates only one thing at a time at one point on the surface. Cadastral maps, as James Scott has described in *Seeing Like a State* (1998), are instruments to simplify local complexities and make them legible – 'precise, schematic, general and uniform', preconditions for a property regime and legible for taxation and conscription. There is a long and widespread history of how these maps have been implicated in disenfranchising local and indigenous people and enabling state and commercial interests to appropriate and exploit resources.

Counter mapping (Rocheleau, 2005) is a term used to describe mapping that seeks to defend the rights and interests of those who are weakened, disenfranchised or deprived by the use made of maps-as-usual by the state and powerful interests. Counter mapping has taken many forms.[10] At first these were described as informal, made by local people without any technology for spatial exactness. A comparison of cases (Borrini-Feyerabend et al, 2004, p149) concluded: 'A key lesson that emerges from these cases is that participatory mapping is an effective method to promote land tenure regularisation, to value local knowledge, and to strengthen cultural identity.' The maps of indigenous peoples as in the early 1990s had a counter legibility but tended to lack legal and bureaucratic credibility. All the same, they could have an impact. In Eritrea, a map and matrix made by three farmers communicated directly to an official from the Land Commission why the proposed consolidation of scattered holdings would not work (see Box 7.1).

Just how potent these forms of community mapping could be was shown in Malaysia. After a community map in Sarawak had been instrumental in the legal victory of an Iban village against a tree plantation corporation, the Government passed a Land Surveyors Law in 2001 which made community mapping illegal (Fox et al, 2006, pp98, 103). There could be few more dramatic indicators of the power of mapping.

This power has been enhanced by aerial photographs, satellite imagery, and GIS and GPS. Maps have then become even more instruments of power than they were. Following a research project in several Asian countries, Jefferson Fox and his colleagues concluded that 'SIT (Spatial Information Technology) transforms the discourse about land and resources, the meaning of geographical knowledge, the work practices of mapping and legal professionals, and ultimately the very meaning of space itself', and argued that 'Communities that do not have maps become disadvantaged as 'rights' and 'power' are increasingly framed in spatial terms' (Fox et al, 2005, pp3, 7). Mapping has become necessary: failing to be on a map corresponds to a lack of proof of existence, and of ownership of land and resources. For many of the marginalized, not engaging ceases to be an option.

By the latter 2000s, combinations of participatory modes and SITs as with PGIS have spread quite extensively as effective forms of counter mapping. They have been facilitated to enable local people to make their own maps and models, and then used by them for their own research, analysis, assertion of rights and

Box 7.1 *Empowerment through mapping: An afternoon in Eritrea*

Resource Map of Village Agroecological Zones
Adi-Ktekla Village, Mendefra, Eritrea

Drawn by 3 Farmers with Chalk on mud floor, then redrawn by them on paper
(reduced from A3)

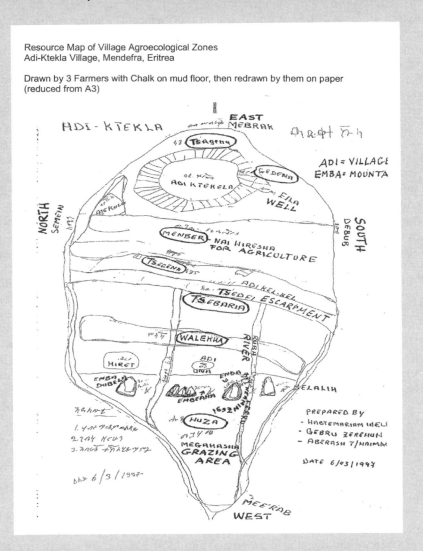

Six of us visited a village. We had all been trained in PRA behaviours and knew to keep quiet. One of us was from the Land Commission. The Government was proposing land consolidation, to bring scattered fields together. We met the village head in his hut. After a discussion we asked him what would be a good land policy for his village. He replied

'Whatever the Government says is right.'

Outside, a woman farmer invited us for tea. The village head and another farmer came with us. We had a long discussion about crops. All of us remained silent except for the facilitator/interviewer. He asked if they could draw a map of the village land, showing agroecological zones. With chalk and enthusiasm they drew a large map on the mud floor, and then redrew it on paper, showing six zones. Then they were asked to count out 100 maize grains, and draw a matrix on the only suitable surface, the bottom of an upturned pan. The matrix had the agroecological zones down the side and the main crops across the top. With much debate, and changes in the scores, the farmers placed the seeds in the matrix. They said they were scoring for importance – a composite score for the crop and zone. This showed tangibly and visibly the complexity of their farming system, and how farmers needed land in different zones.

Table 7.2 *Relative importance of main crops by agroecological zone – Adi-ktekla village, Mendefgra, Eritrea*

	Maize	Barley	Teff	Wheat	Sorghum	Finger millet	Beans and peas	Total
Gedena	3	3	5					11
Member		15	8	6			6	35
Tsagena		4		4			4	12
Tsebaria					9	5		14
Walekha			7		6		6	19
Huza						4	5	9
Total	3	22	20	10	15	9	21	100

Method: Listing after mapping then scoring with 100 maize grains on the matrix drawn with chalk
Analysts: Habtemaria Weldai, Gebru Zerehun, Aberash T/Maimanot

When they had finished, and the spread of scores across the crops and zones could be seen by everyone, the same head of the village turned to the official from the Land Commission and said:

> 'Now you can see why your policy will not work.'

The map and matrix were later debated in policy circles in Asmara.

resolution of conflicts over resources. In many instances they have served to level or reverse power relations with government organizations, politicians and corporations (see e.g. PLA 54, 2006, *passim*). One form of mapping could lead to another: the inhabitants of a Kayapo village in the Amazon gave a political orientation to their cartography as they began to realize the power of their work with satellite imagery. They turned around a research programme from representing their botanical knowledge to producing a political map to represent their territory and rights (The Inhabitants of Moikarakô et al, 2006). Another research project found that these technologies enhanced tenure security in cases studied in Indonesia, Thailand, Cambodia and the Philippines.

Patterns have varied with implications for power relations both within communities and between communities and other powers and organizations (Fox et al, 2005 summarized in Fox et al, 2006). The effects have not always been benign. Conflict can arise through defining boundaries which have previously been flexible. In a case in Sarawak, community leaders used a community map to collude with a corporation's plan to lease customary lands for an oil palm plantation (Fox et al, 2006, p103). But the balance of evidence is that more often local people have gained: through conducting their own research, making their own maps and models, and using these to mediate their relationships with government organizations, politicians and corporations, and to support their management of their own resources.

The pathways and patterns of power through mapping are thus many and varied, and have twists and turns. In Rwanda a key element in the Ubudehe movement (Shah, 2008; Ubudehe seminar, 2006) is participatory social maps made on cloth at the community level. These are reported to have been made in some 9000 rural communities (cellules). They show categories of wealth and poverty, and can also show access to services. They have been used at the national level for ministers to hold each other to account. In the words of one official, 'There is information challenging us daily from Ubudehe. This is not information analysed by some bureaucrat in a cosy office. It's information from the ground by the people themselves. From where I sit as a government official, this is a great planning tool' (Shah, 2008, p3). The Rwandan experience demonstrates the potential for a synergy of power: it shows that not only can local people be empowered, but also officials and politicians who make use of the detail and credibility of their maps. It presents conditions in which participatory mapping can be a positive sum with gains both for communities and for those with official roles in the state.

Facilitation, behaviour, attitudes and ethics

One reason why it took so long for participatory mapping to become a self-spreading movement may be the beliefs, behaviour and attitudes of professionals. Most local people, asked if they can make a map, have in the past said no. Before the early 1990s perhaps few were asked anyway, and if they were, their negative responses were taken at face value. We have learnt that the facilitator has to believe that 'They can do it', and also to allow people time to work out for themselves how to do it. A little initial help drawing with a stick on the ground has sometimes been needed to start things off, but almost always this leads quickly to 'handing over the stick' and then shutting up and letting the process take off. Earlier, these were not normal professional behaviours. Induced disability – the inability of 'lowers' to do things because of the behaviour of 'uppers', is still widespread in development but less than before. And the maps people make affect the perceptions, behaviour and attitudes[11] of those who facilitate or watch.

Ownership and use are pervasive issues related to context, purpose, medium, process, facilitation, behaviour, attitudes and relationships. The challenges are there in every process. Photography is a case heightened and changed by technology. There is a new ease with digital cameras of 'capturing' a map. On the positive side, this can mean that the original map stays with a community, and that prints of the photographs can be returned to them as thanks. On the negative side, it can mean that information is much more easily extracted and removed than before. If the original map was only on the ground, and no photographs are returned, people in the community are left with nothing except that they learnt through the process. Here, as ever, it comes back to personal awareness, commitment and responsibility on the part of facilitators.

With SITs, practical ethical issues are sharpened by the exclusive command, initially at least, of an alien technology by the outsider. There is a danger of disempowering people because, unlike ground and paper mapping, there has to be a period of training which puts the outsider in a dominant, knowledgeable role. Facilitators have been well described as 'technology intermediaries', persons who introduce local people to the technology and enable them to use it. Like other participatory mapping, but more acutely, PGIS and SITs present ethical challenges.

Ethics: The Who? and Whose? questions

Some of these can be expressed as 'who?' and 'whose?' questions. The inclusive checklist that follows serves as a sobering reminder of just how many dimensions of power, intelligibility, usefulness and ownership there can be, and how these relate to the bottom lines of Who gains?, Who loses?, Who is empowered? and Who is disempowered?

Who? and Whose? questions

Source: Rambaldi et al, 2006, p108[12]

Stage 1. Planning
Who participates?
Who decides on who should participate?
Who participates in whose mapping?
And who is left out?

Who identifies the problems?

Whose problems?
Whose questions?
Whose perspective?
And whose problems, questions and perspectives are left out?

Stage 2. The mapping process
Whose voice counts? Who controls the process?

Who decides on what is important?
Who decides, and who should decide, on what to visualize and make public?
Who has visual and tactile access?
Who controls the use of information?
And who is marginalized?

Whose reality? And who understands?

Whose reality is expressed?
Whose knowledge, categories, perceptions?
Whose truth and logic?
Whose sense of space and boundary conception (if any)?
Whose (visual) spatial language?
Whose map legend?
Who understands the physical output?
And who does not?
And whose reality is left out?

Stage 3. Resulting information control, disclosure and disposal
Who owns the output?

Who owns the map(s)?
Who owns the resulting data?
What is left with those who generated the information and shared their knowledge?
Who keeps the physical output and organizes its regular updating?

Whose analysis and use?

Who analyses the spatial information collated?
Who has access to the information and why?
Who will use it and for what?
And who cannot access and use it?

And ultimately...
What has changed?
Who benefits from the changes?
At whose costs?

Who gains and who loses?

Who is empowered and who is disempowered?

Conclusion

The conclusion has to be pluralist: we know that many forms of spatial representation and mapping can empower those who are variously weaker, poorer, vulnerable, marginalized or on the peripheries. There is a place for people's expression of their spatial realities on the ground and on paper. There is a place for aerial photographs and satellite imagery. There is a place for PGIS and GPS. There is a place for participatory 3-D models, both freely fashioned and proportional using GIS. There is a place for cloth maps in every community. There is huge scope for sequences and combinations. None of these is 'the best'. There is no 'best'. Which fits where depends on context, capabilities and purpose. What matters is for those who facilitate to reflect on power and focus on ethics, referring continually to the who questions.

It has to be asked, again and again, how much mapping and modelling empower and enhance equitable local control and how much they disempower and lead to exploitation. This chapter, and most of the published sources, report on good practice. But how much bad practice is there? For the future, the need and the great opportunity is for those who pioneer and adopt good practices to struggle to inform and inspire others, so that what is already a self-spreading movement on a very wide scale will also be self-improving with quality assurance built in. Technologies like coloured chalks on the ground, or GIS from satellites, can fascinate and mesmerize, But they are means not ends. For participatory mapping and modelling to fulfil their promise, technology is secondary. People have to come first. The major challenge remains, with mapping as with other approaches and methods, that those with power and those who facilitate have the vision and commitment to ensure that the processes lead to sustainable gains, not losses, for those who are poorer, more marginalized and less powerful.

Notes

1   Much of this chapter has grown out of a paper (Chambers, 2006) to the International Conference on Participatory Spatial Information Management and Communication: 'Mapping for Change', held in the Kenya College of Communication and Technology, Nairobi 7–10 September 2005. It owes much to the discussions of that conference, the many other contributors and papers, and exchanges on email. I thank all concerned and hope they will understand that it is simply not feasible to acknowledge their individual contributions. Many of the papers have been edited and can be found in *Participatory Learning and Action*, vol 54 (2006), and Peter Mbile (ed) *The Electronic Journal of Information Systems in Developing Countries*, vol 25 (2006). *Participatory Learning and Action* 54 is available from www.iied.org/NR/agbioliv/pla_notes/backissues.html#free. Also available to order in Arabic, Bangla, Chinese (traditional and simplified), English, French, Hindi, Persian-Dari, Portuguese, Spanish, Swahili and Tamil at: www.iied. org/pubs/display.php?o=14524IIED

Accessible sources include www.ppgis.net for an open forum on Participatory Geographic Information Systems and links to other sources (accessed 26.03.08).

2   A meme originally meant an idea, skill, story or any kind of behaviour that is copied from person to person by imitation (Dawkins, 1976, cited in Blackmore, 2003, p22).

3   In March 2006 a conference on Indigenous Cartography and Representational Politics was held at Cornell University. It sought to initiate a critical dialogue between different groups involved with indigenous cartographies, including the tensions between indigenous knowledge and scientific knowledge and social changes in communities resulting from mapping projects. See www.arts.cornell.edu/sochum/mapping

4   Pers. comm. in Chambers (1983) *Rural Development*, p99.

5   Cited in Paul van Mele et al (eds) (2005) *Innovations in Rural Extension*, p69.

6   That participatory mapping took off in India and spread from there is my interpretation. That is what I was aware of. There may have been parallel developments elsewhere. There tends to be a time that is ripe for innovations that then occur in different places at the same time, but one receives more notice and so is thought to have been the originator of the others.

7   When I showed slides of the Kalmandargi model and the Kistagiri maps, all of them created by villagers in at most a few hours and with only light facilitation, at the Remote Sensing Centre in Hyderabad, the Director asked me 'And how long did it take you to train the villagers to do that? One year? Two years?'

8   For a fuller listing of applications with examples see Mukherjee, 2002, pp150–203.

9   I shall be grateful to anyone who can point me to an overview of experience using maps for participatory monitoring and evaluation.

10 For a listing of forms of counter mapping see Rocheleau, 2005.

11 For a fuller treatment of behaviour, attitudes and beyond see Chapter 6 of Chambers, *Ideas for Development* (2005) together with references to sources which I am not repeating here.

12 This list of questions is a lightly edited version of one built up progressively both at the Mapping for Change International Conference on Participatory Spatial Information Management and Communication held at the Kenya College of Communication of Technology, Nairobi, Kenya, 7–10 September 2005 and in subsequent email exchanges between the authors of the paper (Rambaldi et al, 2006) and others.

8

Traps and Liberations

The difficulty lies not so much in developing new ideas, as in escaping from the old ones. (John Maynard Keynes)

I thought I knew about village life as my roots are in the village, and I still visit family in my village from time to time. But I know nothing about what it is like to be poor and how hidden this kind of poverty can be. (Participatory researcher, Views of the Poor, Tanzania, in Jupp, 2004)

Abstract

The challenge is for development professionals to be in touch and up to date. One means is liberation from the Jurassic trap of large multi-purpose questionnaire surveys by inventing and adopting alternatives such as participatory numbers. The urban and capital city trap has become ever more serious, a new black hole with gravity intensified, especially for aid agency and INGO staff, by meetings, negotiations, policy discussions, workshops and the digital tyranny. The many ways to beat the biases of development tourism can be a source of fun as well as insight. Learning face to face with people living in poverty deserves a continued revival. Immersions with overnights are gaining momentum. More needs to be learnt about how to liberate, retaining past learning, improving going to scale, and enabling through values and incentives. Practical ethics are part of pro-poor professionalism. A paradox of power is the win–win that all can gain when those with power over liberate themselves by empowering others.

Context and challenge: To be in touch and up to date

For humankind in the 21st century there are many challenges: global warming, international governance, security, trade justice, tax justice, nuclear armaments and power... The list can be long. Linked with all these, pervasively and persistently, are issues of poverty, inequality and injustice, and what we can call development policies and practice. This book has no pretensions to deal directly with the biggest issues. But indirectly, it points to directions and levers for change. The themes of this chapter are that we, development professionals, are mired in traps, not all of which are well perceived, that we have new paths to liberation, and that following these can be exhilarating, fulfilling and fun.

Part of the background is the litter of errors, each burying its predecessors, in the history of development. The World Bank, in particular, seems to have a periodicity between its damaging dogmas. The most clearly disastrous was structural adjustment, forced on the weakest and most indebted countries to repay their debts: by cutting budgets for education, health, infrastructure and other services, it deprived and further marginalized and intensified the suffering of hundreds of millions of the poorest and most vulnerable people, and may well have led to the premature death of millions of children and adults. Now we have, or have had, the dogmas of neo-liberalism with the spectacular hypocrisy of gargantuan agricultural subsidies to already rich farmers in the North further impoverishing farmers in the South whose subsidies have had to be stopped. Faced with mega errors like these, to concern oneself with the minutiae of modes of inquiry in development conjures up the old clichés: the ostrich with its head in the sand, or fiddling while Rome burns.

These big issues are not confronted head-on in this chapter. At best some of the seeds sown here, many of them collected from others, may germinate to make a difference. This they may do if they contribute to commitment and realism, if through them there are fewer errors and less harm done, and more policies and actions that lead to social justice and better lives for those who are most vulnerable and deprived.

In the past two decades, the case for learning about and from poor people and understanding their conditions and perspectives has become better recognized. In rhetoric, poverty is higher than ever on the development agenda. The complexity and diversity of poverty are better appreciated. At the same time, the realities of poor people are changing fast. The communications revolution has touched many more poor and rural people through television, cassettes, CDs and CDRs, radio, newspapers, telephone networks, mobile phones, email and internet, and has opened windows for them onto other lifestyles, not least those of the urban middle classes. Inequalities have become starker. In many rural and urban areas, livelihood strategies and livelihoods have diversified. For those committed to pro-poor policies and practices, the intensified challenge is continuously to learn and unlearn, to be in touch and keep up to date.

This applies to all development professionals. especially bureaucrats working in governments in the South, academics, consultants, communicators, and most visibly those who work in aid agencies, whether multilateral or bilateral, and in international and national NGOs. They may work in Northern headquarters, in developing countries' capital cities, or outside them.

I shall consider two dimensions. The first is methodological, about inquiry and knowing. The second is personal, about learning, changing and acting: it is no good knowing unless something is done as a result. I want to suggest that together these two dimensions can contribute to an ethic and practice of pro-poor professionalism.

The imagery is traps and liberations: traps of which development professionals are often unaware; and escapes and liberations opened up by participatory approaches and methods. The evidence and arguments are informed by the past and present, and point forward to a future in which change can be expected to be, if anything, faster and faster.

Out of the Jurassic trap: Alternatives to dinosaurs

Chapter 1 argued that many large questionnaires and surveys are pathological – expensive, laborious and misleading – and that 'scientific' methodology was often misplaced. But in the name of sophistication and rigour, many powerful economists, statisticians and scientists persist in complicating their scientific sledgehammer to crack the local nut. They are, as we say these days, visually challenged. If your only optical instrument is a telescope, things close to you look blurred. As this becomes more evident, these normal professionals manifest brick-wallitis: when you bang your head against a brick wall and it does not fall down, bang harder. They add to the questionnaire and increase the size of the sample and of the control. They enlarge the telescope; and the blur gets worse.

As we have seen, there are other, cheaper, faster and more credible modes of inquiry: direct observation (Chapter 3), rapid rural appraisal (RRA) (Chapter 4), participatory rural appraisal (PRA) (Chapter 5), participatory numbers (Chapter 6) and participatory mapping and GIS (Chapter 7). There are many alternatives to large questionnaires and surveys, and most of them can be facilitated in ways which empower local people. The evidence and examples are so many and so credible that as a means to investigate a topic a long questionnaire with a large sample is ripe for extinction (pp13–16).

Complexity underpins the point.

The conventional view, in which I was myself trapped (pp19, 21), has been that for complex topics, multiple causality and multiple potential impacts, long questionnaires were needed to capture and quantify all the relevant details for analysis. This is precisely wrong. Long questionnaires are not open to serendipity; they do not learn; they do not adapt; they generate much garbage; they have, in short, a learning disability. As pointed out in Chapter 1, this is not to argue that censuses and other time series national surveys should necessarily be abandoned.

What we have learnt is that the more complex and multifaceted an issue, the stronger is the comparative advantage of local people using group-visual PRA methods. Repeatedly, they have shown that they can conduct far more complex, grounded, detailed and quicker analysis than is feasible with a conventional questionnaire. Meera Shah and her colleagues (1999a, pp51–53) have illustrated how adolescents can carry out complex analysis of sexual behaviour. Girls listed a typology of sex partners and dimensions of selecting them, and then ranked and scored these against each other in a matrix. 'Such an analysis may seem very complex, and perhaps difficult to understand for the reader, but … it took the girls only 40 minutes to carry out … and discuss the reasons…' (Shah, 1999a, p52).

A parallel point applies with farmers and agricultural scientists. In studying complexity and diversity, farmers have comparative advantages over scientists.

Unconstrained by the reductionist rigidities of conventional research design with its few variables, predetermined treatments, and requirements for replications, farmers can learn quickly from observing and adjusting to a wide range of physical and crop conditions. In the late 1980s this was understood with farmer participatory research. Sumberg and Okali wrote (1989, p112):

> *We contend that farmers' role in technology development becomes more critical and cost effective as the proposed technology becomes more multi-faceted and complex... The need is not to keep the trials 'simple enough for farmers to understand and evaluate' (Farrington and Martin, 1988) nor to develop more sophisticated statistical methods, but rather for research and research institutions to accept the proposition that* **adoption by farmers is validation of a technology,** *one might say by definition, even if we are unable always to identify or quantify the technology's effects.* (Emphasis in the original)

This has been far from the attitudes and behaviour of some leading rice scientists with the System of Rice Intensification (SRI). Some, indeed, have denied its validity despite its exponential adoption by now (2008) probably hundreds of thousands of farmers. One reason why scientists have been so much slower to learn than farmers is that SRI changes six cultivation practices all together and the changes are synergistic. This does not fit into a normal experimental frame. So farmers can innovate, experiment, observe and evolve their practices rapidly in ways impossible for their disabled scientist colleagues. Every farmer is by definition an experimenter, searching for practices that work, and able to try out and learn fast from a multitude of varied practices and from other farmers. NGOs are similarly free: an organization that was training farmers in Orissa tried out 26 varieties (Prasad et al, 2007, p6) on a small field of less than three acres, without the controls that scientists would have been constrained to have. This approach of continuous innovation, observation and learning generates a long further agenda for trials and research (see e.g. Sabarmatee, 2007, p41).

The conclusion is that for studies of complex or sensitive subjects, participatory approaches, whether with visual/tangible and group approaches and methods, or with continuous observation and adaptation of many variables, have many advantages over questionnaires and conventional scientific research. We are not talking here about modes of inquiry that lack rigour. To the contrary, their rigour is often superior – based on personal motivation, observation, group analysis, triangulation, making adjustments, and continuous learning by doing. The main limitations are the inventiveness of those who devise them, the training of facilitators and above all the understanding and support of those with professional, bureaucratic and financial power. If this chapter persuades some of them to see and act differently, it will have served a good purpose.

From urban trap to new black hole

The urban trap (pp26–29) has intensified. Capital cities have become black holes, their gravity too strong for escape. This affects all, including government staff, but is most conspicuous with the staff of aid agencies and INGOs. The trap refers to headquarters in Northern countries as well as capital cities in the South.

Three factors stand out.

First, **the capital trap** itself. In the past, donor and lender agencies had technical assistance personnel and field projects to visit. As these became less fashionable and were more and more abandoned,[1] and as sector-wide approaches, direct budget support and policy dialogue became dominant and prestigious activities, so more and more time came to be spent in meetings – between aid agencies trying to 'harmonize' with each other,[2] between aid agency and government staff, and again between them and a proliferation of partners including civil society.

The problem has been compounded by the absurd self-defeating aid policies of trying to do more with less, meaning higher budgets with fewer staff, who in consequence have less and less time to make visits or for personal and professional development. So spatially centralized are mindsets, that in aid agency parlance 'the field' now usually means the receiving country which in turn usually means the capital city; a field mission from the headquarters of an aid agency is a mission to a capital city, not to the field outside the capital.[3]

In parallel, a pandemic of workshops has spread like a virus through capital cities.[4] Aid instruments and their acronyms have multiplied, demanding more reporting.[5] Nor does a sector-wide focus diminish the trap. Rather, it demands and attracts a flood of consultants who spawn a plethora of reports which pile up in the queue to be read, discussed and acted on: in the four years to 2005, there were 93 consultants' reports on education in Rwanda (pers. comm. Renwick Irvine). The backlog of unread reports preys on the consciences of agency staff and adds to the magnetic hold of the capital where they have to be read and followed up on. And then there are important visitors and visiting missions.

Taken together, all this makes it easier to understand how in an African country, two expatriate social development advisers reportedly never went outside the capital city in the first nine months of their posting, and how in an Asian country another such adviser reportedly only went out of the capital city once in three years. Where there is a security problem, the hold of the capital city is even more severe, especially for those in the UN whose insurance policies may not cover visits to villages: a senior adviser engaged in drafting a national development strategy may never have been outside the capital. For some aid agency staff, perhaps many, rural visits are only possible in their own time at weekends, if then. And these are people whose life and work is meant to be attacking and reducing poverty. Such isolation and ignorance are a pathology.[6]

Second, **digital addictions and tyranny**. Mobile phones make staff accessible wherever they are. The internet has transformed access, information, activities and relationships. To learn about poverty, you now visit a website, not a village. Email has become at the same time resented, addictive and tyrannical, tying staff more and more to their computer screens, and reducing personal contact. Aid agencies are more vulnerable than ever to instant demands from a distant head office. A senior official of a multilateral bank received a long and imperious email from his boss in headquarters just as he was going into a morning of back-to-back meetings. When he came out of these, he found a reminder asking why he was taking so long to reply. This dominating and demoralizing use of email appears to have gone largely unremarked. Blackberry is a Trojan horse of intrusive invasion and erosion of private time and space; someone known to have one cannot hide. Hierarchy can then be strengthened, together with an orientation upwards to authority rather than downwards to poor and marginalized people. And the traps of central places and capital cities close ever tighter.

Third, **the personal dimension**. Aid agency, senior government and NGO staff in capital cities may be allured by the prestige and importance of policy dialogue. This is seductive for almost all of us, not least when early in our careers. That is where power can be exercised; that is how to make a difference. And better it may seem, to be seen and heard speaking well in a meeting than to be unseen listening to and learning from poor people. There may, too, be a reluctance to expose oneself, to be physically or morally uncomfortable, to be confronted by the realities of poverty, or to be, or be thought to be, some sort of poverty voyeur. Understandable though it may be, there is here a psychopathology of avoidance. Better, we can rationalize, to go nowhere near poverty, to shut it out, than to have any exposure that might be blurred, distorted or misleadingly unrepresentative. The biases of the organized visit of rural development tourism can even be an excuse – 'I have heard all about that. I am not going to fall for that', as it has been expressed. It is easy for development professionals in capital cities to find 'good' reasons for not going out and meeting poor people.

But a straw in the wind was the OECD's review of the United Kingdom's development aid (OECD, 2006) when it observed:

> *The Review team would also encourage staff currently working in headquarters to spend more time visiting the field and country office staff to spend more time out of capital cities. Greater efforts should be made in getting key staff closer to the development realities they support...*

Out of the black hole: Beating biases is fun

One solution, easy to recommend, is simply to make more visits away from the workplace, and to make them longer. The decline in rural visits by urban-based professionals is lamentable and demands resolute reversal. Both rural and urban visits will always be ways of keeping in touch and up to date with people, conditions and change. Fighting to find ways to escape traps and to beat biases are not only good things to do; they should also be fun.

With rural development tourism, there are many ways to avoid and offset the biases. 'Old hands' like President Lyndon Johnson (see note 9, p47) have known some of these. Some can involve decisive and undiplomatic interventions. But it can be rude and embarrassing to alter what has been arranged; and if people in communities have been warned of a visit, and barring compelling reasons, it is bad not to go to them as planned. To avoid these and other traps, here are some common-sense ideas of what a visitor can do:

Send messages in advance

- Make your purpose and hopes clear.
- Indicate your hope for informality and willingness to 'rough it'.
- Avoid the frequently visited VIP circuit.[7]
- Consider avoiding lunch.[8]
- Ask for time for just wandering around.[9]
- Ask that no programme be prearranged.[10]

Reflect and offset during a visit

Reflect critically on how the biases are affecting perception and learning, and try to offset them. A longer personal list is better, but some of the more important are:

- Spatial and project: where is being visited and what seen, and where is not being visited and not seen?
- Person: who is being met, seen and heard and who not met, seen and heard – women, children, the sick, the very old, migrants, those who are busy, non-users of services, the marginalized and excluded, and those, of course, who have died?
- Seasonal: what are things like at other times of the year, especially during the rains?
- Diplomatic: what questions are not being asked, where are you not going, whom are you not meeting because of politeness or timidity? Are you striking a good balance between probing and being culturally and gender sensitive?
- Professional: what are you predisposed to notice and ask about, and not to notice or ask about?
- Security: are insecure areas, and people who are insecure, being excluded?

Offset biases and enjoy

- **Take it in turns 'to wear the tie'.** A USAID team took it in turns to be the important person who received the first garland, met the notables, sat at the table, and made the speech. While this was going on, others slipped away and wandered around.
- **Use local and unconventional transport.** Bicycles are brilliant, and can sometimes be hired or borrowed in villages, especially in South Asia. Horses can reach further places faster than walking. Local buses and bicycle rickshaws (in South Asia) have much to recommend them. Nor should helicopters be derided. They do not give the experience of remoteness but their ability to offset spatial biases is unique. In the Ethiopian famine of 1984 they helped reveal the plight of remote communities. Rajiv Gandhi when Prime Minister of India made unannounced visits to inaccessible tribal communities in central India and one imagines may have been able to listen to the local people without the normal high-pressure preparations and interventions of squadrons of officials.

- **Allow an extra day.** Plan in an unplanned day during which you can indeed wander around or follow up on leads. This can be as good as it is difficult to justify to those with normal mindsets and bureaucratic reflexes and who ought to know better. If you are old, or credibly infirm, say you need to rest.

Include the excluded

David Hirschmann (2003), drawing on experience of working within the time and other constraints of being a consultant, has advice for including the excluded:

- **Use rhetorical space.** Make use of donor rhetoric of participation, gender, poverty and so on to open up spaces to give voice to, listen to and learn more about those who are poorer and more excluded, not least women.
- **Reinterpret information.** Take account of the 'unseen', those not included in survey and other data, and consider who has been left out and why and what needs to be done to have them included.
- **Turn the room around.** Tactfully change patterns of seating, meeting and interaction to include and give voice to the excluded and unheard. Separate meetings with women, and more time for them to exert influence, are often needed.

Gender issues deserve underlining. Not only are women often absent or marginalized in meetings, but it is harder for them to find blocks of time, or even places, for meeting undisturbed. The principle of 'Ask them' applies: to ask them the most convenient time and place for them. For rural women in South Asia this is frequently the least convenient time for 'us': after dark, when all their duties are done. And they can show astonishing stamina by continuing their meetings after midnight. And try to assure a gender balance in any visiting group or team.[11]

There are many other ways to offset biases. Many of them can be fun. Being aware of how one is trapped can lead to wry smiles. Inventive improvisation often leads to good learning. Experiences provide stories and jokes to share with colleagues. At all costs, awareness of the limitations of brief visits should not deter but encourage development professionals to go where poor people are, to meet them, to collect and share experiences, and learn to do this better. All of us who are practitioners or victims of development tourism, whether rural or urban, can develop our own ideas for good practice.

My own favourite is advice from the *Alpine Journal*. Designed for ski mountaineering, this applies to much else in life, and equally, if not more, to rural and urban visits:

> Start early
> Don't rush
> Think!

Learning face to face

In the 2000s learning face to face has come to the fore, often with deeper and more insightful learning, sometimes personally transformative. Four forms can be noted: team reality checks; total participatory research; immersions with overnights; and listening and life stories.

Team reality checks

Team visits and interactions with local people have been a key part of RRA. RRAs with officials have transformed views of land tenure and policy in Tanzania (Johansson and Hoben, 1992), and in Madagascar and Guinea (Freudenberger, 1998). Responding to three critical evaluations, United Nations High Commissioner for Refugees (UNHCR) initiated annual participatory assessments with refugees in which the staff of the headquarters in a country go out and meet and listen to refugees. An evaluation (Groves, 2005) found it to be 'extremely positive and useful tool in that it brings staff closer to the realities of the people of concern'. In the words of one staff member:

> *There has been a big effect for me personally and for the implementing partners that I work with. Before, we knew that there were differences between sex and age groups but we didn't realise to what extent. There has been a total change in implementing partners' attitudes.*

The Swedish International Development Agency (Sida) in Bangladesh began in 2007 to pioneer a new form of reality check. This is designed to listen to poor people's realities on primary healthcare and primary education. It will be conducted with the same households at the same time of the year, October/November, when conditions are often at their most difficult for poor people, repeated each year for five years. It combines immersions (living with the poor) with more conventional participatory approaches. It stresses listening and learning the perspectives of poor people themselves. The findings will feed into annual policy reviews (Sida, 2007; Jupp with others, 2007b).

Total participatory research

Swiss Agency for Development and Cooperation (SDC) undertook a remarkable activity in Tanzania in which some of its staff were trained in participatory research and then spent a whole day living and working each with a very poor family (SDC, 2003; Jupp, 2004a). Dee Jupp, who facilitated it, has written: 'The outcomes of the exercise were extraordinary. Not only was a wealth of insights into the life of poor households gathered, but the experience turned out to be transformational for many of the research team' (Jupp, 2007a). In spite of this, the approach has not, to my knowledge, ever been repeated. Participants said 'The image of the baby crying all day with hunger will always be with me', 'I've worked in rural villages for more than twenty years, but I have never had an experience like this', 'We heard the untold stories. It was an eye-opener as families shared their problems that would never be aired in group meetings', and 'Even village leaders could not tell you what we experienced for ourselves'.

The insights gained included that poor people gave higher priority to their shelter and housing than had been thought, and that some did not know about services provided free by the state. The outcomes of this participatory research included photographs taken by poor people which were later exhibited in Bern. The main benefit, though, was personal experiential learning, and its contribution to SDC planning and priorities.

Immersions with overnights

Immersion is the term commonly used to describe an outsider being hosted by a family and staying in a community for a few days with overnights. As a practice it has been growing, and may be near a tipping point. Immersions are now well documented.[12] Staying in communities as a guest, as a person, and not as an official or bringer of benefits, opens up a range of experiences and insights otherwise inaccessible. For one thing, much changes after dark. People relax and talk more freely. There is no rush to finish off and leave. There is less awareness of personal differences. People talk about other things – family and relationships, what matters to them, and subjects otherwise too sensitive like corruption, exploitation, local conflicts, and the wider world... The guest is less likely to be treated prudently with chosen words and information. The overnight stay is subject to its own pressures – to stay not with a poor family but with one which is better off, as may be felt appropriate by community members themselves; or to camp in the school, or in a tent outside the village; or not to stay in the community at all but to put up at a nearby government rest house. The decent reflexes of hospitality on the part of those organizing a visit for the stranger deserve to be respected, but can also be politely but firmly resisted.

The essence of the immersion with overnights is that the visitor is not an important person but a fellow human being and can become a friend. She or he spends nights living in a community, taking part and helping in life, and experiencing and learning as a participant. There are many forms of immersion and many ways of arranging them. They can be spontaneous, on an impulse or seizing an opportunity; but more usually they are prepared and facilitated as reflective experiences. They can be unstructured, or they can be designed to explore a theme.

Immersions have been pioneered, adopted and promoted in varied forms (Eyben, 2004; Irvine et al, 2004, 2006; PLA, 2007). For some social anthropologists, they have long been professional practice. Pioneers have included Karl Osner with the Exposure and Dialogue Programme (EDP) in which typically groups of senior officials and politicians together have a period of orientation, a few days staying with a host family, and then a time of individual and joint reflection. (By 2008 there had been some 77 EDPs with almost 1000 participants.) Other organizations practising immersions are the World Bank with its programme for senior managers introduced by James Wolfensohn; the very large trade union SEWA (the Self Employed Women's Association) in India using immersions for the induction of its own staff and organizing them for others; and ActionAid International. Among bilateral agencies, Sida is leading. Senior staff (Göran Holmqvist and Staffan Herrström) set an example with their own immersions, and then in 2007 Sida became the first bilateral agency to make immersions officially approved and encouraged as practice for its staff (Nilsson et al, 2007).

The benefits of immersions are repeatedly affirmed and illustrated by the reflections of those who have experienced them. In the words of an official of an international aid agency:

> *I have asked myself what would have happened if I had spent one week per year in a village somewhere over the last decade ... ten different contexts, and a number of faces and names to have in mind when reading, thinking, writing, taking decisions and arguing in our bureaucracy.*

One wonders whether the lethal policies of structural adjustment would have been imposed so harshly on indebted countries if those responsible had spent a few days and nights hosted by poor communities in those countries. Immersions should be highly cost-effective ways of enhancing the realism and impact of pro-poor policy and practice and reducing the risk of gross errors. Through their reality checks, they hold the potential to discharge responsibility and accountability both upwards to funders and taxpayers, and downwards to poor people themselves. The question now is not how an organization can afford the time and other resources for immersions for its staff. It is how, if it is seriously pro-poor, it can possibly not do so.

Listening and life stories of people living in poverty

Oral histories have a long pedigree. Recent examples have shown how empathetic interaction and listening can be a source of insight, personal learning and inspiration. Harsh Mander's (2001) *Unheard Voices: Stories of Forgotten Lives* is the stories of forgotten women and men, girls and boys, in contemporary India – street children, sex workers, women, *dalit* and tribal survivors of atrocities, riot victims, especially women, homeless and destitute people, scavengers of night soil, and those living with leprosy and HIV. Their narratives show not only how they survive and cope; they bring out their endeavour to overcome, with rare and humbling courage, resilience, optimism, humanism and hope. In the same spirit and genre, ActionAid researchers in Asia listened to and recorded 250 life stories in Vietnam, Pakistan, Nepal, India and Bangladesh. As the editors of the resulting volume *Listening to People Living in Poverty* (Parasuraman et al, 2003) write, the book '...presents quintessentially the worm's eye view of the experiences of poverty and its impact, against the bird's eye view that dominates the present discourses on poverty'. They provoke and challenge us with their reflection (p26) that 'In a world overwhelmed by bits of floating information, introducing emotions into the reflective process frees meaning-making in creative ways.' Kumaran, one of the researchers, concludes a powerful paper 'Listening as a Radical Act' (2003, p14) by saying that

> *Life story collection is much more than a research method. It is an attitude of mind, a disposition of heart ... by privileging this method of collecting data, we have given legitimacy and significance to different ways of being a researcher and a person. Soon the alternative ways of doing research may come to complement other conventional ways, and hopefully create a radically new development researcher...*

Learning how to liberate

These forms of learning face to face can be experienced as liberating – through new ways of knowing, being and relating. Many of the other approaches and methods considered in this book can also liberate by opening up new and better ways of learning. The more participatory of these methods, when facilitated well, are also empowering for local people. For quality and scale, three challenges stand out:

1 Recovering and reviving the good already known

So many methods, approaches and lessons learnt get silted over by whatever is new. Some like questionnaires respond to a demand, and have a frame and momentum that assure reproduction and survival. Others like participatory mapping are so versatile, powerful and popular that they persist. Other methods and approaches such as some of those of RRA, like being observant (Chapter 3) and semi-structured interviewing (Chapter 4), have been largely buried and forgotten. In part this has been because PRA visual methods have been so powerful and attractive. Also, in any training there is only so much that can be covered, and when PRA methods have primacy others are pushed off the agenda.

The challenge is revolving to retain and augment a full repertoire. This has become more exacting with the proliferation of participatory methodologies. But the flip side of the coin is that the repertoire is now so rich that we have opportunities for inventiveness and versatility that are without precedent, as we shall explore in Chapter 9.

2 Retaining quality with going to scale

PRA, and, though less well known, RRA before it, usually deteriorated when they were taken to scale. They shared this unfortunate experience with innumerable other methodologies. We need to learn better how to build self-reinforcing quality into methodologies. The literature on the subject is not sparse, and usually advocates steady expansion and good training, but if the liberations of participatory approaches are to spread well, much needs to change.

The challenge is to learn much more about how to retain and enhance quality when going to scale, and to put lessons learnt into practice.

3 Enabling incentives and values

Institutional change is often needed, from a top–down control orientation to a more democratic enabling orientation. This is painfully well known, and often stressed. But many organizations still trap, confine and constrain their staff.

The challenge is to learn more about the interactions of the institutional and the personal dimensions, and the liberating incentives and values which make space for and reward creative diversity in a participatory mode.

Whose trap? Whose liberation? Issues of Ethics

The flip side of thinking about traps and liberations is to ask about local and poor people. Do participatory approaches and methods trap them? There are many questions of practical ethics.

Ethical issues with research have always been there and have received much attention. RRA, PRA and PLA have generated their own concerns. Some who use participatory approaches in an extractive mode have been much preoccupied with abuses and ethical dilemmas:

- **Taking people's time.** The time of poor people is, contrary to common professional belief, often very precious, especially at difficult times of the year (such as commonly during the rains). Rural people are often polite, hospitable and deferential to outsiders, who do not realize the sacrifices of time they are making. A day of weeding lost at a critical period can have high hidden costs in a smaller harvest.
- **Raising expectations.** Any process of analysis facilitated by an outsider is liable to raise expectations of some benefit, even when the outsider goes to pains to explain that they have nothing to offer and nothing will follow from their visit. Disappointment and disillusion with visitors and organizations outside the community then follow.
- **Extracting information only for the outsiders' benefit without this being clear to those who provide it.** This is familiar and can apply to almost any outsiders. The information taken away may take various forms such as a map which is removed, or local knowledge, for example of medicinal or other plants. This is a major issue with knowledge of commercial value.
- **Extracting information which will be used against people.** I cannot cite cases but this must surely occur.
- **Exposing people to danger.** Street children who made maps in Cairo in all innocence showed where the drug dealers operated: this could have got them in trouble if the authorities had learnt and taken action. Urban dwellers in Jamaica analysing violence had to be stopped once for their own safety when

local thugs began to take a suspicious interest. Children in a refugee camp inadvertently showed the market where they went with their parents to sell relief food illegally.

- **Repeating activities.** Some (doubtless accessible) villages in Malawi are said to have been 'carpet-bombed' with PRA, and reportedly intercept visitors and negotiate with them before allowing them to enter, while more 'remote' villages are never visited.
- **Causing tensions or violence in a community.** This has occurred especially with women who take part in participatory activities, and who are later abused and beaten by their husbands when the outsiders have left. This can apply to any 'lower' group in a community.

To tackle these, a code of ethics has been drafted for those who use such methods to obtain numbers.[13]

The paradox of power: Reversals for pro-poor professionalism

Power can be seen to have four forms (VeneKlasen and Miller, 2002, p45):

Power over (others)
Power to (choose and do things, agency)
Power with (others, collective power)
Power within (self worth and confidence)

A paradox of power is that the exercise of power over can be a trap. It can go with responsibility, worry and stress. It can be part of a syndrome of control from above that diminishes and disempowers those below. All this is well known. What is less recognized is how fulfilling it can be for those with power over when they empower others. This can liberate by diminishing stress for those with power over. It can also give many satisfactions from learning what those empowered discover and show they can do. In terms of liberation, it can be a win–win.[14]

The paradox of this reversal of normal thinking and practice is overarching. It applies to all the traps and liberations. In every case, in every dimension, those with power over have the power to free and empower others. They can make space for and support alternatives to large questionnaire surveys. They can seize and make space for themselves and others to escape the traps of headquarters and capital cities. They can promote learning face to face. They can set an example with immersions themselves, encouraging others, and making time and providing resources for them to do likewise. They can open all this up through example, incentives and rewards.

This is all part of the fulfilment of a responsible pro-poor professionalism. It already has pioneers and champions with the vision and guts to show a lead. It needs many more. Above all, it needs more who seek out direct learning, face to face. For that is how to keep up with the changing realities of people living in poverty; that is how to be more in touch and up to date; and that is how to rekindle passion in the fight for a fairer and better world.

Notes

1   See for example, Groves (2004). The abandonment of projects was often unethical, and reflected the ignorance and insensitivity of donors isolated in aided countries' capital cities, and more so in their headquarters in their home countries. Had they been more in touch, in some of the ways suggested in this paper, they might have behaved better.
2   Harmonization can mean instructions from home headquarters to influence more powerful lenders or donors in an aided country. '...the fashionable joint funding schemes which are supposed to support harmonisation and supposedly create greater efficiency, seem to me to do the opposite – endless time spent in meetings trying to harmonise with folk who simply do not see things the same way and do not have the same set of values' (pers. comm. Dee Jupp).
3   See for example, the usage in the Paris Declaration (DAC, 2005) of 'missions to the field' and 'field missions'.
4   On a visit to Ghana in 2003, the only time when aid agency staff could be met was at breakfast. Some of those who came left early because of a World Bank workshop on the PRSP (attended by at least 200 people). And there were at least two other major development-related workshops going on in parallel.
5   For example, the World Bank requires what Wilks and Lefrançois (2002) characterize as an 'assessment overload' of up to 16 analytical reports in its client countries, each of which is liable to accentuate the capital trap as officials, consultants and others struggle to complete them. Intentions to harmonize demands for reports were articulated in the Declaration adopted at the High-Level Forum on Harmonisation in Rome in February 2003, and in the Paris Declaration on Aid Effectiveness (DAC, 2005) adopted in March 2005.
6   In these strictures I do not pose as 'holier than thou'. In several respects, my own isolation and ignorance can also be described as sick.
7   If you are given a visitor's book to sign, with signatures of the great and good, or supposedly so, smile wryly and chalk up a failure.
8   Formal arrangements for this often superfluous meal can be tiresome for hosts, complicate itineraries, limit the time spent seeing, listening and learning, and again and again curtail visits. If there are bananas, you can say bananas are fine. Or at most sandwiches, samosas or their local equivalents. But use your judgement on this. Lunch can provide opportunities for conversations otherwise denied; in three days of field visits near Kabul in May 2006, I was able to have only one conversation with a woman. She was a social organizer. In the open she wore a full burka and was an unperson. Once seated in a curtained-off area for lunch, she removed the cover to reveal an animated and enthusiastic woman with whom I was able to have a fascinating talk. Without lunch, I would have missed this privilege, so rare, I was told, for a male visitor

in Afghanistan.

9   This request is often not effective, but making it establishes the point that you want this, and puts a foot in the door even if it does not always open it. In a community outside Kabul, a spare hour after the formal meeting was invaluable for meeting some of the poorer people.

10   This, too, may not work. I have made the request and arrived to be courteously presented with a detailed itinerary of visits to people who would be waiting for me. As an officer of the Indian Administrative Service, Anil C. Shah (pers. comm.) was able to avoid this. When visiting an area he would choose on a map where to go, and pick a village which was far to reach. Arriving unexpectedly, his findings were stark, revealing and embarrassing for the local staff.

11   This is precisely hardest in those societies where women are most subjugated; in only one of three days of field visits from Kabul in May 2006 did we have a woman in the party who was able to talk to women's groups! And for men to talk to them was utterly out of the question. The male bias was spectacular.

12   The best starting point for sources on immersions is *Participatory Learning and Action* 57, 2007. It contains history, personal accounts, advice and experience on organization, and reflections on process and learning. It is available online at www.iied.org/NR/agbioliv/pla_notes/backissues.html. Other websites are www.exposure-dialog.de/english/ for the Exposure and Dialogue programme, www.actionaid.org for immersions organized by ActionAid International, and www.praxisindia.org for more general information.

13   A code of ethics was drawn up by the Participatory Numbers group (see note 1, p131) in the UK. It was long and appears lost. A shorter, succinct statement is needed.

14   I have tried to explore further how acts of empowering others can be a win–win in 'Transforming Power: From zero-sum to win-win?', Chambers, 2006a.

9

Participatory Methodologies: Drivers for Change

Revolutions should be described not in terms of group experience but in terms of the varied experiences of individual group members. Indeed, that variety itself turns out to play an essential role in the evolution of scientific knowledge.
(Thomas Kuhn, 1993)

Reality is far too complex to be understood from one particular frame.
(William Savedoff, 2008)

...it is essential to keep on discovering new ways of finding out... It is not innovation but innovativeness ... that needs to be nurtured. (Dee Jupp, 2007, p122)

...since we are in a world of permanent *white water, we are going to be beginners indefinitely.* (Peter Vaill, 1996, p81. Emphasis in original)

Abstract

With astonishing speed, the journey has brought us new modes of inquiry, most recently with the flowering, proliferation and spread of participatory methodologies (PMs). With the pluralism and diversity of PMs we are in a new space: with a vastly enhanced repertoire; with a new eclectic creativity; and with a wealth of innovations specific to context and purpose.

Theory is implicit and emergent in this book. It is part of the pervasive paradigmatic shift from things to people. Theories of chaos, complexity and emergence resonate with, shed light on and underpin the evolution and spread of PMs. To these can be added eclectic pluralism, with a coherence and complementarity between context (local, complex and diverse) and eclecticism (adaptive, creative and pluralist).

PMs can be drivers and means to personal, institutional, professional and social change. Many blocks impede their recognition, evolution and adoption. Practical priorities are: to foster methodological diversity and enrich the repertoire; to make time and space for reflection, unlearning and innovation; to identify and multiply innovators and facilitators; to help people in funding agencies understand what they can do; to transform modes of teaching especially in tertiary education; and to institutionalize critical reflection and focused brainstorming.

The emergent paradigm informs and resonates with an immanent ideology and a new professionalism. At the core are principles and commitments to equity, respect, diversity, and human rights. **Who** *finds out,* **who** *learns, and* **who** *is empowered are core questions. The challenge and opportunity are for participatory methodologies to provide entry points for confronting and changing relationships and power. As long as there is a human race and organized society, participatory methodologies will remain frontiers for inquiry and drivers for personal, institutional and professional transformations. For those who wish and are willing, the scope is boundless. The exhilaration, fun and fulfilment of innovation and change for the better should never end.*

The journey so far

Our journey in this book has covered experiences and developments over some four decades. It has the limitations of a personal view. I have tried to describe the main features and currents of change in those parts of the streams where I have found myself. Others have had other experiences. Anyone else would have written a different book. Much else has been significant. Still, in this last chapter I will try to express what it seems to me has been happening, how it can be understood in terms of theory, why it has been so little recognized, its potentials, and ways forward and what this could mean for our world. I shall argue that the flowering of a multiplicity of participatory methodologies now presents us, humankind, with opportunities that are without precedent.

The journey that began with the dinosaurs of massive multi-subject questionnaires and with the biased empiricism of brief rural visits led through the search for better modes of inquiry to the repertoire and principles of rapid rural appraisal (RRA). This in turn evolved, fed by other flows, into the marvellous excitements of early participatory rural appraisal (PRA), its exponential spread, its widespread misuse, and its diffusion and subsuming in the broader family of participatory methodologies (PMs) and participatory learning and action (PLA). These in turn have now evolved, cross-fertilized and spread during the past decade with an exhilarating diversification and creativity, spawning innumerable forms and varieties. In the mid-1990s we were coming to terms with the spread of PRA. In the latter 2000s the challenge is to comprehend the astonishing range and implications of a new multiplicity of PMs. This is much more than collecting stamps or catching, classifying and naming butterflies. It is trying to see the range of potentials of the proliferating diversity of PMs, and to understand and nurture the conditions and processes that support the dispersed creativity and performance through which they continue to emerge and evolve.

Methodological diversity and pluralism

Methodological monocultures or fundamentalisms confine and cramp creativity. On its own, the large multi-subject questionnaire survey is unimodal, a reflex for moving on a flat Earth. For many, it remains as a knee-jerk, embedded as an automatic choice as method for inquiry. The same can be said of some other monocultures. For a time, there were even PRA fundamentalists, consultants who proselytized and sold PRA as a standard solution for every problem.

Some fundamentalisms survive. But increasingly they are passé, overtaken by the burgeoning multiplicity of participatory options of the 21st century. The diverse pluralism of these options has three dimensions.

The first is the rich range of tried and tested PMs. In the early and mid-1990s there was a proliferation of named methodologies, a few of them originating earlier. Many had short lives or spread little. The survivors have diverse and distinctive characteristics. The selection of PMs outlined in Chapter 5 were:

- farmer participatory research (itself a family of PMs)
- farmer field schools and integrated pest management
- Reflect
- Stepping Stones
- Internal Learning System (ILS)
- the Participatory Action Learning System (PALS)
- Community-Led Total Sanitation (CLTS).

Others with distinct characteristics include:

- Participatory Technology Development (Haverkort et al, 1991; PTD, 2005)
- Open Space (Owen, 1997)
- Planning for Real (Gibson, 1996)
- Participatory Poverty Assessments (Norton et al, 2001; Robb, 2002)
- Theatre-based approaches (Abah, 2004; McCarthy and Galvão, 2004; Guhathakurta, 2008)
- Participatory Geographic Information Systems (Chapter 7)
- Outcome Mapping (Earl et al, 2001)
- Most Significant Change (Davies and Dart, 2005; Willetts and Crawford, 2007)
- Appreciative Inquiry (AI) (Ludema and Fry, 2008)
- ALPS (the Accountability, Learning and Planning System of ActionAid) (ActionAid International (AAI), 2006c)
- Participatory video (Lunch and Lunch, 2006)
- Star (Nakiboneka, 2008)
- Participatory Vulnerability Analysis (AAI, 2008)
- Negotiated learning (Guijt, 2007b)
- Participatory Appraisal of Competitive Advantage (PACA, 2008).

In addition there are two large families:

- Participative Inquiry and Practice (Reason and Bradbury, 2008), embracing many approaches to action research which have been largely separate from the streams described in this book. Examples are action learning (Pedler and Burgoyne, 2008), cooperative inquiry (Heron and Reason, 2008) and participatory action research (Swantz, 2008; Rahman, 2008).
- Participatory democracy for which there has been an explosion of PMs, especially in India and South America, including citizen's juries (Wakeford et al, 2008), participatory budgeting, budget tracking, monitoring of service delivery, responsibility mapping, report cards, holding officials to account, social audits and related applications of digital and internet technology (pers. comm. John Gaventa).

And there are surely many more. Together with PRA/PLA (Chapter 5) and participatory methods that generate numbers (Chapter 6) these present an extraordinary collection of methods and ideas which have worked. The range of recipes, ingredients and how these can be combined has expanded and continues to expand it would seem exponentially.

The second dimension is ease of borrowing and adapting methods and approaches. This can be understood in terms of the visibility, divisibility and porosity of named PMs. As far as I know, there is open access to details of all the PMs listed above. They are global commons. At least as important, they are divisible, that is dimensions and elements of them can be picked out and adapted and used. This is true not only of those that are broader approaches (like AI) but also of those that are methodologically more internally integrated as systems (like ILS): from AI it is possible to take the idea of asking people first to show what they are proud of, and from ILS the idea of the visual diary. Porosity – having permeable boundaries, no copyright, no exclusive ownership – permits and encourages the borrowing and adapting.

The third dimension is innovation as a way of working and being, inventing and improvising anew for each purpose and context. More and more consultants, facilitators, researchers and activists have become eclectic and innovative pluralists who devise sequences and combinations of methods to fit each case. To do this they draw on more and more experiences, ideas and sources. The potential for mixed methods has proliferated at the same time as the more creative practitioners have been able and willing to explore and exploit it. They draw on multiple repertoires and put together and improvise sequences fitting for purpose and context. What they do is new each time. At its best this is a performance, an art form. And what they do is often not named.

All this can apply in participatory workshops and with participatory field research.

Eclectic combinations and sequences, combined with improvisation, are a part of many participatory workshops. Unfortunately, these are rarely recorded and published. An exception is a two-day workshop for participants from Middle Eastern countries facilitated by two of my colleagues. In the words of one of them:

Peter Taylor and I facilitated a journey of discovery over a couple of days that combined personal recall of experiences with creative writing, theatrical enactment, conceptual sense-making and practical application during field visits. (Pettit, 2006, p76)

One wonders how many similar experiences are never shared.

More numerous are accounts of ad hoc invention for participatory field research. We have seen (Chapter 6, pp116–117) how, in Malawi, Sarah Levy and her colleagues evolved an ingenious sequence of participatory methods combining social mapping, household listing, and food security sorting and piling, in order to find what categories of people had benefited from the Targeted Inputs Programme. Many of such PMs devised by creative consultants for context and purpose are one-off. We can learn here from the work of Dee Jupp. Four of the PM innovations she has led (Jupp, 2007a)[1] have been:

- a Participatory Poverty Assessment in Bangladesh (UNDP, 1996) in which focus groups of poor women and men discussed and ranked their priorities for changes which were doable and would make a difference to their lives
- a Participatory Human Rights Assessment with visuals (Jupp, 2007a, pp108–109)
- participatory research with very poor people in Tanzania (SDC, 2003; Jupp, 2004)
- a giant wall mind-map developed in a Somali peace-building process (Jupp, 2007a, p113).

These could be applied in many places. Yet none has to my knowledge been used elsewhere. One wonders how many goldmines like these lie untapped. Consultants have to go on to other work. Sponsoring agencies have got what they paid for. Donor staff have to get on with spending their budgets: they are not rewarded for recognizing and disseminating PMs. And they too move on. A thousand flowers have bloomed, faded and died. Only a few have seeded or hybridized. Big opportunities have been missed.

Implicit and resonant theory

As we saw in Chapter 5, PRA/PLA-related theory has been induced from practice rather than the other way round. This has been described in terms of three domains: first, attitudes, behaviours and mindsets; second, methods especially those involving groups, visuals and tangibles; and third, sharing and relationships. Moving from PRA and PLA to participatory methodologies more generally, three other underlying dimensions of theory can be discerned, explaining and underpinning what has been happening. They are: the shift from a paradigm of things to one of people; theories of chaos, complexity and emergence; and creative and eclectic pluralism.

Paradigms: From things to people[2]

Tensions and changes in development thinking, procedures and practices can be interpreted in terms of paradigms: one associated with things, and one with people. Paradigm here refers to a mutually reinforcing pattern of concepts, values and principles, methods, procedures and processes, roles and behaviours, relationships and mindsets, and orientations and predispositions.

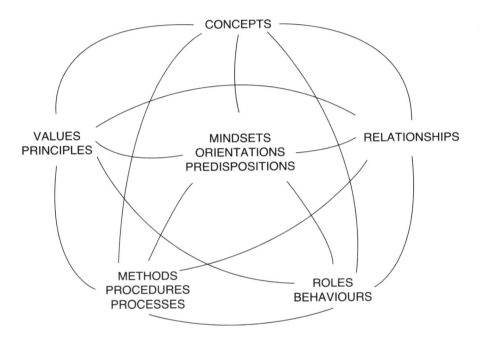

Figure 9.1 *Dimensions of a paradigm*

Two contrasting paradigms, of things and of people, can illuminate significant differences and are relevant to the argument here.

The two paradigms are contrasted for emphasis. But dichotomies can distort and caricature by polarizing and presenting elements that are often complementary or continua as though they are mutually exclusive. It is not a question of bad/good or either/or. Each has its fitting context. We need good physical infrastructure on the things side and good relationships and capabilities on the people side. Moreover, much good practice straddles and combines the two.

That said, the paradigm of things comes from, fits and works with the physical world: it is top–down, centralized, standardized, simplified and reductionist; it values measurement; and its outputs are physical things such as infrastructure and reports. The paradigm of people comes from, fits and works with the social

Table 9.1 *Contrasting paradigms of things and people*

Generative basis	Things and procedures	People and processes
Orientation, planning and access	Top–down Centralized Controlling	Bottom–up Decentralized Empowering
Key words	Planning Design Blueprint	Participation Emergence Process
Methods	Standardized Reductionist Universal Fixed	Performative Inclusive Contextual Flexible
Embodying Expressing	Rules Conventions	Principles Values
Implicit assumptions about causality and change	Linear Controllable Predictable	Non-linear Uncontrollable Unpredictable
Valuing and relying for rigour and quality on	Regulation Precision Measurement Statistical analysis	Responsibility Fitness Judgement Triangulation
Roles and behaviours	Supervising Enforcing	Facilitating Enabling
Typical procedure and processes	Questionnaires Randomized control trials Logframes	Participatory methodologies
Mode and ethos	Hierarchical	Democratic

world: it is bottom–up, decentralized, diverse, complex and inclusive; it values judgement, and has outputs that are social such as capabilities and relationships. Much development practice can be interpreted as in tension between the norms of these two paradigms, and a struggle to shift from the historically dominant 'things' set of economists and engineers, to the 'people' set, in principle the domain of all disciplines, in practice mainly of social scientists. Methodologically, questionnaires, randomized control trials, sampling, statistical probabilities and logframes belong on the things and procedures side, while participatory methodologies belong on the side of people and processes.

Self-organizing systems: Chaos, complexity and emergence

The paradigm of people resonates with the theories of chaos (Gleick, 1988), complexity (Waldrop, 1994), emergence (Johnson, 2002), and ideas of deep simplicity underlying complexity, diversity, dynamism and unpredictability (Gribbin, 2004). These have rarely been considered in development (but now see Ramalingam et al, 2008).[3] Concepts and insights of systems theory and complexity science can illuminate realities that are obscured or misperceived through linear, control-oriented, standardized, top–down approaches. For example, interconnected and interdependent elements and dimensions, feedback processes, non-linearity, and sensitivity to initial conditions are all found in development processes. Messy partnerships (Guijt, 2008)[4] and relationships and unpredictable outcomes are commonplace.

Perhaps the most relevant concept is that of self-organizing systems on the edge of chaos. The edge of chaos is the zone of diverse, self-organizing and emergent complexity which lies between top–down rigidity and random chaos. Computer simulations have provided insights. In this zone systems manifest complex behaviour based on simple rules. For example, random blobs on a computer screen can be programmed with three rules so that they form flocks and fly around together (Resnick, 1994), behaviour that could never be programmed in a conventional top–down manner.

In many contexts in the natural world there is similar complex behaviour without a central authority: besides birds flocking and fish shoaling, ant colonies are much cited. Slime moulds are perhaps the most iconic example. They at times exist as dispersed individual cells, invisible to the naked eye: at others they come together as visible aggregates. For 20 years mycologists searched for specialized 'pacemaker' cells that they believed must be determining this behaviour. The alternative explanation, now accepted, of widespread responses of individual cells to changes in the environment, was for long met with scepticism. And it is this scepticism that is of prime interest, for it expresses our deeply rooted mindsets that look for explanations in a central authority, what Steven Johnson (2002, pp29–67) calls 'the myth of the ant queen', the idea that the complex and continuously emergent behaviour of ants in a colony must be controlled by the queen.

The shift to a mindset that recognizes such forms of self-organization has been gradual and is far from complete. It has been a revolution in the way we think about the world and many of its systems (Johnson, 2002, pp54–55). Its logic is bottom–up. Applied to human society, it takes the form of emergent, complex and unpredictable behaviour generated by active agents bound variously by simple rules, conventions, principles and/or values. In an obvious form, based on rules, this logic can be found in games, football and chess for example.

Participatory methodologies manifest this bottom–up logic. In understanding behaviours in PMs, it helps to distinguish between rules and conventions, which are lower-level, specific and detailed determinants, and principles and values which are higher-level general guides. Rules and conventions are to be followed, to be obeyed; principles and values are to be interpreted, to be embodied. With

PMs, good performance is based less on rules and conventions, and more on principles and values.

This point is illustrated by manuals. Typically, these instruct in detail what to do and in what sequence. In the early days of Reflect, a large Mother Manual was produced. When it was interpreted too literally as rules, it had to be replaced with a loose-leaf sourcebook of ideas which are ingredients rather than a recipe (Archer and Newman, 2003). Users had to exercise judgement (based implicitly on principles and values) in choosing and interpreting what to do. This spawned a proliferation of local innovation and ownership (Box 9.1).

Box 9.1 *Reflect: From Mother Manual to multiplicity*

After the piloting of Reflect, in Bangladesh, El Salvador and Uganda in 1993/4 and its early evolution, experience was brought together in a Mother Manual. This was intended as a resource for the introduction and development of Reflect in other places and countries. It recommended adaptation of its participatory tools to address critical local issues. But it was interpreted literally as detailed rules, resulting in routinised and inappropriate application. It was withdrawn and more emphasis was placed on selecting and training facilitators, and shifting the balance of activity to give less prominence to literacy and more to critical analysis and empowerment. This spawned more creativity and variety of local practice. In an evaluation in 2001, of 134 organisations surveyed, 28 were still using the Mother Manual, 17 had regional or national manuals, 55 local manuals, and 34 no manual (CIRAC, 2001, p47).

For me, a fascinating and similar discovery has been an inverse relationship between rules and instructions on the one hand, and commitment and creative diversity on the other. In PRA training I used for years to take 20 minutes or so to 'teach' how to do matrix scoring. Trainees would then practise, and we would walk around and comment. I would point out who had done it 'right' and where they had got it 'wrong'. I slowly realized that this froze out spontaneity, creativity, diversity and discovery. I now take two or three minutes to show a rough example, give a minimal framework and resources, and tell groups to form themselves and get on with it. One result has been that I have come to learn many methods for matrix scoring that I had never imagined! Another is that participants learn experientially for themselves, from their own inventions, practice, mistakes and reflective critiques.

Bimal Phnuyal had already gone down this road. When conducting a PRA training he had used to give a long background of PRA to participants before they went to practise in the field. He would describe the key features and steps for each technique. Participants as well as trainers wanted to 'clarify' everything before practice. Then in a training of facilitators in El Salvador, in 1998, they went straight into mapping. Participants produced a beautiful community map. They were then asked to reflect on and write down how they had done it. 'We as trainers benefited more from this experience, we could learn how we can learn by doing, and why it is not necessary to give theory first. Participants can theorize from their own practice' (Pers. comm. 1998).

As with many PRA methods in group situations in communities, starting conditions may be influenced by a facilitator, and suggestions made, but when the stick, if held at all, is metaphorically or literally handed over, actors then invent processes for themselves.

A practical illustration of self-organizing systems is known as SOSOTEC (self-organizing systems on the edge of chaos). This provides and expresses principles for participatory workshops, teaching and learning (Chambers, 2002, pp93–94, 105, 123–128). The predisposing conditions are first, commitment by actors to common goals – like learning about a subject, or sharing and collecting insights, or meeting together for a common interest; and second, simple enabling principles or rules. In a participatory workshop, SOSOTEC can be effective for many decentralized activities, like rearranging furniture, meeting and greeting one another, and open-ended activities with self-forming groups as in Open Space (Owen, 1997). Often this bottom–up logic of enablement engages and releases energy and interaction leading to learning and understanding. And principles and rules or guidelines can and often are made in a participatory mode by participants themselves.

In a SOSOTEC mode, there is power to empower. This can be exercised either through power over, or through power with (Chapter 8, p164). The mode is to convene and set minimum enabling principles or non-negotiables. An example is women's savings groups in South India, convened and facilitated by the NGO MYRADA. There were only two non-negotiable principles: first, that accounting should be competent and transparent; second, that leadership and the holding of offices should regularly rotate. Beyond that, the over 2000 groups were free to make their own rules and procedures. They then looked not upwards and outside for authority, but to themselves, and took ownership and pride in their self-organizing and adaptive systems.

Participatory methodologies can be seen through this lens. They generate self-organizing systems with emergent properties, the detail of which cannot be foreseen. Whether it is matrix scoring or mapping, or the formation of women's savings groups, or any one of most if not all participatory methods or methodologies, we find that active adaptive agents, interacting together within a few common values, principles and rules, manifest behaviours and realities that are both complex and unpredictable.

Pluralism: Eclectic, versatile and creative

These frames or theories combine to support and understand what is happening, the flowering and spread of a new eclectic, versatile and creative pluralism based on principles and values found and expressed in behaviours, attitudes and mindsets. These can include mutual respect, humility, listening, sensitivity, courage, awareness, integrity, curiosity, playfulness, humour, originality, critical reflection... They are qualities of good facilitators and innovators.

This eclectic pluralism is antithetical to exclusive branding and the ego of ownership. It also extends the PRA principle of sharing without boundaries. That originally was thought of as sharing freely the approaches and methods of PRA. But now it applies to all methodologies. For a time there was a multiplicity of brands, ownerships and associated egos. But as methodologies have continued to proliferate, so the boundaries have become more porous and less significant. Pervasively the spirit now is one of seeking, finding, borrowing, adopting, adapting, cross-fertilizing and inventing. There is no territory, no ownership, no copyright. Like Linux and Wikipedia there is open access, and anyone can use and contribute. As a courtesy the originator of an idea, process or method may be acknowledged. But in mixing, matching, adapting, inventing and creating methodologies there are no intellectual property rights or patents. There are no permissions to be sought.

That said, it is reasonable that those who have evolved a tradition which bears a label can seek to minimize its misuse or abuse as it spreads. They may indicate minimum empowering ground rules and sequences, and principles and values. But when others adopt, adapt and use well what they have developed, instead of resentment and dismay they should feel pride and pleasure. And this pride and pleasure can be most fulfilling when they are not even known to have been the source.

The case for eclectic pluralism has two foundations.

First, eclecticism is for flexibility, creativity, diversity, hybridization, and local and contextual fit. A method or methodology may prove to be one-off, as with the Dee Jupp examples above: opportunities for wider adaptation and use may be lost; or it may be that what was tailor-made for a context and purpose was fitting but not amenable to spread. However, the needs here are to share and spread not just methodological innovations but more so the attitudes, behaviours and mindsets that are vital to processes of innovation, and beyond that to multiply innovators.

Second, pluralism contrasts with any methodological monoculture, like sometimes that of questionnaires. The now defunct monoculture of the mechanistic Training and Visit system for agricultural extension (Benor and Harrison, 1977) contrasts with the creative pluralism of a project for innovations in rural extension in Bangladesh which had 45 sub-projects, many of these with their own methodology (van Mele et al, 2005). Paradigmatically, pluralism has to be part of innovation systems (van Mele and Braun, 2005). Practically, for inquiry, methodological pluralism, as in mixed methods approaches, contributes cross-checking and triangulation and multiplies insights.

The combination of these in eclectic pluralism is an affirmation of the paradigm of people and process. Creative, emergent and to a degree unpredictable, it opens up almost infinite variation in modes of inquiry through adaptations, mixes, inventions and improvisations of methods and approaches. When methods and PMs are improvised anew to fit each context and purpose, the range of potentials appears almost without limit. The scope for innovation and discovery for any facilitator is unbounded. Resources of ideas and experiences are global and increasingly shared and accessible; and the potentials and opportunities for creativity are multiplying. Eclectic and creative pluralism should become a major dimension of many modes of inquiry in the 21st century.

Potential to transform: PMs and their facilitation as drivers for change

These theories link and support each other. Emergence and self-organizing systems on the edge of chaos fit with the people paradigm of bottom–up logic, empowerment and enhancing capabilities. Eclectic pluralism then offers new versatility and scope, through the endless combinations and adaptations it promises for local and social relevance. And the resulting participatory methodologies are about so much more than the inquiry with which this journey started. For they facilitate transformations of power. They enable local people and lowers generally to appraise and analyse the complexity and diversity of their realities. And beyond that they can nurture critical awareness and action to transform power and claim social justice. PMs can then be a fertile seedbed not only for methodological innovation but also for social change.

Interventions to change a paradigm (Figure 9.1) can be with any of its components – concepts; values and principles; methods, procedures and processes; roles and behaviours; or relationships. Through critical self-awareness and reflection, they can also start with mindsets, orientations and predispositions.

Figure 9.2 now takes us into another space and invites us to approach from another direction, starting with participatory methodologies as drivers of change.

Change can start in any circle and spread through the arrows, or it can start with PMs.

Empirically, for any PM, the causal links of the diagram present an agenda of questions, asking case by case to what extent and how it has or could influence change. Reviewing the range of PMs described in this book, I find that all of them entail approaches, methods and processes, all of them imply sharing and influence relationships, and all of them affect behaviour, attitudes and mindsets, and these in turn become part of professional, institutional and personal change. The links are clearer and more marked with some PMs than others, and they vary in the balance and strength of their drives and how these feed through into the professional, institutional and personal domains. Stepping Stones, Reflect and Star, for example, are strong in the field context on behaviour, attitudes, mindsets, sharing, relationships and personal change but less so on professional and institutional change. But they can also entail and generate changes that are professional in terms of training and orientation and institutional in the norms of supporting and implementing organizations.

The personal dimension is primary. Much has been written about the dynamics of personal learning and change. Learning cycles are variously

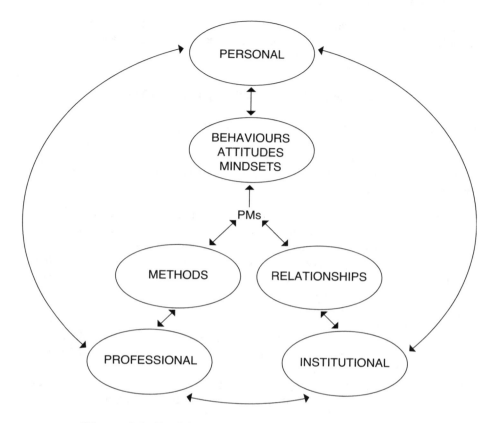

Figure 9.2 *Participatory methodologies as drivers for change*

expressed as sequences, for example action – experience – reflection – learning – planning – action–reflection ... and so on. In Figure 9.2 this experiential learning takes place largely in the behaviours, attitudes and mindsets circle, but can then extend into the others. All but the most transient and superficial PMs entail experiential learning and change for those who facilitate or take part, the more so when critical reflection is part of them: behaviours generate experiences and relationships, which in turn influence orientations and perceptions. Facilitators and participants often state that something has changed for them, and some describe the effects as transformative. Some reflective practitioners say that their family life is affected as well as their work.

At the core of PMs as potential drivers for change, is facilitation and the orientation and the personality of the facilitator. 'Asked who are the most important persons in the development, spread and evolution of high-quality PMs, without hesitating I will respond that it is the facilitator' (Nandago, 2007, p37). Facilitation can be a mode of interaction in almost every human relationship and context. It is part of a participatory paradigm, feeding into and being informed and itself transformed by the experiences of process. For professional, institutional and personal change, PMs and facilitation appear potent points of entry. The big question is whether on a large scale and over decades they could be significantly transformative in our world.

Blocks to realizing potentials

Whatever the answer to that question, and whatever the participatory rhetoric, the spread of PMs and facilitation faces formidable blocks. There is more than a blind spot here; in some professions and organizations, it is more like a dark night (though one may hope, just before a dawn). Blind spots and dark nights cry out for explanation. With PMs, some of the reasons seem to be:

*   Powerful people, especially economists in global and central organizations, call the shots (Chapter 1) concerning methodology. They are known to expect traditional and inappropriate 'scientific' and medical research designs, such as the so-called 'gold standard' of randomized control trials. Others are obliged and willing to accept grants and fees to feed them with fodder harvested and prepared in familiar forms.
*   Most faculties in universities, colleges and training institutes have been socialized into and are trapped in top–down didactic modes of teaching. For them to change would be challenging personally, professionally and in-stitutionally, would require effort and imagination, and would entail risks to career and so to income and family.
*   Many have been trained and socialized into the ideas, values, methods, behaviours, mindsets and relationships of the linear paradigm of things, and regard these as the only forms of rigour.
*   Top–down categories, language, mindsets and requirements impede in-novation and the expression of local diversity and complexity. The logframe is but one example of such a restraint (Wallace, 2006).
*   Staff in funding agencies – governments, aid agencies, INGOs and founda-tions – are only familiar with traditional methodologies and are neither willing nor able to invest time in changing the approaches of those they fund. Nor are they prepared or able to allow enough time and space for the development and pilot testing of PMs. (Exceptions are mainly in South Asia, and with some of the more imaginative, flexible and innovative bilateral funders, such as Swedish International Development Agency (Sida), Swiss Agency for Development and Cooperation (SDC), and foundations like Ford and Rockefeller.)
*   PMs are vulnerable to the withdrawal of funding, especially when they are evaluated according to the norms of the things paradigm, as tragically hap-pened with Stepping Stones in several African countries (Welbourn, 2007 and pp95–96).
*   Creative and eclectic consultant-facilitators are still relatively few.[5] Many of those who have the abilities are trapped in bureaucracies with other re-sponsibilities. There is no training anywhere, to my knowledge, in how to be creatively eclectic and inventive with PMs.

- Many innovations pass unnoticed. Consultants are not paid to disseminate their innovations. Those who sponsor them rarely budget for dissemination.

Weighing the massive interacting inertia of these blocks, it is scarcely surprising that PMs are not more widely recognized, promoted and adopted. At the same time, the challenge is clear and the opportunity immense.

So the questions are: what have we learnt? And what should be done and by whom?

Lessons of experience and ways forward

Looking back, lessons can be sought in the experiences with RRA, farmer first and PRA. In all these cases establishing contacts and networks of innovators, convening workshops and conferences, and publishing the outcomes contributed to establishment and spread. Professional innovators marginalized in their own institutions met others similarly isolated and drew comfort from their common experience and the new collegiality of a marginalized minority. Later, publications in prestigious (international, peer-reviewed) journals contributed to acceptance and respectability.

With PMs these activities – networking, workshops and conferences, publications in prestigious journals, and collegiality among marginalized innovators – are all needed and are taking place. Other key lessons of experience apply to actors and organizations. Seven seem salient, each pointing to action:

I The personal dimension: Innovators, facilitators, disseminators

With PMs, the personal dimension is central. Multiplication, spread and quality require innovators, disseminators and facilitators. Some people have 'got it': as innovators and facilitators they are creative and sensitive; have an inner conviction and confidence; enjoy taking risks; love new ideas; learn from being wrong; ever try new things; and bounce back from failure full of new energy. Remembering Dr Zeuss's dictum that 'Adults are obsolete children', they are adults who can still play like children.[6] A good facilitator of Community-Led Total Sanitation should be able to dance and sing[7] (pers. comm. Kamal Kar). We need more such people with the time, space, encouragement and daring to innovate and facilitate, and champions to support them.

The scarcer resource is not funds but people. Innovators, disseminators and facilitators may be different people. But perhaps an ideal is combinations in the same person or group. Creative innovators are the rarest. The key is finding them, helping them gain experience, and supporting them, and doing these on a larger scale. Many are trapped in organizations and need to be liberated. We need many more of those with the flair for PMs to be given more space by their organizations or to be able to break out from them.

The shortage of innovators and facilitators is the major constraint on the quality and scale of PMs. Innovators are needed but in fewer numbers than facilitators. PRA training was all the rage in the first half of the 1990s. Some of it, particularly by IIED and by Indian trainers who travelled to other countries, was of very high quality, but much of it was poor, even execrable. More recently, again and again, for example with Reflect, Stepping Stones, IPM and STAR, the identification and selection, training, orientation, mentoring and support of facilitators has been stressed as the key to quality (see e.g. Nandago, 2007).

The potential of training people in facilitation, and encouraging them to practice it in everyday life, is at the early stages of being explored. The ILAC (Institutional Learning and Change) initiative in the CGIAR (Consultative Group for International Agricultural Research) has convened three-day workshops of scientists and managers, conducted by Sam Kaner (see Kaner et al, 1996). Those who have been through the experience have returned to their organizations with new orientations and behaviours, leading, for example, to more democratic and participatory conduct of meetings. The quality of this training may be exceptional, but there may be seeds here of an approach which over years could, through many pathways, help to transform power and relationships in many organizations.

2 Time and space for creativity

The past two decades have seen an accelerating proliferation of innovations in methodology. Especially where these have sought to generate participatory numbers, they have demanded weeks or months, not days, for puzzling, experimenting, failing and succeeding, and trying out new ideas, sequences and combinations, in a process of crafting a combination and sequence of methods that seems to work. The participatory research on starter packs in Malawi took three weeks for a team of three, testing, brainstorming, and trying different methods and mixes, before they were able to evolve an adequate methodology (pers.comm. Fiona Chambers). Anirudh Krishna took six months of trial and error to develop the stages of progress methodology. For years, the problem of comparability between communities with wealth ranking appeared insoluble, and was only cracked in South Africa after much effort and numerous trials (Hargreaves et al, 2007; Anton Simanowitz, pers. comm.). Reflect similarly went through trials for many months, in three different countries. Alice Welbourn (2007, p133) records that Stepping Stones took much longer to produce than originally envisaged and than any normal organizational planning would allow. Examples are legion.

These experiences show that time and space are needed for creativity if what is done is to fit purpose and context. Lack of time and resources allowed by sponsors and funders is one reason for the default knee-jerk of the questionnaire. All too often, even now, there is too little time and no space to debate approach and methods, and then for open-ended experimentation. Logframes, targets and budgets needing to be spent compound the problem and constrain or stifle creativity. The time allowed needs to be optimized. The relationship between time and creativity can even be a U-shaped curve – high with little time, and high with plenty. Dee Jupp has pointed out that as a consultant with a time-bound contract she has been impelled to be extremely creative. Some pressure can surely sometimes help. Creativity can be intense in a crucible of crisis. But this depends on the eclecticism, creativity and confidence of the pioneer, the ambient conditions, and the nature of the methodology. And methodologies evolved under time pressure may be precisely those that do not spread, whereas those that take longer do. For those that entail social change, and need to seed movements, time and patience may always be needed, as was the case with Reflect and Stepping Stones, both for evolving the core methodology, and for its local evolution and adaptation.

3 Methodological diversity: Enriching the repertoire

For creators and facilitators part of this is simply enriching a personal repertoire. A good chef may specialize in the dishes of one region, country or culture. An excellent chef will have a wider expertise. And the greatest of all will have improvised and invented new dishes.[8] Every meal, too, is for them a work of art and even love. The analogy is too obvious to labour. But one difference may be that a good creator and facilitator will take more risks, and expect more learning from mistakes, than a cook; for what the facilitator is doing is more different each time, and less under control. People in a process do not behave like cooking ingredients on a stove.

For facilitators this implies a lifetime of learning, gaining skills and confidence, trying different ways of doing things, searching for alternatives, and adding continuously to the repertoire on which they draw. There are many sources, not least colleagues and co-facilitators. The internet harbours amazing treasures, but many facilitators are addicted to action and prefer that to searching.

One way to enrich the repertoire is to rediscover and revive from the past. There are many elements in the heritage that can be adopted, adapted, mixed and further evolved to fit current and future needs. Dogmatic rejection is also itself to be rejected: for all eclectic pluralism is by definition inclusive and needs to draw on past experience.

4 Funders[9]

Funders are crucial actors. They are powerful. They may mean well but repeatedly they do damage in two ways.

The first is too much money in too short a time. For what is needed, there may be no shortage of funds. The problem increasingly is too much money, too few staff to be able dispense it sensitively in small packets, and too tight a time frame. In development aid, this is part of the chronic pathology of bilateral and multilateral agencies driven and driving hard in the wrong direction, increasing disbursements and decreasing staff, all in the name of efficiency. It is difficult to understand how so many intelligent people can be so stupid. Community-Led Total Sanitation (Kar refs, pp96–97 and Box 9.2) in Bangladesh was not helped by an excessive grant to an INGO which then had for years to focus its attention on recruiting staff and gearing up to spend the money, when what was needed was more immediate training, mentoring and support for facilitators.[10]

The second is conditions that come with the money. The creator of Stepping Stones, Alice Welbourn, has written (2007, p131):

> *Increasingly donors expect us to define clearly in advance what all our outputs and outcomes are going to be, and who the funding is or is not going to be spent on. So there is no investment in creativity, there is no faith in us as creative agents of change, nor in the people with whom we might work, as independent thinkers who might come up with new good ideas themselves, based on their own experiences, along the way. The set agenda which allows no room for exploration or experimentation is stifling critical opportunities for learning.*

Box 9.2 *Transformative action by funding organizations*

Kamal Kar, a freelance participatory facilitator, together with partners in Bangladesh (VERC and Water Aid), evolved a participatory methodology known as Community-Led Total Sanitation (CLTS). This turns much conventional wisdom on its head, notably about subsidies for individual household toilets in rural areas, and spends less for greater benefits to communities. Staff of the Water and Sanitation Programme (WSP) of the World Bank recognized this, and sponsored international visits of key decision-makers to Bangladesh, and of Dr Kar to India, Pakistan, Indonesia and other countries to conduct training. These visits were seminal for the international spread of CLTS. Without them, CLTS might have been stillborn, or very limited and slow in its scope. The vision and commitment of the WSP staff, and later of other organizations such as Plan International and UNICEF, have been critical.

In contrast, some of the early activities in PRA were supported with funding from the Aga Khan Foundation, ODA (DFID as it is now), the Ford Foundation, NOVIB, SDC and SIDA (now Sida), among others. The grants were generous but not on a scale that made it difficult to spend them reasonably well. And the conditions were flexible: what was actually done never corresponded with what it was thought at the outset would be done,[11] and the funders understood and appreciated this.

The potential contribution of funders is as great as the danger that they will do damage. The questions and challenges are whether they can:

- recruit and support creators. These are often consultants
- make small enough grants over long enough periods
- be patient and allow enough time for PM development and piloting
- provide for support, experiential learning, mentoring and rewards for facilitators
- make provision for writing up and dissemination

and, most difficult

- find and support organizations and processes that select, socialize and support creators, facilitators and disseminators.

5 Transforming university and college teaching

Transforming the cultures and practices of universities and colleges is, in the long term, the most important task. Mostly, they are deserts for methodological innovation, which is little recognized as an academic activity;[12] and van Mele and Braun (2005, p153), reviewing innovations in agricultural extension, write: 'It is difficult to see how such innovations might have arisen in a research institute or university, where staff advancement depends on academic publications.' But modes and styles of teaching are a more serious problem. As long as teaching is didactic, those taught will be didactic in turn: they will be magnetized to carry top–down teaching and instructing into their working lives and careers. The overused but apposite metaphor is fishing babies from a river without going upstream to stop the person who is throwing them in. Many, perhaps most, perhaps at times almost all, lecturers and courses in universities are, through their top–down teaching styles, throwing the babies in. I have heard it remarked of students that 'By the time they leave university the damage has been done.' The PhD process can be the most harmful. Rehabilitating those who have been disabled by the experiences of education is tackling the problem too late. We have to go upstream and stop the harm at source.

Participatory learning has many manifestations. Despite this, higher education faces severe obstacles: the embedded and entrenched habits of lecturing; unwillingness to experiment; fear of being ridiculed by colleagues or marginalized for promotion; the legacies of dead architects who built tiered auditoria which inhibit or prevent discussion; sclerotic curricula; tight timetables; huge classes to be lectured to, in one case at Makerere University in Uganda, 500 at a time; and the embedded conservatism, too, of some students who prefer listening to (or dozing through) lectures to proactively finding out for themselves.

Many participatory alternatives have been and are being evolved. There are islands of innovation. In March 2007 a two week e-forum on teaching and learning with large numbers harvested many alternatives, ideas and tips. This encourages the long-term hope that teaching and learning can be transformed, that teachers will become much more coaches and facilitators, and that participatory workshops[13] will become more the mode of learning, with students learning by talking, by teaching each other, and above all by experiencing. All of this points towards our need to learn more about learning and changing.

6 Experiential learning, critical reflection and brainstorming

One pathway is critical reflection. Repeatedly development professionals, whether in aid agencies, agricultural research, NGOs or academia, talk of their need for time to stop, think and reflect. In part this is an expression of the human condition: there is never enough time. In part it is a symptom of lack of self-discipline and personal organization. In part too it is often an indicator of addiction to overwork and long hours. For all that, both subjectively and objectively, it is a real need. Nor is it adequately provided for by most organizations.

At the personal level it needs critical reflection on one's conditioning, mindset, frames for making meaning, and predispositions. Beyond that it requires time and openness. Koy Thompson (2008), reflecting on his immersion experience with a family in northern Ghana, celebrates:

> *...doing nothing in order to unlearn. Why unlearn? Because unlearning is a state of mind that encourages critical thinking and openness. Because to unlearn, you have to drop your professional defences, the position of power you have over other people by virtue of your money, knowledge, experience, and status, and become vulnerable.*

Professionally we are pointed towards teaching and learning. Our professions, professional bodies, universities and colleges do not run courses on unlearning. Nor has anyone, to my knowledge, written a book on the unlearning organization.

An exception, indeed an extreme one, is the Community Development Resource Association (CDRA) in Cape Town which devotes one week in four to review, reflection and planning. As a civil society support organization that conducts workshops and training it is exceptional; and many would find such an allocation of time excessive. But it is a discipline and an experience that has enabled it to make outstanding contributions to development understanding and practice, not least through its annual 'reports', which are really not reports at all but insightful reflections.[14]

Another example is the practice, which may be on the increase, of staff of an organization taking a week away together for guided reading and reflection.[15] One variant of this is the immersion, when development professionals are hosted by a poor community and stay and live and experience with them quite often for some three days and nights, preceded by orientation and followed by reflection.

Group immersions for brainstorming are a strange gap in development practice. I refer here to a group of people dedicating a number of days together totally to tackling a problem, opportunity or need and coming up with a creative way forward. The only case that comes to mind led to the ALPS (Accountability,

Learning and Planning System) of ActionAid International (David and Mancini, 2004; David et al, 2006). Two attempts to reduce the burden of reporting in ActionAid had failed. The Chief Executive gave six people, including the Chief Finance Officer, five days to come up with a solution. They met in Harare. They were undisturbed. The solution had to be radical. It was. It has evolved to become integral not just to how AAI does its business and seeks to relate to partners, but also to its culture and how it sees itself.

The wonder is that we, development professionals, do not do this more often. Consider the following candidates for similar creative brainstorming that could lead to proposed participatory procedures or programmes, and add your own to the list:

- non-linear alternatives to the logframe
- more alternatives to questionnaires
- internalizing facilitation as a way of relating in an organization
- how to find people who 'have got it' with PMs, and support, encourage, train and mentor them for eclectic and creative pluralism
- devising ways in which funding agencies could support the dissemination of new participatory methodologies the creation of which they have sponsored
- participatory learning with large groups (e.g. 100 students).

Could five or six well-selected people spending a few days together in a retreat mode on any of these subjects come up with proposals that would be as transformative as ALPS was for ActionAid? And if they might why are we so poorly organized that this is so rare as a practice?

7 Combinations and sequences: Personal, institutional and professional

The listing above leaves out the crucial synergies and power of combinations and sequences. So it is fitting to conclude with an example which should be a wave of the future, inspiring and showing ways forward for many disciplines. This is veterinary participatory epidemiology (PE) in East Africa (Catley, 2007). In the mid-1990s participatory approaches and methods of RRA and PRA were widely used in small-scale community-based livestock projects, but not by research centres, veterinary schools or government veterinary services. By mid-2007 PE was professionally accepted and substantially established and integrated into these organizations and spreading to other countries and other applications such as the surveillance of avian flu.

The strategy to institutionalize PE began with a survey to understand the concerns of veterinarians working throughout Africa, and then efforts to address these. A deliberate attempt was made to create a branch of RRA/PRA that veterinarians could call their own. Studies to 'play the numbers game' explored and established the validity and reliability of PE (Catley, 2007; Abebe et al, 2007).

Complementarities were identified and exploited between PE and established epidemiology; and publications were sought and gained in respected international peer-reviewed journals. A key event was a two-week training course on PE for national government epidemiologists and senior academic staff from veterinary schools in seven East African countries with an initial focus on attitudes and behaviour and including field-testing of PE methods face to face with livestock keepers during the training. This was followed up with support to Masters students in veterinary schools leading to Masters theses and publications. Over time PE was evolved and adapted creatively and diversified into a range of impact assessments and other applications.

The success of this strategy illustrates synergies of changes which are personal, professional and institutional. For these, participatory methodologies can be a key point of entry. But on their own they are not a panacea. For them to be transformative demands long-term engagement, sensitivity to professional concerns, institutionalization in universities, research organizations and government departments, and throughout and above all sustained and creative personal commitment.

The story of participatory epidemiology in East Africa is not over. Many challenges remain. But enough has been achieved to encourage and inspire others in other professions and disciplines, and in other countries, to evolve and use participatory methodologies creatively as a means of personal, professional and institutional transformation. It shows ways forward. The challenge is to make it indeed a wave of the future.

Coda: Visionary realism

The journey of this book started with 'us', development professionals and our modes of inquiry. It was we who investigated, visited, observed and analysed. The path then took us through RRA, discovering better modes of inquiry, and then to PRA and enabling local, and especially poor, people themselves to appraise, analyse, plan and act. PRA became one of the inclusive PLA family of participatory methodologies. We have seen that PMs and their facilitation have been evolved and applied in innumerable human contexts, demonstrating an extraordinary versatility. And now these are more than ever part of the common melting pot in which methods and approaches mix and merge and from which methodologies are created. The journey has been from extractive inquiry to empowerment, from owned and branded methodologies to open access and eclectic pluralism.

This has also been a journey into a new paradigm. Three decades ago elements of it were there, but inchoate. Now they cohere. There is congruence between the professional, the institutional and the personal: the professional shift of methods, values and behaviours from those of things, rules and top–down planning to those of people, principles and bottom–up participation; the institutional shift from confining controls to empowering supports, making space for creative diversity; and the personal change from regulator and controller to coach and facilitator.

Central to these transformations are combinations of personal reflexivity and institutional change. Changes in institutions, especially in organizational norms, values, procedures, rewards and relationships, complement personal change and vice versa. Congruence between the personal and the institutional is a predisposing condition for participatory processes in groups and communities, and for the continuous discovery together of ways of doing things which fit local contexts. And, as I have argued, participatory methodologies are themselves seminal points of entry for good change.

The new paradigm informs and resonates with an immanent ideology and a new professionalism. At the core are principles and commitments to equity, respect, diversity, human rights and changing power relations. Who finds out, who learns, who is empowered are again and again local people and whoever are 'lowers'. We now know that their knowledge, capabilities and potentials usually exceed their own expectations and those of others. We are driven then to turning on their heads the normal mindsets, methods, behaviours and attitudes of professionals and those with power.

The potentials are awesome. If PMs can change power and power relations; if they can apply in almost every domain; if the potential for their invention and use is greater than ever; if they can improve gender and other social relations; if their use is often fulfilling and fun, and adds spice and quality to the experience of living and being – if these are realities, what then are the limits to the changes they can spark and support? Introduced and evolved more and more in all domains of human relationships – teaching and learning, government, NGO and other organizations and their management and procedures, families, religious practices, the private sector, international relations and meetings, political processes, how we bring up children … can participatory methodologies, and facilitation as a way of being and relating, be drivers for deep and lasting change, transforming our world for the better, not just now but over decades and centuries to come?

The journey enters new territory. As long as there is a human race and organized society, adventures of inquiry, of empowering others and of eclectic and creative pluralism, will continue. PMs for inquiry, revealing realities and generating insights, will always be a frontier for innovation. But the challenge is far more than this. It is for PMs and facilitation to go beyond inquiry, to be an entry point and means to transform power and relationships, and so our world. For those who wish and are willing, the scope is boundless. The opportunities presented by PMs will for ever open up. The exhilaration, fun and fulfilment of innovation and change for the better should never end.

Notes

1   Let me recommend Dee Jupp's (2007) contribution 'Keeping the art of participation bubbling: Some reflections on what stimulates creativity in using participatory methods' in Brock and Pettit (eds) *Springs of Participation*, pp107–122 for evidence and ideas which support much of the argument of this chapter.

2   For fuller explication of the things and people paradigms and the shift between them see Chambers (1997), pp36–38.

3   Ramalingam et al (2008) is a useful and comprehensive review of potential implications of complexity science for development and humanitarian work. That paper has contributed to these paragraphs. Among the concepts the authors present and analyse are: system characteristics and behaviours emerging from simple rules of interaction; non-linearity; attractors; chaos and the edge of chaos; adaptive agents; self-organization; and co-evolution.

4   Irene Guijt's (2008) book *Seeking Surprise* breaks new ground in rethinking monitoring and argues for transforming its 'DNA'. Elements in this include messy partnerships as collective cognitive agents, distributed cognition, sense-making and cognitive dissonance or 'surprise'. Guijt argues that it is through the new configurations of messy partnerships and other types of alliances that institutional transformation must increasingly unfold.

5   However, I can think of half a dozen of the most creative who left their organizations in order to devote themselves to participatory approaches and methods full time.

6   Children learn fast – they make and correct mistakes. They fall down again and again but rarely hurt themselves badly. Adults have further to fall and often hurt themselves when they do. Do we need to be closer to the ground and more adventurous, and risk falling more often?

7   It is foolhardy to quote this, lest it be used against me. Dancing is fine, but I dread those international parties where everyone is more or less forced to sing a song. We are all different and all have a basic human right (which I exercise on such occasions) not to participate.

8   The highly successful New York restaurateur Danny Meyer 'wants the kitchens of his restaurants to be scenes of rampant and collegial improvisation… Cardoz [one of the chefs] often works without recipes, wielding some twenty-one different spices. "I just play", he has said of his approach to creating dishes' (Abrahamson and Freedman, 2006, p195).

9   For a fuller statement see Chambers (2007) 'Creating, evolving and supporting participatory methodologies: Lessons for funders and innovators', in Brock and Pettit (eds) *Springs of Participation*, pp177–189. This includes practical advice.

10   When it was clear that CLTS had huge potential, a bilateral agency sent out a mission. When I learnt that it was proposing a grant of £3 million, I protested that that was far too much. The mission returned with proposals for £17.5 million. It is simply very difficult, I think, for those who work in these agencies to recognize the disservice they do to participatory approaches and methodologies by either throwing too much money at them, or failing to give consistent support at much lower levels.

11   For example, I was astonished to see that in my proposal to AKF, DFID and the Ford Foundation for two years in India 1989–91, a major part of my work was to concern agricultural research! But what was exciting and important was the way people, especially in Indian NGOs, were pioneering PRA, and that was where I concentrated. There was never a murmur from

my sponsors. In later budgets I included a substantial item for 'Unanticipated opportunities'. Again and again, this proved invaluable. To give a recent example, it allowed the Participation Group at IDS to engage with and support Community-Led Total Sanitation in its early, and unforeseen, days. Could 10 or 20 per cent of a budget be accommodated for 'Unanticipated opportunities' in a logframe? Why not? But the tightening conditions of donors are diminishing, not enhancing, the impact they are so keen to have measured.

12   I know I should not, but I cannot restrain myself from mentioning my own experience. In 1988 I argued in an IDS retreat that we should exploit our comparative advantage in methodological innovation. Not a single one of my colleagues even commented. Admittedly it was hot at the end of a hard day, and the bar was opening, but all the same...

13   See for example Chambers (2002).

14   The annual reports of CDRA are posted at www.cdra.org.za

15   Research institutions rarely have residential facilities for groups of visitors to come on retreats. Yet for the partnerships and relationships of the 21st century, these would provide wonderful opportunities for interaction and mutual learning and understanding. The Institute of Development Studies, Sussex, at the time of writing, alone among development studies centres in the UK, does have accommodation and the opportunity to convert this into a specially designed retreat centre.

References

Aashray Adhikar Abhiyan (AAA) (2002) 'Basere ki Kahani (Story of Shelter): A study of the problems in the night shelters in Delhi using participatory research', www.hic-sarp. org/documents/HIC-2.pdf (accessed 14 December 2006)

Abah, O. S. (2004) 'Voices aloud: Making communication and change together', *Participatory Learning and Action*, 50: 45–52

Abbott, J., Chambers, R., Dunn, C., Harris, T., de Merode, E., Porter, G., Townsend, J. and Weiner, D. (1998) 'Participatory GIS: Opportunity or oxymoron' *PLA Notes* 23: 27–34

Abebe, D., Catley, A., Admassu, B. and Bekele, G. (2007) 'Using Participatory Impact Assessment (PIA) to Inform Policy: Case studies from Ethiopia', paper to Farmer First Revisited Workshop, Institute of Development Studies, Sussex, December

Abel, N. and Stocking, M. (1979) 'Rapid Aerial Survey Techniques for Rural Areas', paper for RRA conference, 4–7 December, Institute of Development Studies, Sussex

Abeyasekera, S. (2001) *Analysis Approaches in Participatory Work Involving Ranks or Scores*, Statistical Services Centre, University of Reading, Reading

Abrahamson. E. and Freedman, D. H. (2006) *A Perfect Mess: The Hidden Benefits of Disorder*, Weidenfeld and Nicolson, London

Absalom, E. et al (1995) 'Participatory methods and approaches: Sharing our concerns and looking to the future', *PLA Notes*, 22: 5–10

ActionAid International (AAI) (1991) 'Jamkhed: Participatory Rural Appraisal in identifying major illness, healthcare providers and costs', ActionAid, Bangalore

ActionAid International (AAI) (2008) 'Participatory Vulnerability Analysis: A step-by-step guide for field staff', www.actionaid.org/assets/pdf/PVA%20final.pdf (accessed 26 February 2008)

ActionAid International (AAI) (2006a) 'From Services to Rights: A review of ActionAid International's participatory practice', ActionAid International, Private Bag X31, Saxonwold 2132, South Africa, www.reflect-action.org (accessed 14 December 2006)

ActionAid International (AAI) (2006b) 'Immersions: Making poverty personal', www. actionaid.org/1063/immersions_making_poverty_personal.html (accessed 14 December 2006) for information on forthcoming immersions

ActionAid International (AAI) (2006c) *ALPS Accountability, Learning and Planning System*, Actionaid International, Private Bag X31, Saxonwold 2132, Johannesburg

ActionAid-Nepal (1992) *Participatory Rural Appraisal Utilisation Survey Report Part 1: Rural Development Area Sindhupalchowk*, Kathmandu: Monitoring and Evaluation Unit, ActionAid-Nepal

Adams, A. (1979) 'An open letter to a young researcher', *African Affairs*, 78: 313, 451–479

Adato, M. and Meinzen-Dick, R. (eds) (2007) *Agricultural Research, Livelihoods and Poverty: Studies of Economic and Social Impacts in Six Countries*, The Johns Hopkins Press, Baltimore, Maryland

Adato, M. and Nyasimi, M. (2002) 'Combining Qualitative and Quantitative Techniques in PRA to Evaluate Agroforestry Dissemination Practices in Western Kenya', draft, International Food Policy Research Institute, Washington DC

Akerkar, S. (2001) 'Gender and participation: Overview report', in *Gender and Participation: Cutting Edge Pack*, BRIDGE, IDS, Brighton www.bridge.ids.ac.uk/ (accessed 14 December 2006)

Altieri, M. A. (1989) *Agroecology: The Scientific Basis of Alternative Agriculture*, Westview Press, Boulder and IT Publications, London

Amanor, K. (1989) '340 Abstracts on Farmer Participatory Research', Network Paper 5, Agricultural Administration (Research and Extension) Network, ODI, June

Ampt, P. R. (1988) 'Rapid Rural Appraisal', Forbes Shire, Initial Report, School of Crop Sciences, University of Sydney

Ampt, P. R. and Ison, R. L. (1988) 'Report of a Rapid Rural Appraisal to Identify Problems and Opportunities for Agronomic Research and Development in the Forbes Shire, NSW', School of Crop Sciences, University of Sidney

Ampt, P. R. and Ison, R. L (1989) 'Rapid Rural Appraisal for the Identification of Grassland Research Problems', Proceedings of the 16th International Grassland Congress, Nice, France, 1291–1292

Appleton, J. (1992) 'Notes from a food and nutrition PRA in a Guinean fishing village', *RRA Notes* 16: 77–85, IIED, London

Appleyard, B. (1992) *Understanding the Present: Science and the Soul of Modern Man*, Pan Books, London

Archer, D. (2007) 'Seeds of success are seeds of potential failure: Learning from the evolution of *Reflect*', in Brock, K. and Pettit, J. (eds) *Springs of Participation*, 15–28

Archer, D. and Goreth, N. M. (2004) 'Participation, literacy and empowerment: The continuing evolution of Reflect', *Participatory Learning and Action*, October, pp35–44

Archer, D. and Nandago, M. G. (2004) 'Participation, literacy and empowerment: The continuing evolution of *Reflect*', *PLA Notes* 50: 35–44

Archer, D. and Newman, K. (compilers) (2003) 'Communication and Power: *Reflect* practical resource materials', ActionAid, London www.reflect-action.org/ (accessed 14 December 2006)

Argyris, C., Putnam, R. and McLain Smith, D. (1985) *Action Science: Concepts, Methods and Skills for Research and Intervention*, Jossey-Bass Publishers, San Francisco and London

Ashby, J. A. (1990) 'Evaluating Technology with Farmers: A handbook', IPRA Projects, Centro Internacional de Agricultura Tropical (CIAT), AA 6713, Cali, Colombia

Ashe, J. (1979) *Assessing Rural Needs: A Manual for Practitioners*, VITA (Volunteers in Technical Assistance), 3706 Rhode Island Avenue, Mt Rainier, Maryland 20822, USA

Barahona, C. (2005) 'Experience and Innovation: How the research methods evolved', in Levy, S. (ed) *Starter Packs*: 77– 92

Barahona, C. and Levy, S. (2003) 'How to Generate Statistics and Influence Policy Using Participatory Methods in Research: Reflections on work in Malawi 1999–2002', *IDS Working Paper 212*, IDS, Brighton

Barahona, C. and Levy, S. (2007) 'The best of both worlds: Producing national statistics using participatory methods', *World Development*, 35.2: 326–341

Barnett, A. (1979) 'Rapid Rural Appraisal: A personal view of the first IDS workshop', *RRA* 2, IDS, Brighton

Bawden, R. J., Macadam, R. D., Packham, R. J. and Valentine, I. (1984) 'Systems thinking and practice in agricultural education', *Agricultural Systems*, 13: 205–225

Bayer, W. (1987) 'Browse Quality and Availability in a Farming Area and a Grazing Reserve in the Nigerian Subhumid Zone', Report to the ILCA Subhumid Zone Programme, Kaduna, Nigeria, Gottingen

Bayer, W. (1988) 'Ranking of browse species by cattlekeepers in Nigeria', *RRA Notes* 3, 4–10, IIED, London

Beck, T. (1989) 'Survival strategies and power among the poorest in a West Bengal village', *IDS Bulletin*, 20.2: 23–32

Beebe, J. (1987) 'Rapid Appraisal: The evolution of the concept and the definition of issues', in *KKU Proceedings*, 47–68

Beebe, J. (2001) *Rapid Assessment Process: An Introduction*, Altamira Press, Walnut Creek, Lanham, New York, Oxford

Belshaw, D. G. R (1981a) 'Village viability assessment procedures in Tanzania: Decision-making with curtailed information requirements', *Public Administration and Development*, 1.1, 3–13

Belshaw, D. G. R. (1981b) 'A theoretical framework for data-economising appraisal procedures with applications to rural development planning', in R. Longhurst (ed) *IDS Bulletin*, 12.4: 12–22

Benor, D. and Harrison, J. Q. (1977) *Agricultural Extension: The Training and Visit System*, World Bank, Washington

Bentley, M. E., Pelto, G. H., Straus, W. L., Schumann, D. A., Adegbola, C., de la Pena, E., Oni, G. A., Brown, K. H. and Huffman, S. L. (1988) 'Rapid Ethnographic Assessment: Applications in a diarrhoea management program', *Social Science in Medicine*, 27.1, 107–116

Bernadas, C. N. Jr (1991) 'Lesson in upland farmer participation: The case of enriched fallow technology in Jaro, Leyte, Philippines', *Forests, Trees and People Newsletter*, 14: 10–11

Bevan, P. and Joireman, S. F. (1997) 'The perils of measuring poverty: Identifying the "poor" in rural Ethiopia', *Oxford Development Studies*, 26.4: 315–343

Biggs, S. D. (1979) 'Timely analysis in programmes to generate agricultural technologies', *RRA* 2, Brighton: IDS

Biggs, S. (1980) 'Informal R & D', *Ceres*, 13.4: 23–26

Biggs, S. (1988) 'Resource-poor Farmer Participation in Research: A synthesis of experiences from nine national agricultural research systems', ISNAR (International Service for National Agricultural Research), The Hague

Blackburn, J., Brocklesby, M. A., Crawford, S. and Holland, J. (2004) 'Operationalising the rights agenda: Participatory Rights Assessment in Peru and Malawi', *IDS Bulletin*, 36.1: 91–99, IDS, Brighton

Blackmore, S. (2003) 'Consciousness in meme machines', *Journal of Consciousness Studies*, 10.4–5: 19–30

Blurton Jones, N. and Konner, M. J. (1976) '!Kung knowledge of animal behaviour (or: The proper study of mankind is animals)', in Lee, R. B. and DeVore, I. (eds), *Kalahari Hunter-Gatherers: Studies of the !Kung San and Their Neighbors*, Harvard University Press, Cambridge, Mass

Booth, D., Holland, J., Hentschel, J., Lanjouw, P. and Herbert, A. (1998) 'Participation and Combined Methods in African Poverty Assessment: Renewing the agenda', Social Development Division, Africa Division, DFID, London, February

Booth, D. (2003) 'Towards a better combination of the quantitative and the qualitative: Some design issues from Pakistan's Participatory Poverty Assessment', in R. Kanbur (ed) *Q-Squared*, 97–102

Borrini-Feyerabend, G., Pimbert, M., Taghi Farvar, M., Kothari, A. and Renard, Y. (2004) 'Sharing Power: Learning by doing in co-management of natural resources throughout the world', IIED and IUCN/CEESP/CMWG, Cenesta, Tehran

Boserup, E. (1965) *The Conditions of Agricultural Growth: The Economics of Agrarian Change Under Population Pressure*, George Allen and Unwin, London

BRAC (1983) 'The Net: Power structure in ten villages', Bangladesh Rural Advancement Committee, 66 Mokhahali Commercial Area, Dhaka 12

Bradbury, H. and Reason, P. (eds) (2001) *Handbook of Action Research: Participative Inquiry and Practice*, Thousand Oaks, London and Sage Publications, New Delhi

Bradley, P. N., Chavangi, N. and van Geldar, A. (1985) 'Development research and planning in Kenya', *Ambio*, 114.4–5: 228–236

Bradley, S. M. (1992) 'Visual Literacy: A review with an annotated bibliography', mimeo, IIED, London

Broad, R. (2006) 'Research, knowledge, and the art of "paradigm maintenance": The World Bank's Development Economics Vice-Presidency (DEC)', *Review of International Political Economy*, 13:3, August, 387–419

Brock, K. (1999) (unpublished) 'Analysis of Consultations with the Poor : Wellbeing ranking and causal diagramming data', Participation Group, Institute of Development Studies, University of Sussex, Brighton

Brock, K. and Pettit, J. (eds) (2007), *Springs of Participation: Creating and Evolving Methodologies for Participatory Development*, ITDG Publications, London

Brokensha, D., Warren, D. and Werner, O. (eds) (1980) *Indigenous Knowledge Systems and Development*, University Press of America, Lanham, Maryland

Brosius, J. P., Lowenhaupt-Tsing, A. and Zerner, C. (eds) (2005) *Communities and Conservation: Histories and Politics of Community-based Natural Resource Management*, Altamira Press

Brown, D., Howes, M., Hussein, K., Longley, C. and Swindell, K. (2002) *Participation in Practice: Case Studies from the Gambia*, Overseas Development Institute, London

Buchanan-Smith, M. (1992) 'Finding Out how People Prioritize Their Food Security Problems in Chad: The challenges of RRA at national level', mimeo, Brighton: IDS

Bunch, R. (1985) 'Two ears of corn: A guide to people-centered agricultural improvement', *World Neighbors*, 5116 North Portland, Oklahoma City, Oklahoma 73112

Burn, R. W. (2000) *Quantifying and Combining Causal Diagrams*, Statistical Services Centre, University of Reading, UK

Byerlee, D. et al (1979) 'On-farm Research to Develop Technologies Appropriate to Farmers', paper presented at *the Conference* of *the International Association of Agricultural Economists*, Banff, Canada

Campbell, G. J., Shrestha, R. and Stone, L. (1979) 'The Use and Misuse of Social Science Research in Nepal', Research Centre for Nepal and Asian Studies, Tribhuvan University, Kirtipur, Kathmandu

Carden, F. (2002) *Building, Learning and Reflection into Development Programs*, International Development Research Centre, Ottawa

Carruthers, I. (1979a) 'A Mental Construct for Unstructured On-farm Interviews', *RRA* 2, IDS, Brighton

Carruthers, I. (1979b) 'Breadth, Depth or Replications? – Sampling problems with insufficient time, money or background', *RRA* 2, IDS, Brighton

Carruthers, I. and Chambers, R. (1981) 'Rapid appraisal for rural development', *Agricultural Administration*, 8.6: 407–422

Catley, A. (2007) 'From Marginal to Normative: Institutionalizing participatory epidemiology', paper to Farmer First Revisited Workshop, Institute of Development Studies, Sussex, December 2007

Catley, A. and Mariner, J. (2002) 'Where there is no data: Participatory approaches to veterinary epidemiology in pastoral areas in the horn of Africa', *Drylands Programme Issue Paper 110*, IIED, London

CBCRM (2003a) *Fisheries Management in Community-based Coastal Resource Management*, Oxfam GB and the CBCRM Resource Center, Quezon City, Philippines

CBCRM (2003b) *Participatory Monitoring and Evaluation in Community-based Coastal Resource Management*, Oxfam GB and the CBCRM Resource Center, Quezon City, Philippines

Cernea, M. (ed) (1985) *Putting People First: Sociological Variables in Development Projects*, The Johns Hopkins Press, Baltimore

Chambers, R. (1973) 'Practices in Social Science Research: Some heresies', paper to conference at the Agrarian Research and Training Institute, Colombo, unpublished

Chambers, R. (1974a) *Managing Rural Development: Ideas and Experience from East Africa*, Scandinavian Institute of African Studies, Uppsala

Chambers, R. (1974b) 'Opportunism in Rural Research', unpublished paper to the Seminar, Project on Agrarian Change in Rice-Growing Areas of Tamil Nadu and Sri Lanka, St John's College, Cambridge

Chambers, R. (1978) 'Project selection for poverty-focused rural development: Simple is optimal', *World Development*, 6.2: 209–219

Chambers, R. (1979) 'Health, agriculture and rural poverty: Why seasons matter', *Discussion Paper 148*, IDS, Brighton

Chambers, R. (1981) 'Rapid Rural Appraisal: Rationale and repertoire', *Discussion Paper 155*, IDS, Brighton

Chambers, R. (1983), *Rural Development: Putting the Last First*, Longman, Harlow, UK

Chambers, R. (1986) 'Normal Professionalism, New Paradigms and Development', *Discussion Paper 227*, IDS, Brighton

Chambers, R. (1989) 'A New Administration: Beyond Henry Fordism and the self-deceiving state', paper for the IDS Retreat, 11–12 December 1989

Chambers, R. (1993) *Challenging the Professions: Frontiers for Rural Development*, Intermediate Technology Publications, London

Chambers, R. (1994) 'The origins and practice of participatory rural appraisal', *World Development*, 22.7: 953–969

Chambers, R. (1997) *Whose Reality Counts? Putting the First Last*, Intermediate Technology Publications, London

Chambers, R. (2002) *Participatory Workshops: A Sourcebook of 21 Sets of Ideas and Activities*, Earthscan, London and Sterling VA

Chambers, R. (2004) 'Reflections and Directions: A personal note', *Participatory Learning and Action*, 50: 23–34

Chambers, R. (2005) *Ideas for Development*, Earthscan, London and Sterling VA

Chambers, R. (2006a) 'Transforming power: From zero sum to win-win?', in R. Eyben, C. Harris and J. Pettit (eds) *Exploring Power for Change*, 99–110

Chambers, R. (2006b) 'Creating, evolving and supporting participatory methodologies: Lessons for funders and innovators', in Brock, K. and Pettit, J. (eds) *Springs of Participation*, 177–189

Chambers, R. (2006c) 'Participatory Mapping and Geographic Information Systems: Whose map? Who is empowered and who disempowered? Who gains and who loses?', in P. Mbile (ed) *EJISDC*, 54, pdf size 55.2 KB

Chambers, R. and Harriss, J. (1977) 'Comparing twelve South Indian villages: In search of practical theory', in B. H. Farmer (ed) *Green Revolution? Technology and Change in Rice Growing Areas of Tamil Nadu and Sri Lanka*, 301–322

Chambers, R. and Jiggins, J. (1986) 'Agricultural Research with Resource-poor Farmers: A parsimonious paradigm' *Discussion Paper 220*, IDS, Brighton

Chambers, R. and Leach, M. (1989) 'Trees to meet contingencies: Savings and security for the rural poor', *World Development*, 17.3: 329–432

Chambers, R. and Wickremanayake, B. W. E. (1977) 'Agricultural extension: Myth, reality and challenge' in B. H. Farmer (ed) *Green Revolution? Technology and Change in Rice Growing Areas of Tamil Nadu and Sri Lanka*, 155–167

Chambers, R., Longhurst, R., Bradley, D. and Feachem, R. (1979) 'Seasonal Dimensions to Rural Poverty: Analysis and practical implications', *Discussion Paper 142*, IDS, Brighton

Chambers, R., Longhurst, R. and Pacey, A. (eds) (1981) *Seasonal Dimensions to Rural Poverty*, Frances Pinter, London

Chambers, R., Pacey, A. and Thrupp, L. A. (eds) (1989a) *Farmer First: Farmer Innovation and Agricultural Research*, Intermediate Technology Publications, London

Chambers, R., Saxena, N. C. and Shah, T. (1989b) *To the Hands of the Poor: Water and Trees*, Oxford and 11311, New Delhi and IT Publications, London

Chandler, D. and Torbert, W. (2003) 'Transforming inquiry and action: By interweaving 27 flavors of action research', *Journal of Action Inquiry*, 1.2: 133–152

Chawla, L. and Johnson, V. (2004) 'Not for children only: Lessons learnt from young people's participation', *Participatory Learning and Action*, 50: 63–72

Checkland, P. B. (1981) *Systems Thinking, Systems Practice*, John Wiley & Sons, Chichester

Chen, C., Chowdhury, A. K. M. A. and Huffman, S. (1978) 'Classification of Energy-protein Malnutrition by Anthropometry and Subsequent Risk of Mortality', International Centre for Diarrhoea Disease Research, Bangladesh

Chung, K., Haddad, L., Ramakrishna, J. and Riley, F. (1997) *Identifying the Food Insecure: The Application of Mixed-Method Approaches in India*, IFPRI, Washington DC

Cinderby, S. (1999) 'Geographic Information Systems (GIS) for participation: The future of environmental GIS?' *International Journal of Environment and Pollution*, 11.3: 304–315

Cinderby, S. and Forrester, J. (forthcoming) 'Facilitating the local governance of air pollution using GIS for participation', *Applied Geography*

CIRAC (2001) *Global Survey of Reflect*, International Reflect Circle (CIRAC), CIRAC Paper Two, August, International Education Unit, ActionAid, London N19 5PL

Clay, E. J. (1978) 'Direct and Indirect Methods of Observation in Rapid Rural Appraisal', *RRA* 1, IDS, Brighton

Cobb, R., Hunt, R., Vandervoort, C., Bledsoe, C. and McClusky, R. (1980) *Impact of Rural Roads in Liberia*, Project Impact Evaluation No. 6, June, Agency for International Development, Washington

Colbert, E. H. (1951) *The Dinosaur Book: The Ruling Reptiles and Their Relatives*, 2nd edition, McGraw Hill, New York, London, Toronto

Collinson, M. (1979) 'Understanding Small Farmers', *RRA* 2, IDS, Brighton

Collinson, M. (1981) 'A low cost approach to understanding small farmers', *Agricultural Administration*, 8.6: 433–450

Conklin, H. C. (1957) 'Hanunoo Agriculture: A report on an integral system of shifting cultivation in the Philippines', FAO Forestry Development Paper 12, Rome

Conlin, S. (1979) 'Baseline Surveys: An escape from thinking about research problems and, even more, a refuge from actually doing anything', *RRA* 2, IDS, Brighton

Conroy, C. (2005) *Participatory Livestock Research: A Guide*, ITDG Publishing, Bourton-on-Dunsmore, Warwickshire UK

Convergence (1975) 7.2, (1981) 14.2 and (1988) 21.2 and 3: special issues on participatory research

Conway, G. (1985) 'Agroecosystem analysis', *Agricultural Administration*, 20: 31–55

Conway, G. (1986) 'Agroecosystem Analysis for Research and Development', Winrock International Institute for Agricultural Development, PO Box 1172, Nana Post Office, Bangkok 10112

Conway, G. (1987) 'Rapid rural appraisal and agroecosystem analysis: A case study from Northern Pakistan', *KKU Proceedings*, 228–254

Conway, G. (1988) 'Rainbow over Wollo', *New Scientist*, 5, May

Conway, G. (1989) 'Diagrams for Farmers', in Chambers, R., Pacey, A. and Thrupp, L. R. (eds) *Farmer First*, 77–86

Conway, G., Sajise, P. and Knowland, W. (1989) 'Lake Buhi: Resolving conflicts in a Philippines development project', *Ambio*, 18.2: 128–135

Cooke, B. (2004) 'Rules of thumb for participatory change agents', in Hickey, S. and Mohan, G. (eds) *Participation: From Tyranny to Transformation?*, 42–55

Cooke, B. and Kothari, U. (eds) (2001) *Participation: The New Tyranny?*, Zed Books, London

Corbett, J., Rambaldi, G., Kyem, P., Weiner, D., Olson, R., Muchemi, J., McCall, M. and Chambers, R. (2006) 'Overview: Mapping for change – the emergence of a new practice', *Participatory Learning and Action*, 54: 13–19

Cornwall, A. (1992) 'Body Mapping in Health RRA/PRA', *RRA Notes* 16: 69–76, IIED, London

Cornwall, A. (2003) 'Whose voices? Whose choices? Reflections on gender and participatory development', *World Development*, 31.8: 1325–1342

Cornwall, A. and Guijt, I. (2004) 'Shifting perceptions, changing practices in PRA: From infinite innovation to the quest for quality', *Participatory Learning and Action*, 50, 160–167

Cornwall, A. and Pratt, G. (eds) (2003) *Pathways to Participation: Reflections on PRA*, Intermediate Technology Publications, London

Cornwall, A. and Welbourn, A. (eds) (2002*) Realizing Rights: Transforming Approaches to Sexual and Reproductive Well-being*, Zed Books, London

Cox, S. and Robinson-Pant, A., with B. Elliott, D. Jarvis, S. Lawes, E. Milner and T. Taylor (2003) 'Empowering Children Through Visual Communication', School of Education and Professional Development, University of East Anglia, Norwich NR4 7TJ, UK, www.uea.ac.uk (accessed 18 December 2006)

Cox, S., Currie, D., Frederick, K., Jarvis, D., Lawes, S., Millner, E., Nudd, K., Robinson-Pant, A., Stubbs, I., Taylor, T. and White, D. (2006) 'Children Decide: Power, participation and purpose in the primary classroom', School of Education and Lifelong Learning, University of East Anglia, Norwich NR4 7TJ, UK, www.uea.ac.uk (accessed 18 December 2006)

Cresswell, T. (1992) 'Unemployment and Health: The development of the use of PRA in identified communities in Staveley, North Derbyshire', *RRA Notes* 16: 27–30 IIED, London

Cromwell, E., Kambewa, P. Mwanza, R. and Chirwa, R. with KWERA Development Centre (2001) 'Impact Assessment Using Participatory Approaches: "Starter Pack" and sustainable agriculture in Malawi', *Network Paper No 112*, Agricultural Research and Extension Network, Overseas Development Institute, London

Daane, J. R. V. (1987) 'Quelle méthode pour l'analyse de systèmes de production en Zone Rurale Tropicale: le dilemme entre démarche quantitative peu fiable et démarche qualitative peu généralisable', contribution au 8ème Seminaire d'Économie Rurale, CIRAD, France

DAC (2005) 'Paris Declaration on Aid Effectiveness: Ownership, Harmonisation, Alignments, Results and Mutual Accountability', Development Advisory Committee of the OECD, Paris

David, R. and Mancini, A. (2004) 'Going Against the Flow: The struggle to make organisational systems part of the solution rather than part of the problem – the case of ActionAid's Accountability, Learning and Planning System', *Lessons for Change Series*, 8, Brighton: IDS

David, R., Mancini, A. and Guijt, I. (2006) 'Bringing systems into line with values: The practice of accountability, learning and planning system (ALPS)', in R. Eyben (ed) *Relationships for Aid*, 133–153

Davies, R. and Dart, J. (2005) *The 'Most Significant Change' (MSC) Technique: A Guide to its Use*, www.mande.co.uk/docs/MSCGuide.pdf (accessed 14 February 2008)

Davis Case, D'A. (1990) 'The Community's Toolbox: The idea, methods and tools for participatory assessment, monitoring and evaluation in community forestry', *Community Forestry Field Manual*, 2, FAO, Rome

Dawkins, R.(1976) *The Selfish Gene*, Oxford University Press, Oxford (new edition with additional material, 1989)

Desai, V. and Potter, R. B. (eds) (2005) *Doing Development Research*, Thousand Oaks, London and Sage, New Delhi

Devavaram, J., Nalini, Vimalnathan, J., Sukkar, A., Krishnan, Mayandi, A. P. and Karunanidhi (1991) 'PRA for rural resource management', *RRA Notes* 13: 102–111, IIED, London

Devitt, P. (1977) 'Notes on Poverty-orientated Rural Development', *Extension, Planning and the Poor*, Agricultural Administration Unit Occasional Paper 2, Overseas Development Institute, London

Dewees, P. (1989) Aerial photography and household studies in Kenya, *RRA Notes* 7: 9–12, London: IIED

Dilts, R. (2001) 'From farmers' field schools to community IPM', *LEISA*, 17.3: 18–21

Dilts, R. and Hate, S. (1996) 'IPM farmer field schools: Changing paradigms and scaling-up', *Agricultural Research and Extension Network*, 596, ODI, London

Doyle, Arthur Conan (1891) 'A Scandal in Bohemia', in *The Adventures of Sherlock Holmes*

Dreze, J. (1990) 'Poverty in India and the IRDP delusion', *Economic and Political Weekly*, September 29: A95–A104

Drinkwater, M. (1993) 'Sorting fact from opinion: The use of a direct matrix to evaluate finger millet varieties', *RRA Notes* 17: 24–28

Dunn, A. M. (1991) 'New Challenges for Extensionists: Targeting complex problems and issues', paper for the 10th European Seminar on Extension Education, Universidade de Tras-os-Montese Alto Douro, Vila Real, Portugal

Dunn, T. and McMillan, A. (1991) 'Action Research: The application of Rapid Rural Appraisal to learn about issues of concern in landcare areas near Wagga Wagga, NSW', paper presented to a Conference on Agriculture, Education and Information Transfer, Murrumbigee College of Agriculture, NSW

Earl, S., Carden, F. and Smutylo, T. (2001) 'Outcome Mapping: Building learning and reflection into development programs', International Development Research Centre, Ottawa, www.idrc.ca/en/ev-9330-201-1-DO_TOPIC.html (accessed 8 April 2008)

Education Action (1994–2006) ongoing, issues1–20, ActionAid, London, www.reflect-action.org (accessed 19 December 2006)

Edwards, M. and Gaventa, J. (eds) (2001) *Global Citizen Action*, Lynne Rienner, Boulder, Colorado

EEC (2007) 'The Importance of a Methodologically Diverse Approach to Impact Evaluation – specifically with respect to development aid and development interventions',
European Evaluation Society, December, www.europeanevaluation.org (accessed
31 January 2008)

Ekins, P., Hillman, M. and Hutchinson, R. (1992) *Wealth Beyond Measure: An Atlas of
New Economics*, Gaia Books, London

Eldridge, C. (1995) 'Methodological Notes, Instructions to Facilitators, Household
Responses to Drought Study in Malawi, Zambia, and Zimbabwe', Save the Children,
UK

Eldridge, C. (1998) 'Summary of the Main Findings of a PRA Study on the 1992 Drought
in Zimbabwe', Save the Children, UK

Eldridge, C. (2001) 'Investigating Change and Relationships in the Livelihoods of the Poor
Using an Adaptation of Proportional Piling', Save the Children, UK

Elliott, C. M. (1970) 'Effects of ill-health on agricultural productivity in Zambia', in
Bunting, A. H. (ed) *Change in Agriculture*, Duckworth, London, 647–655

Elliott, C. (1999) 'Locating the Energy for Change: An introduction to appreciative
inquiry', International Institute for Sustainable Development, 161 Portage Avenue East,
Winnipeg, Manitoba, info@iisd.ca

Ellman, A. (1979) 'Cost effectiveness of rapid appraisal for rural project preparation',
RRA 2, Brighton: IDS

ERCS (1988) 'Rapid Rural Appraisal: A closer look at life in Wollo', Ethiopian Red Cross
Society, Addis Ababa and IIED, London

Estrella, M. and Gaventa, J. (1997) *Who Counts Reality? Participatory Monitoring and
Evaluation: A Literature Review*, Participation Group, Institute of Development Studies,
University of Sussex, Brighton

Estrella, M. with J. Blauert, D. Campilan, J. Gaventa, J. Gonsalves, I. Guijt, D. Johnson and
R. Ricafort (eds) (2000) *Learning from Change: Issues and Experiences in Participatory
Monitoring and Evaluation*, IT Publications, London

Eyben, R. (2004) 'Immersions for policy and personal change', *IDS Policy Briefing*, Issue
22, Brighton: IDS

Eyben, R. (ed) (2006) *Relationships for Aid*, Earthscan, London and Sterling VA

Eyben, R., Harris, C. and Pettit, J. (eds) (2006) 'Exploring power for change', *IDS Bulletin*,
37.6, November, Brighton: IDS

Fakih, M., Rahardjo, T. and Pimbert, M. with A. Sutoko, D. Wulandari and T. Prasetyo
(2003) 'Community Integrated Pest Management in Indonesia: Institutionalising
participation and people centred approaches', *Institutionalising Participation Series*,
IIED: London and Brighton: IDS

Fallon, P. (1979) Comments on Mick Moore's 'Denounce the gang of statisticians, etc.',
see *RRA* 2

Fals-Borda, O. and Rahman, Md. A. (eds) (1991) *Action and Knowledge: Breaking the
Monopoly with Participatory Action-Research*, ITDG Publications, London

Farmer, B. H. (ed) (1977) *Green Revolution? Technology and Change in Rice-growing Areas
of Tamil Nadu and Sri Lanka*, Macmillan, London and Basingstoke

Farrington, J. (ed) (1988) *Experimental Agriculture*, 24, part 3

Farrington, J. and Martin, A. (1988) 'Farmer Participation in Agricultural Research: A
review of concepts and practices', *Agricultural Administration Unit Occasional Paper 9*,
Overseas Development Institute, London

Feuerstein, M. T. (1979) 'Establishing rapport', *RRA Notes* 2, IIED, London

Forests, Trees and People Newsletter, International Rural Development Centre, Swedish
University of Agricultural Sciences, Box 7005, 750 07 Uppsala, Sweden

Forrester, J. (1999) 'The logistics of public participation in environmental assessment', *International Journal of Environment and Pollution*, 11.3: 316–330

Forrester, J. and Cinderby, S. (2005) 'Geographic Information Systems for participation', in Leach, M., Scoones, I. and Wynne, B. (eds) *Science and Citizens*: 232–236

Fowler, A. (2007) 'Civic Driven Change and International Development: Exploring a complexity perspective', Contextuals no 7, Context International Cooperation, Utrecht

Fox, J., Suryanata, K. and Hershock, P. (eds) (2005) *Mapping Communities: Ethics, Values, Practice*, East-West Center, Honolulu, Hawaii

Fox, J., Suryanata, K., Hershock, P. and Pramono, A. H. (2006) 'Mapping power: Ironic effects of spatial information technology', *Participatory Learning and Action*, 54: 98–105

Francis, S., Devavaram, J. and Erksine, A. (1991) 'Workshop on Participatory Rural Appraisal for Planning Health Projects', 2–5 October 1991, SPEECH, Madurai

Francis, S., Devavaram, J. and Erskine, A. (1992) 'Training workshop on Participatory Rural Appraisal for planning health projects', *RRA Notes* 16: 37–47, London: IIED

Franzel, S. and Crawford, E. (1987) 'Comparing formal and informal survey techniques for farming systems research: A case study from Kenya', *Agricultural Administration*, 27, 13–33

Freire, P. (1970) *Pedagogy of the Oppressed*, The Seabury Press, New York

Freudenberger, S. K. (1995) 'The historical matrix: Breaking away from static analysis', *Forests, Trees and People Newsletter*, 26/27: 78–79, April

Freudenberger S. K. (1998) 'The use of RRA to inform policy: Tenure issues in Madagascar and Guinea', in J. Holland and J. Blackburn (eds) *Whose Voice? Participatory Research and Policy Change*, Intermediate Technology Publications, London, 67–88

Friis-Hansen, E. and Sthapit, B. (eds) (2000) 'Participatory Approaches to the Conservation and Use of Plant Genetic Resources', International Plant Genetic Resources Institute, Rome

FSRU (1991) 'Structural Adjustment and Communal Area Agriculture in Zimbabwe: Case studies from Mangwende and Chivi communal areas: A report of a rapid rural appraisal exercise', Farming Systems Research Unit, Department of Research and Specialist Services, Ministry of Lands, Agriculture and Rural Settlement, Harare, Zimbabwe, November

FSSP (1987) 'Diagnosis, Design and Analysis in Farming Systems Research and Extension', Volumes I, II and III, and Trainer's Manual, Farming Systems Support Project, Institute of Food and Agricultural Sciences, University of Florida, Gainesville, Florida 32611

Funtowicz, S. O. and Ravetz, J. R. (1990) 'Global Environmental Issues and the Emergence of Second Order Science', Commission of the European Communities, Luxembourg

Galbraith, J. K. (1979) *The Nature of Mass Poverty*, Harvard University Press, Cambridge, Mass. and London, UK

Galpin, M., Dorward, P. and Shepherd, D. (2000) *Participatory Farm Management Methods for Agricultural Research and Extension Needs Assessment: A Manual*, Departments of Agricultural Extensions and Rural Development, University of Reading, UK, cited in Marsland et al (2000)

Ganewatta, P. (1974) 'Socio-economic factors in rural indebtedness', *Occasional Publication Series*, 7, Agrarian Research and Training Institute, Columbo

Gaventa, J. (1980) *Power and Powerlessness: Rebellion and Quiescence in an Appalachian Valley*, University of Illinois Press, Chicago

Gaventa, J. (1993) 'The powerful, the powerless and the experts: Knowledge struggles in an information age', in P. Park, B. Hall and T. Jackson (eds) *Participatory Research in North America*, Bergin and Hadley, Amherst MA

Gaventa, J. and Cornwall, A. (2008) 'Power and knowledge', in Reason, P. and Bradbury, H. (eds) *Action Research*, 172–189

Gaventa, J. and Horton, B. (1981) 'A citizens' research project in Appalachia, USA', *Convergence*, 14.3: 30–42

Gaventa, J. and Lewis, H. (1991) 'Participatory education and grassroots development: The case of rural Applachia', *Gatekeeper Series No 25*, London: IIED

Gibbs, C.(1987) 'Rapid Rural Appraisal: An overview of concepts and applications', *KKU Proceedings*, 193–206

Gibson, T. (1991) 'Planning for Real: The approach of the Neighbourhood Initiatives Foundation in the UK', *RRA Notes* 11: 29–30, London: IIED

Gibson, T. (1996) *The Power in Our Hands: Neighbourhood Based – World Shaking*, Jon Carpenter, Charlbury

Gilbert, E. H., Norman, D. W. and Winch, F. E. (1980) 'Farming Systems Research: A critical appraisal', *MSU Rural Development Paper No 6*, Department of Agricultural Economics, Michigan State University, East Lansing, Michigan 48824

Gill, G. (1991) 'But how does it compare with the real data?', *RRA Notes* 14: 5–14, London: IIED (also Research Report Series Number 16, HMG Ministry of Agriculture-Winrock International, Kathmandu, January 1992)

Gill, G. J. (1993) 'O.K., The Data's Lousy, But It's All We've Got (Being a Critique of Conventional Methods)', *Gatekeeper Series* No 38, London: IIED

Gleick, J. (1988) *Chaos: Making a New Science*, Sphere Books, Penguin Group, London

Glöckner, H., Mkanga, M. and Ndezi, T. (2004) 'Local Empowerment Through Community Mapping for Water and Sanitation in Dar es Salaam', *Environment and Urbanization*, 16: 185–198, April

Gonsalves, J. et al. (eds) (2005) 'Participatory research and development for sustainable agriculture and natural resource management: A sourcebook', in Volume 1: *Understanding Participatory Research and Development, International Potato Center-Users' Perspectives with Agricultural Research and Development*, Laguna, Philippines and IDRC, Ottawa, Canada

Gordon, G. (1979) 'Finding out about child (0–5 years) feeding practices', *RRA 2*, Brighton: IDS

Gordon, G. and Cornwall, A. (2004) 'Participation in sexual and reproductive well-being and rights', *Participatory Learning and Action*, 50: 73–80

Gosselink, P. and Strosser, P. (1995) 'Participatory Rural Appraisal for Irrigation Management Research: Lessons from IIMI's experience', *Working Paper No 38*, International Irrigation Management Institute, Colombo

Gould, P. and White, R. (1974) *Mental Maps*, Harmondsworth, Penguin Books, UK

Govinda, R. (1999) *Reaching the Unreached through Participatory Planning: School Mapping in Lok Jumbish, India*, International Institute for Educational Planning, Paris and National Institute of Educational Planning and Administration, New Delhi

Grandin, B. (1988) *Wealth Ranking in Smallholder Communities: A Field Manual*, Intermediate Technology Publications, London

Grandstaff, T. B. and Grandstaff, S. W. (1987a) 'Semi-structured interviewing by multi-disciplinary teams in RRA', *KKU Proceedings*, 129–143

Grandstaff, T. B. and Grandstaff, S. W. (1987b) 'A conceptual basis for methodological development in Rapid Rural Appraisal', *KKU Proceedings*, 69–88

Grandstaff, S. W., Grandstaff, T. B. and Lovelace, G. W. (1987) 'Summary report', *KKU Proceedings*, 3–30

Greenwood, D. J. and Levin, M. (1998) *Introduction to Action Research: Social Research for Social Change*, Thousand Oaks, London and Sage Publications, New Delhi

Gribbin, J. (2004) *Deep Simplicity: Chaos, Complexity and the Emergence of Life*, Penguin Books, London

Groenfeldt, D. (1989) 'Guidelines for Rapid Assessment of Minor Irrigation Systems in Sri Lanka', *Working Paper No 14*, International Irrigation Management Institute, Sri Lanka

Groves, L. (2004) 'Questioning, learning and "cutting edge" agendas: Some thoughts from Tanzania', in Groves, L. and Hinton, R. (eds) *Inclusive Aid*, 76–86, Earthscan, London

Groves, L. (2005) 'UNHCR's Age and Gender Mainstreaming Pilot Project 2004: Synthesis report', United Nations High Commissioner for Refugees, Evaluation and Policy Analysis Unit, Geneva at www.unhcr.org/epau (accessed 21 December 2006)

Groves, L. and Hinton, R. (eds) (2004) *Inclusive Aid: Changing Power and Relationships in International Development*, Earthscan, London and Sterling VA

Guba, E. G. and Lincoln, Y. S. (1989) *Fourth Generation Evaluation*, Sage Publications, Newbury Park, London, New Delhi

Gueye, B. and Freudenberger, S. K. (1991) *Methode Accelerée de Récherché Participative*, London: IIED

Guhathakurta, M. (2008) 'Theatre in Participatory Action Research: Experiences from Bangladesh', in Reason, P. and Bradbury, H. (eds) *Action Research*, 510–552

Guijt, I. (1998) 'Participatory Monitoring and Impact Assessment of Sustainable Agriculture Initiatives: An introduction to the key elements', Sustainable Agriculture and Rural Livelihoods Programme, *Discussion Paper No 1*, London: IIED

Guijt, I. (2000) 'Methodological issues in Participatory Monitoring and Evaluation', in M. Estrella with others (eds) *Learning from Change*, IT Publications, London, 201–216

Guijt, I. (2007a) 'Rethinking Monitoring for Collective Learning in Rural Resource Management', paper to Farmer First Revisited Workshop, Institute of Development Studies, Sussex, December 2007

Guijt, I. (2007b) *Negotiated Learning: Collaborative Monitoring in Forest Resource Management*, Resources for the Future, Washington DC

Guijt, I. (2008) 'Seeking Surprise: Rethinking monitoring for collective learning in rural resource management', published PhD Thesis, Wageningen University, Wageningen, the Netherlands

Guijt, I. and van Veldhuizen, L. (1998) 'What Tools? Which Steps? Comparing PRA and PTD', *Issue Paper no 79*, IIED

Guijt, I. and Shah, M. K. (1998) *The Myth of Community: Gender Issues in Participatory Development*, IT Publications, London

Guijt, I., Manneh, K., Martin, M. and Sarch, T. (1992) 'Reflections on the training: Process and prospects', in *From Input to Impact: Participatory Rural Appraisal*, ActionAid, The Gambia and IIED, London, 1–19

Gujja, B., Pimbert, M. and Shah, M. K. (1998) 'Village voices challenging wetland management policies: PRA experiences from Pakistan and India', in J. Holland and J. Blackburn (eds) *Whose Voice?*, 57–66

Gulati, L. (1981) *Profiles in Female Poverty: A Study of Five Poor Working Women in Kerala*, Hindustan Publishing Corporation (India), Delhi 110007

Gupta, A. K. (1989). 'Scientists "views of farmers" Practices in India: Barriers to effective interaction', in Chambers, R., Pacey, A. and Thrupp, L. R. (eds) *Farmer First*, 24–31

Gupta, A. and IDS workshop (1989) 'Maps drawn by farmers and extensionists', in Chambers, R., Pacey, A. and Thrupp, L. R. (eds) *Farmer First*, 86–92

Gypmantasiri et al and Conway, G. (1980) *An Interdisciplinary Perspective of Cropping Systems in the Chiang Mai Valley: Key Questions for Research*, Multiple Cropping Project, Faculty of Agriculture, University of Chiang Mai, Thailand, June

Hadjipateras, A., Akuilu, H., Owero, J., de Fatima Dendo, M. and Nyenga, C. (2006) 'Joining Hands: Integrating gender and HIV/AIDS', Report of an ACORD Project using Stepping Stones in Angola, Tanzania and Uganda, ACORD, Kampala, London and Nairobi hasap@acord.org.ug ; info@acord.org.uk ; info@acordnairobi.org

Hahn, H. (1991) 'Apprendre avec les yeux, s'exprimer avec les mains: Des paysans se forment à la gestion du terroir', *AGRECOL*, Oekozentrum, CH-4438 Langenbruck, Switzerland

Hammond, S. A. and Royal, C. (eds) (1998) *Lessons from the Field: Applying Appreciative Inquiry*, Practical Press, PO Box 260608, Plano TX 75026-0608, USA

Hargreaves, J. R., Morison, L. A., Gear, J. S. S., Makhubele, M. B., Porter, J. D. H., Buzsa, J., Watts, C., Kim, J. C. and Pronk, P. M. (2007) '"Hearing the voices of the poor": Assigning poverty lines on the basis of local perceptions of poverty: A quantitative analysis of qualitative data from participatory wealth ranking in rural South Africa', *World Development*, 35.2: 212–229

Harrison, P. (1987) *The Greening of Africa: Breaking Through in the Battle for Land and Food*, Paladin Grafton Books, London

Harriss, J. (1977) 'Bias in the perception of agrarian change in India', in B. H. Farmer (ed) *Green Revolution? Technology and Change in Rice-growing Areas of Tamil Nadu and Sri Lanka*, Macmillan, London and Basingstoke, 30–36

Harwood, R. (1979) *Small Farm Development: Understanding and Improving Farming Systems in the Humid Tropics*, Westview Press, Boulder, Colorado

Hatch, J. K. (1976) 'The Corn Farmers of Motupe: A study of traditional farming practices in Northern Coastal Peru', Land Tenure Center Monographs No. 1, Land Tenure Center, 1525 Observatory Drive, University of Wisconsin, Madison, Wisconsin 53706

Haverkort, B., van der Kamp, J. and Waters-Bayer, A. (1991) *Joining Farmers' Experiments: Experiences in Participatory Technology Development*, Intermediate Technology Publications, London

Heron, J. and Reason, P. (2008) 'Extending epistemology within a cooperative inquiry', in Reason, P. and Bradbury, H. (eds) *Action Research*, 366–380

Herring, R. J. (n.d., c. 2003) 'Data as social product', in R. Kanbur (ed) *Q-Squared*, 141–151

Heslop, M. (2002) *Participatory Research with Older People: A Sourcebook*, HelpAge International, PO Box 32832, London N1 9ZN

Heyer, J. (1989) 'Landless agricultural labourers' asset strategies', *IDS Bulletin*, 20.2: 33–40

Hickey, S. and Mohan, G. (eds) (2004) *Participation: From Tyranny to Transformation? Exploring New Approaches to Participation in Development*, Zed Books, London, New York

Hildebrand, P. (1978) 'Motivating Small Farmers to Accept Change', paper for the Conference on Integrated Crop and Animal Production to Optimize Resource Utilization on Small Farms in Developing Countries, Bellagio

Hildebrand, P. (1979a) 'Summary of the sondeo methodology used by ICTA', *RRA 2*

Hildebrand, P. (1979b) 'Comments about multidisciplinary team efforts', *RRA 2*

Hildebrand, P. (1981) 'Combining disciplines in rapid appraisal: The sondeo approach', *Agricultural Administration*, 8.6: 423–432

Hill, P. (1972) *Rural Hausa: A Village and a Setting*, Cambridge University Press, Cambridge

Hirschmann, D. (2003) 'Keeping "The Last" in mind: Incorporating Chambers in consulting', *Development in Practice*, 13.5: 487–500

Holland, J. and Blackburn, J. (eds) (1998) *Whose Voice? Participatory Research and Policy Change*, Intermediate Technology Publications, London

Holland, J. and Campbell, J. (2005) *Methods in Development Research*, ITDG Publishing, Bourton-on-Dunsmore, Rugby, UK

Holmes, T. (2001) 'A Participatory Approach in Practice: Understanding fieldworkers' use of PRA', in ActionAid The Gambia, *IDS Working Paper 123*, Brighton: IDS

Holmes, T. (2002) 'Rapid spread through many pathways', in *Pathways to Participation: Critical Reflections on PRA*, Brighton: IDS, 4–5

Honadle, G. (1979) 'Rapid Reconnaissance Approaches to Organizational Analysis for Development Administration', *Working Paper No. 1*, prepared under AID Contract No. DSAN–C–0065, Development Alternatives, Inc., 1823 Jefferson Place, N.W., Washington DC 20036

Hoogerbrugge, I. D. and Fresco, L. (1993) 'Home Garden Systems: Agricultural characteristics and challenges', *Gatekeeper Series No 39*, London: IIED

Hope, A. and Timmel, S. (1984) *Training for Transformation: A Handbook for Community Workers*, (set of 3 books), Mambo Press, Harare (republished by IT Publications, London, 1996)

Howes, M. (1979a) 'The uses of indigenous technical knowledge in development', in IDS (1979)

Howes, M. (1979b) 'Stratifying a rural population: Trade-offs between accuracy and time, *RRA 2*, Brighton: IDS

Howes, M. (1980) 'A Year in the Life of a Poor Farming Household', background paper for Inner London Education Authority Schools Project, mimeograph, Brighton: IDS

IDS (1979) 'Rural development: Whose knowledge counts?', *IDS Bulletin*, 10.2, Brighton: IDS, February

IIED (1989) 'Patchy Resources in African Drylands: A review of the literature and an agenda for future research and development', a proposal of the Drylands Programme, London: IIED

IIED and Farm Africa (1991) 'Farmer Participatory Research in North Omo', Ethiopia Report on a training course in Rapid Rural Appraisal, London: IIED

ILO (1981) *Zambia: Basic Needs in an Economy under Pressure*, International Labour Office, Jobs and Skills Programme for Africa, Addis Ababa (available from ILO Publications, ILO, CH-1211, Geneva 22)

Inglis, A. S. (1990) 'Harvesting Local Forestry Knowledge: A field test and evaluation of rapid rural appraisal techniques for social forestry project analysis', dissertation presented for the degree of Master of Science, University of Edinburgh

International HIV/AIDS Alliance (2006a) 'All Together Now! Community mobilisation for HIV/AIDS', International HIV/AIDS Alliance, Brighton, UK, www.aidsalliance.org

International HIV/AIDS Alliance (2006b) 'Tools Together Now! 100 participatory tools to mobilise communities for HIV/AIDS', International HIV/AIDS Alliance, Brighton, UK, www.aidsalliance.org

Irvine, R., Chambers, R. and Eyben, R. (2004) 'Learning from poor people's experiences', *Lessons for Change in Policy and Organisations*, 13, Brighton: IDS

Irvine, R., Chambers, R. and Eyben, R. (2006) 'Relations with people living in poverty: Learning from immersions', in R. Eyben (ed) (2006) *Relationships for Aid*, 63–79

Ison, R. I. (1990) 'Rapid Rural Appraisal: A participatory "problem" identification method relevant to Australian agriculture', School of Crop Sciences, University of Sydney 2006

Iyengar, S. and Hirway, I. (eds) (2001) *In the Hands of the People: Selected papers of Anil C. Shah*, Gujarat Institute of Development Research, Ahmedabad, Centre for Development Alternatives, Gujarat, Development Support Centre, Gujarat

Jackson, C., Mandal, S. and Carruthers, I. (1978) 'Notes on rapid land ownership and management studies', *RRA 1*

Jamieson, N. (1987) 'The paradigmatic significance of Rapid Rural Appraisal', *KKU Proceedings*, 89–102

Jayakaran, R. (1991) 'PRA camp at Mahilong, Bihar, 27–30 November 1990: Krishi Gram Vikas Kendra', *RRA Notes* 13: 118–122 London: IIED

Jayakaran, R. (2002) *The Ten Seed Technique*, World Vision, China, download at www.fao.org/Participation/ft show.jsp?ID=1981

Jayakaran, R. (2003) *Participatory Poverty Alleviation and Development: A Comprehensive Manual for Development Professionals*, World Vision, China

Jayakaran, R. (2007) 'New Participatory Tools for Measuring Attitude, Behaviour, Perception and Change' (an overview of some of the new participatory tools being used for assessment and evaluation) Ravi_Jayakaran@online.com.kh and Ravi@Jayakaran.com

Johansson, L. and Hoben, A. (1992) 'RRAs for land policy formulation in Tanzania', *Forests, Trees and People Newsletter*, 14/15: 26–31

Johnson, S. (2002) *Emergence: The Connected Lives of Ants, Brains, Cities and Software*, Penguin Books, London

Johnson, V., Ivan-Smith, E., Gordon, G., Pridmore, P. and Scott, P. (1998) *Stepping Forward: Children and Young People's Participation in the Development Process*, Intermediate Technology Publications, London

Jones, C. (1996a) *PRA Methods*, Topic Pack, Participation Group, Brighton: IDS

Jones, C. (1996b) 'Matrices, Ranking and Scoring: Participatory appraisal "methods" paper', Participation Group, Brighton: IDS

Jonfa, E., Tebeje, H. M., Dessalegn, T., Halala, H. and Cornwall, A. (1991) 'Participatory modelling in North Omo, Ethiopia: Investigating the perceptions of different groups through models', *RRA Notes* 14: 24–25, December

Joseph, S. (1991) 'Lead Time, Lag Time: RRA/PRA in ActionAid', ActionAid Postbox 5406, 2 Resthouse Road, Bangalore 560001

Joseph, S. (1994) 'Mapping a relationship' [planning village water and sanitation], *Participation in Action*, ActionAid, Bangalore, Issue 1, September

Joseph, T. and Joseph, S. (1991), 'PRA in Malda District, West Bengal: Report of a training workshop for ActionAid India and Tagore Society for Rural Development', *RRA Notes* 13: 95–101, London: IIED

Joseph, S. and 31 others (1994) 'Programme review/evaluation', October, ActionAid Somaliland c/o ActionAid, Hamlyn House, London N195PG

Juma, C. (1987) 'Ecological Complexity and Agricultural Innovation: The use of indigenous genetic resources in Bungoma, Kenya' paper for the Workshop on Farmers and Agricultural Research: Complementary Methods, IDS 26–31 July, cited in Chambers, R., Pacey, A. and Thrupp, L. R. (eds) *Farmer First*, 32–34

Jupp, D. (2004) 'Views of the Poor: Some thoughts on how to involve your own staff to conduct quick, low cost but insightful research into poor people's perspectives' (available on request from djupp@btinternet.com) (accessed 23 June 2006)

Jupp, D. (2007a) 'Keeping the art of participation bubbling: Some reflections on what stimulates creativity in using participatory methods', in Brock, K. and Pettit, J. (eds) *Springs of Participation*, 107–122

Jupp, D. With 13 others (2007b) 'Reality checks: First reflection', *Participatory Learning and Action*, 57: 121–125

Kabutha, C. and Ford, R. (1988) 'Using RRA to formulate a village resources management plan, Mbusanyi, Kenya', *RRA Notes* 2, October, 4–11, London: IIED

Kagugube, J., Ssewakiryanga, R., Barahona, C. and Levy, S. (submitted 2007) 'Integrating qualitative dimensions of poverty into the third Uganda National Household Survey (UNHS III)', *Journal of African Statistics*

Kanbur, R. (n.d., c.2003) *Q-Squared: Combining Qualitiative and Quanititative Methods of Poverty Appraisal*, Permanent Black, D-28 Oxford Apartments,11, I.P. Extension, Delhi 110092

Kanbur, R. and Shaffer, P. (eds) (2006) 'Q-squared in practice: Experiences of combining quantitative and qualitative approaches in poverty analysis', *World Development*, Special Issue

Kaner, S., with J. Lind, C. Toldi, S. Fisk and D. Berger (1996) *Facilitator's Guide to Participatory Decision-Making*, New Society Publishers, Gabriola Island, BC, Canada, www.newsociety.com

Kanji, N. (2004) 'Reflection on gender and participatory development', *Participatory Learning and Action*, 50: 53–62, October

Kapadia-Kundu, N. and Dyalchand, A. (2007) 'The Pachod Paisa Scale: A numeric response scale for the health and social sciences', *Demography India*, June

Kaplinsky, R. (1991) 'From Mass Production to Flexible Specialization: A case study from a semi-industrialized economy', *IDS Discussion Paper 295*, Brighton: IDS, November

Kar, K.(2003) 'Subsidy or Self-respect? Participatory total community sanitation in Bangladesh', *Working Paper 184*, Brighton: IDS, September

Kar, K. (2005) 'Practical Guide to Triggering Community-Led Total Sanitation (CLTS)', Brighton: IDS, November

Kar, K. and Bongartz, P. (2006) 'Update on Some Recent Developments in Community-Led Total Sanitation', Brighton: IDS, April

Kar, K. with Chambers, R. (2008) *Handbook for Community-Led Total Sanitation*, Plan International, UK, London

Kar, K. and Datta, D. (1998) 'Understanding market mobility: Perceptions of smallholder farmers in Bangladesh', *PLA Notes* 33: 54–58

Kar, K. and Pasteur, K. (2005) 'Subsidy or Self-Respect? Community Led Total Sanitation: An update on recent developments', *Working Paper 257*, Brighton: IDS, November

Kassam, Y. and Kemal, M. (eds) (1982) *Participatory Research: An Emerging Alternative Methodology in Social Science Research*, Society for Participatory Research in Asia, 45 Sainik Farm, Khanpur, New Delhi 110 062

Kearl, B. (ed) (1976) *Field Data Collection in the Social Sciences: Experiences in Africa and the Middle East*, Agricultural Development Council Inc, New York

Kendall, M. (1887) *Dreams to Sell*, Kessinger Publishing, Whitefish, MT

Khon Kaen University (1987) *Proceedings of the 1985 International Conference on Rapid Rural Appraisal*, Rural Systems Research and Farming Systems Research Projects, Khon Kaen University, Thailand

Kipling, Rudyard , 'The elephant's child', in *The Just So Stories*

Kochendörfer-Lucius, G. and Osner, K. (1991) 'Development Has Got a Face: Lifestories of thirteen women in Bangladesh on people's economy, results of the International Exposure and Dialogue Programme of the German Commission of Justice and Peace and Grameen Bank in Bangladesh, 14–22 October 1989', *Gerechtigkeit und Frieden* Series, Deutsche Kommission Justitia et Pax, Kaiserstrasse 163, D-5300 Bonn 1

Kolarkar, A. S., Murthy, K. N. K. and Singh, N. (1983) 'Khadin – A method of harvesting water for agriculture in the Thar Desert', *Journal of Arid Environments*, 6: 59–66

Kolavalli, S. and Kerr, J. (2002a) 'Mainstreaming participatory watershed development', *Economic and Political Weekly*, 19 January, 225–242

Kolavalli, S. and Kerr, J. (2002b) 'Scaling up participatory watershed development in India', *Development and Change*, 33.2: 213–235

Konde, A., Dea, D., Jonfa, E., Folla, F., Scoones, I., Kena, K., Berhanu, T. and Tessema, W. (2001) 'Creating gardens: The dynamics of soil-fertility management in Wolayta, Southern Ethiopia', in I. Scoones (ed) *Dynamics and Diversity*, 45–77

Koti, F. and Weiner, D. (2006) '(Re) defining peri-urban residential space using Participatory GIS in Kenya', in P. Mbile (ed) *EJISDC*, 25.8: 1–12

Krishna, A. (2004) 'Escaping poverty and becoming poor: Who gains, who loses and why?' *World Development*, 32.1: 121–136

Krishna, A. (2005) 'Why growth is not Enough: Household poverty dynamics in Northeast Gujarat, India', *Journal of Development Studies*, 41.7: 1163–1192

Krishna, A. (2006) 'Subjective Assessments, Participatory Methods and Poverty Dynamics: The stages of progress method', draft paper for Workshop on concepts and Methods for Analyzing Poverty Dynamics and Chronic Poverty, 23–25 October 2006, University of Manchester, UK

Kuhn, T. S. (1962) *The Structure of Scientific Revolutions*, University of Chicago Press, Chicago and London

Kuhn, T. (1993) 'Foreword' to Hoyningen-Huene, P. *Reconstructing Scientific Revolutions: Thomas S. Kuhn's Philosophy of Science*, xiii, from the *Oxford Dictionary of Scientific Quotations*

Kumar, A.(1992) 'Trends in health care', *RRA Notes* 16: 48–52, London: IIED

Kumar, S. (1991) 'Anantapur experiment in PRA training', *RRA Notes* 13: 112–117, London: IIED

Kumar, S. (ed) (1996) 'ABC of PRA: Attitude and behaviour change', a report on a South-South Workshop on PRA: Attitudes and Behaviour in Bangalore and Madurai, PRAXIS, 12 Patliputra Colony, Patna 800013, Bihar, India

Kumar, S. (2002) *Methods for Community Participation: A Complete Guide for Practitioners*, Vistaar Publications (a division of Sage Publications), New Delhi

Kumaran. R. (2003) 'Listening as a Radical Act', *India Working Paper Series*, ActionAid India, New Delhi

Ladejinsky, W. (1969a) 'The Green Revolution in Punjab: A field trip', *Economic and Political Weekly*, 4.26, 28 June

Ladejinsky, W. (1969b) 'The Green Revolution in Bihar – the Kosi area: A field trip', *Economic and Political Weekly*, 4.39, 27 September

Leach, M., Scoones, I. and Wynne, B. (eds) (2005) *Science and Citizens: Globalization and the Challenge of Engagement*, Zed Books, London and New York

Ledesma, A. J. (1977) 'The Sumagaysay family: A case study of landless rural workers', *Land Tenure Center Newsletter*, 55, January–March, Land Tenure Center, University of Wisconsin

Leonard, D. K. (1977) *Reaching the Peasant Farmer: Organization, Theory and Practice in Kenya*, University of Chicago Press, Chicago and London

Levy, S. (2003) 'Are we targeting the poor? Lessons from Malawi', *PLA Notes* 47: 19–24, August

Levy, S. (ed) (2005) *Starter Packs: A Strategy to Fight Hunger in Developing Countries?* CABI Publishing, Wallingford

Levy, S. (2007) 'Using numerical data from participatory research to support the Millennium Development Goals: The case for locally owned information systems', in Brock, K. and Pettit, J. (eds) *Springs of Participation*, 137–149

Lewis, J. P. (1974) 'Notes of a rural area development tourist', *Economic and Political Weekly*, Review of Agriculture, June

Lewis, O. (1959) *Five Families: Mexican Case Studies in the Culture of Poverty*, Basic Books, New York

Leyland, T. (1994) 'Planning a community animal health care programme in Afghanistan', *RRA Notes* 20: 48–50

Li, X., Wang, G., Remenyi, J. and Thomas, P. (2003) *Training Manual for Poverty Analysis and Participatory Planning for Poverty Reduction*, China International Books, Beijing

Li, X. and Remenyi, J. (forthcoming 2007) 'Whose poverty? Making poverty mapping and poverty monitoring participatory', *Journal of Development Studies*

Liebermann, S. and Coulson, J. (2004) 'Participatory mapping for crime prevention in South Africa: Local solutions to local problems', *Environment and Urbanization*, 16: 125–134, October

Lightfoot, C., de Guia Jr, O., Aliman, A. and Ocado, F. (1987) 'Letting Farmers Decide in On-farm Research', paper to Workshop on Farmers and Agricultural Research: Complementary Methods, Brighton: IDS, 26–31 July

Lightfoot, C., Garrity, D., Singh, V. P., Singh, R. K., Axinn, N., John, K. C., Mishra, P., Salman, A. and Chambers, R. (1991) 'Training Resource Book for Participatory Experimental Design', Narendra Dev University of Agriculture and Technology, Faizabad, UP, India; International Center for Living Aquatic Resources Management, Manila, Philippines; International Rice Research Institute, Manila, Philippines

Limpinuntana, V. (1987) 'Conceptual Tools for RRA in Agrarian Society', *KKU*, 144–173 (*KKU* is the Proceedings of the RRA Conference)

Lincoln, Y. S. and Guba, E. G. (1985) *Naturalistic Inquiry*, Sage Publications, Newbury Park, London, New Delhi

Longhurst, R. and Payne, P. (1979) 'Seasonal Aspects of Nutrition: Review of evidence and policy implications', *Discussion Paper 145*, Brighton: IDS

Longhurst, R. (1979) 'Assessing economic stratification in rural communities', *RRA 2*, Brighton: IDS

Longhurst, R. (ed) (1981) 'Rapid Rural Appraisal: Social structure and rural economy', *IDS Bulletin*, 12.4

Ludema, J. D. and Fry, R. E. (2008) 'The practice of appreciative inquiry', in Reason, P. and Bradbury, H. (eds) *Action Research*, 280–296

Lunch, N. and Lunch, C. (2006) 'Insights into Participatory Video: A handbook for the field', Insight UK Office, 3 Maidcroft Road, Oxford OX4 3EN, UK and Insight French Office, Les Illes, 1120 Montlaur, France, www.insightshare.org

Lynn, H., Ward, D., Nugent, C., Potts, L., Skan, L. and Conway, N. (n.d.) 'Putting Breast Cancer on the Map', The Women's Environment Network, 87 Worship St, London EC2A 2BE artemis@gn.apc.org www.gn.apc.org/wen

MacGillivray, A., Weston, C. and Unsworth, C. (1998) *Communities Count! A Step By Step Guide to Community Sustainability Indicators*, New Economics Foundation, London

Mander, H. (2001) *Unheard Voices: Stories of Forgotten Lives*, Penguin Books, India

Manandhar, D. S., Osrin, D., Shrestha, B. P. et al (2004) 'Effect of a participatory intervention with women's groups on birth outcomes in Nepal: Cluster-randomised controlled trial', *The Lancet*, 364: 970–979, 11 September

Manoharan, M., Velayudham, K. and Shunmugavalli, N. (1993) 'PRA: An approach to find felt needs of crop varieties', *RRA Notes* 18: 66–68

Mans, G. G. (2006) 'Using PGIS to conduct community safety audits', in P. Mbile (ed) *EJISDC*, 25.7: 1–13

Marsland, N., Wilson, I. M., Abeyasekera, S. and Kleih, U. K. (2000) *A Methodological Framework for Combining Quantitative and Qualitative Survey Methods*, Statistical Services Centre, University of Reading, Reading

Mascarenhas, J. (1990) 'Transects in PRA', *PALM Series IV E*, MYRADA, 2 Service Road, Domlur Layout, Bangalore 560 071

Mascarenhas, J. and Kumar, P. (1991) 'Participatory mapping and modelling: User's notes', *RRA Notes* 12: 9–20, London: IIED

Mascarenhas, J., Shah, P., Joseph, S., Jayakaran, R., Devavaram, J., Ramachandran, V., Fernandez, A., Chambers, R. and Pretty, J. (eds) (1991) 'Proceedings of the February 1991 Bangalore PRA Trainers Workshop', *RRA Notes* 13, August, London: IIED and MYRADA, Bangalore

Matthews, H. (1995) 'Culture, environmental experience and environmental awareness: Making sense of young Kenya children's views of space', *The Geographical Journal*, 161.3, November, 285–295

Maurya, D. M., Bottrall, A. and Farrington, J. (1988) 'Improved livelihoods, genetic diversity and farmer participation: A strategy for rice-breeding in rainfed areas of India', *Experimental Agriculture*, 24.3: 311–320

Maxwell, S. (1989) 'Rapid food security assessment: A pilot exercise in Sudan', *RRA Notes* 5, London: IIED

Mayoux, L. (2003a) 'Thinking It Through: Using diagrams in impact assessment', www.enterprise-impact.org.uk

Mayoux, L. (2003b) 'Participatory Action Learning System: An empowering approach to monitoring, evaluation and impact assessment', Manual, draft, June, www.enterprise-impact.org.uk

Mayoux, L. (2003c) Grassroots Action Learning: Impact assessment for downward accountability and civil society development, www.enterprise-impact.org.uk

Mayoux, L. (2004) 'Intra-household Impact Assessment: Issues and participatory tools', available online at www.enterprise-impact.org.uk/informationresources/toolbox/intra-householdIA.shtml

Mayoux, L. (2005) 'Quantitative, qualitative or participatory? Which method, for what and when?', in Desai, V. and Potter, R. B. (eds) *Doing Development Research*, 115–129

Mayoux, L. (2007) 'Road to the foot of the mountain, but reaching for the sun: PALS adventures and challenges', in Brock, K. and Pettit, J. (eds) *Springs of Participation*, 93–106

Mayoux, L. and ANANDI (2005) 'Participatory Action Learning in Practice: Experience of Anandi, India', *Journal of International Development*, 17: 211–242

Mayoux, L. and Chambers, R. (2005) 'Reversing the paradigm: Quantification, participatory methods and pro-poor impact assessment', *Journal of International Development*, 17: 271–298, published online in Wiley InterScience, www.interscience.wiley.com

Mbile, P. (ed) (2006) *Electronic Journal of Information Systems in Developing Countries*, 25, Special Issue on Participatory Geographical Information Systems and Participatory Mapping, www.ejisdc.org

McCarthy, J. and Galvão, K. (2004) *Enacting Participatory Development: Theatre-based technique*, Earthscan, London and Sterling: VA

McCracken, J. A. (1988) 'Participatory Rapid Rural Appraisal in Gujarat: A trial model for the Aga Khan Rural Support Programme (India)', November, IIED, London

McCracken, J. (1989) 'Participatory RRA in Gujarat', *RRA Notes* 4: 16–21, February

McCracken, J. A., Pretty, J. N. and Conway, G. R. (1988) 'An Introduction to Rapid Rural Appraisal for Agricultural Development', IIED, London

McIlwaine, C. and Moser, C. O. N. (2004) 'Drugs, alcohol and community tolerance: An urban ethnography from Colombia and Guatemala', *Environment and Urbanization*, 16.2: 49–62

Mduma, E. K. (1982) 'Appropriate technology for grain storage at Bwakira Chini Village', in Kassam, Y. and Kemal, M. (eds) *Participatory Research*, 198–213

Mearns, R. (1989) 'Aerial photographs in rapid land resource appraisal, Papua New Guinea', *RRA Notes* 7: 12–14A

Mearns, R. (1991) 'Environmental Implications of Structural Adjustment: Reflections on scientific method', *Discussion Paper 284*, IDS, Brighton, February

Mearns, R., Shombodon, D., Narangerel, G., Turul, U., Enkhamgalan, A., Myagmarzhav, B., Bayanjargal, A. and Bekhsuren, B. (1992) 'Direct and indirect uses of wealth ranking in Mongolia', *RRA Notes* 15: 29–38, IIED, London

Meinzen-Dick, R., Adato, M., Haddad, L. and Hazell, P. (2004) 'Science and Poverty: An interdisciplinary assessment of the impact of agricultural research', IFPRI Food Policy Report, International Food Policy Research Institute, Washington DC, October

Mikkelsen, B. (1995) (2nd edition 2005) *Methods for Development Work and Research: A New Guide for Practitioners*, Sage Publications, New Delhi and Thousand Oaks, California and London

Mikkelsen, B. (2005) *Methods for Development Work and Research: A New Guide for Practitioners*, 2nd edition, Sage Publications, New Delhi and Thousand Oaks, London

Mollison, B. (1990) *Permaculture: A Designers' Manual*, Deccan Development Society and Permaculture – India, Hyderabad

Moore, M. (1979a) 'Beyond the tarmac road: A (nut) shell guide for rural poverty watchers', *RRA 2*, IDS, Brighton

Moore, M. (1979b) 'Denounce the gang of statisticians. Struggle against the sample line. Unite the researching masses against professional hegemony', *RRA 2*, IDS, Brighton

Moore, M. (1981) 'Beyond the tarmac road: A guide for rural poverty watchers', in *Rapid Rural Appraisal: Social Structure and Rural Economy, IDS Bulletin*, 12.4: 47–49

Moore, M. P. and Wickremesinghe, G. (1980) *Agriculture and Society in the Low Country (Sri Lanka)*, Agrarian Research and Training Institute, Colombo

Moris, J. R. (1970) 'Multi-Subject Farm Surveys Reconsidered: Some methodological lessons', paper for the East African Agricultural Economics Society Conference, 31 March – 4 April, Dar es Salaam

Morris, C. (1984) *Selections from William Cobbett's Illustrated Rural Rides 1821–1832*, Webb and Bower, Exeter

Morrow, A. L. and Dawodu, A. (2004) 'Influencing birth outcomes in Nepal', *The Lancet*, 364, 11 September, 914–915

Moser, C. (2003) '"Apt Illustration" or "Anecdotal Information"? Can qualitative data be representative or robust?', in R. Kanbur (ed) *Q-Squared*, 79–89

Moser, C. and Holland, J. (1997) *Urban Poverty and Violence in Jamaica*, World Bank Latin American and Caribbean Studies Viewpoints, World Bank, Washington DC

Moser, C. A. and Kalton, G . (1971) *Survey Methods in Social Investigation*, 2nd edition, Heinemann Educational Books Ltd, London

Moser, C. and McIlwaine, C. (2000a) *Urban Poor Perceptions of Violence and Exclusion in Colombia*, Latin American and Caribbean Region, Environmentally and Socially Sustainable Development Sector Management Unit, World Bank, Washington DC

Moser, C. and McIlwaine, C. (2000b) *Violence in a Post-Conflict World: Urban Poor Perceptions from Guatemala*, Latin America and Caribbean Region, Environmentally and

Socially Sustainable Development Sector Management Unit, World Bank, Washington DC

Moser, C. and McIlwaine, C. (2004) *Encounters with Violence in Latin America: Urban poor perceptions from Colombia and Guatemala*, Routledge, New York and London

Mukherjee, N. (1992) 'Villagers' perceptions of rural poverty through the mapping methods of PRA', *RRA Notes* 15: 21–26, IIED, London

Mukherjee, N. (1995) *Participatory Rural Appraisal and Questionnaire Survey: Comparative Field Experience and Methodological Innovations*, Concept Publishing Company, New Delhi

Mukherjee, N. (2002) 'Participatory learning and action with 100 field methods', *Studies in Rural Participation 4*, Concept Publishing Company, New Delhi 110059

Mukherjee, N. and Jena, B. (eds) (2001) *Learning to Share: Experiences and Reflections on PRA and other Participatory Approaches*, Concept Publishing Company, New Delhi

Nagasundari, S. (2007) 'Evolution of the Internal Learning System: A case study of the New entity for Social Action', in Brock, K. and Pettit, J. (eds) *Springs of Participation*, 81–91

Nakiboneka. E. (2008) 'STAR for Literacy and HIV AIDS Prevention, Care and Support', *Education Action*, 22.12. For STAR also see www.actionaid.org/main.aspx?PageID=119

Nandago, M. (2007) 'Training and facilitation: The propellers of participatory methodologies', in Brock and Petit (eds) *Springs of Participation*, 29–39

Narayan, D. (producer) (c.1996) *The Poverty Experts: A Participatory Poverty Assessment in Tanzania*, video, Social Policy and Resettlement Division, Environment Department, The World Bank, Washington DC

Narayan, D. Chambers, R., Shah, M. K. and Petesch, P. (2000) *Voices of the Poor: Crying Out for Change*, Oxford University Press, Oxford, for the World Bank

Narendranath, D. (2007) 'Steering the boat of life with the Internal Learning System: The oar of learning', in Brock and Pettit (eds) *Springs of Participation*, 67–79

NES (1990) *Participatory Rural Appraisal Handbook*, National Environment Secretariat, Kenya; Clark University; Egerton University; and the Center for International Development and Environment of the World Resources Institute, February

Newman, K. (2007) 'Can an international NGO practice what it preaches in participation? The case of ActionAid International', in Brock and Pettit (eds) *Springs of Participation*, 41–52

Nierras, R. M. (2002) 'Generating Numbers with Local Governments in the Philippines', working draft, IDS, Brighton

Nilsson, E., Sandkull, O. and Sundberg, M. (2007) 'Taking onboard immersions within Sida', *Participatory Learning and Action* 57: 118–120

Ninez, V. K. (1984) 'Household Gardens: Theoretical considerations on an old survival strategy', International Potato Center (CIP), Lima, Peru

Noponen, H. (2007) 'It's not just about the pictures! It's also about principles, process and power: Tensions in the development of the Internal Learning System', in Brock and Pettit (eds) *Springs of Participation*, 53–65

Norman, D. W. (1975) 'Rationalizing Mixed Cropping Under Indigenous Conditions: The example of Northern Nigeria', *Samaru Research Bulletin 232*, Institute for Agricultural Research, Samaru, Ahmadu Bello University, Zaria, Nigeria (also *Journal of Development Studies* (n.d.), 3–21)

Norton, A. with B. Bird, K. Brock, M. Kakande and C. Turk (2001) 'A Rough Guide to PPAs: Participatory Poverty Assessment: An introduction to theory and practice', Overseas Development Institute, London

NRI, DFID and SSC (2001) *Combining Quantitative and Qualitative Survey Work: Methodological Framework, Practical Issues, and Case Studies*, Natural Resources Institute, Chatham Maritime, DFID London, and Statistical Service Centre, University of Reading

OECD (2006) *United Kingdom (2006): DAC Peer Review: Main Findings and Recommendations* at www.oecd.org

Okali, C., Sumberg, J. and Farrington, J. (1994) 'Farmer Participatory Research: Rhetoric and reality, intermediate technology', Publications on behalf of the Overseas Development Institute, London

Osner, K., Kochendörfer-Lucius, G., Muller-Glodde, U. and Warning, C. (1992) 'Exposure-und Dialogprogramme': Eine Handreichnung fur Teilnehmer und Organisatoren, Justitia et Pax, Kaiserstrasse 163, 5300 Bonn 1

Osner, K. (2004) 'Using exposure methodology for dialogue on key issues', in *Reality and Analysis: Personal Reflections on the Working Lives of Six Women*, Cornell-SEWA-WIEGO Exposure and Dialogue Programme, available at www.arts.cornell.edu/poverty/kanbur/EDPCompendium.pdf (accessed 23 June 2006)

Owen, H. (1997) *Open Space Technology: A User's Guide*, 3rd edition, Berrett-Koehler, San Francisco, CA

PACA (2008) *Participatory Appraisal for Competitive Advantage*, www.paca-online.de (accessed 14 February 2008)

Pacey, A. (1979) 'Rural appraisal in sanitation programmes: A technology case-study', *RRA 2*, Brighton: IDS

Pacey, A. and Cullis, A. (1986) *Rainwater Harvesting: The Collection of Rainfall and Runoff in Rural Areas*, Intermediate Technology Publications, London

PALM Series 1–5, MYRADA, 2 Service Road, Domlur Layout, Bangalore 560 071

Paoletti, M. (ed) (2005) *Ecological Implications of Minilivestock: Role of Insects, Rodents, Frogs and Snails for Sustainable Development*, Science Publishers, Inc., Enfield (NH) USA and Plymouth, UK

Parasuraman, S., Gomathy, Kumaran, R. and Fernandez, B. (2003) *Listening to People Living in Poverty*, Books for Change, Bangalore www.booksforchange.net

'Paris Declaration on Aid Effectiveness – Ownership, Harmonisation, Alignment, Results and Mutual Accountability', High Level Forum, Paris, 28 February to 2 March 2005, DAC of the OECD

Parker, B. and Kozel, V. (2007) 'Understanding poverty and vulnerability in India's Uttar Pradesh and Bihar: A Q-squared approach', *World Development*, 35, 2: 296–311

Pathways to Participation (c. 2001) 'Critical Reflections on PRA', Participation Group, Brighton: IDS

Pawson, R., Greenhalgh, T., Harvey, G. and Walshe, K. (2005) 'Realist review: A new method of systematic review designed for complex policy interventions', *Journal of Health Services Research Policy*, 10, supplement 1, July, 21–34

Payne, P. (1979) 'Assessment of nutrition problems: What do we look at and what do we measure?', *RRA 2*, Brighton: IDS

Pedler, M. and Burgoyne, J. (2008) 'Action learning', in Reason, P. and Bradbury, H. (eds) *Action Research*, 319–332

Pelto, P. J. and Pelto, G.H. (1978) *Anthropological Research: The Structure of Inquiry*, 2nd edition, Cambridge University Press

Peters, T. (1987) *Thriving on Chaos: Handbook for a Management Revolution*, Alfred A. Knopf, New York

Pettit, J. (2006) 'Power and pedagogy: Learning for reflective development practice', in R. Eyben, C. Harris and J. Pettit (eds) *Exploring Power for Change, IDS Bulletin*, 37.6: 69–78, November

Phnuyal, B. K. (1999) 'Rejecting "the Manual" for more critical and participatory analysis: REFLECT's experience in El Salvador', *PLA Notes* 34: 68–72, February

PID and NES (1989) 'An Introduction to Participatory Appraisal for Rural Resources Management', Program for International Development, Clark University, Worcester Mass. and National Environment Secretariat, Ministry of Environment and Natural Resources, Nairobi, November

Pimbert, M. (2004) 'Natural resources, people and participation', *Participatory Learning and Action*, 50: 131–139, October

Pimbert, M. and Pretty, J. (1997) 'Parks, people and professionals: Putting "participation" into protected area management', in K. B. Ghimire and M. Pimbert (eds) *Social Change and Conservation: Environmental Politics and Impacts of National Parks and Protected Areas*, Earthscan, London, 297–330

PLA Notes, see PLA

PLA Notes (1997) 'Methodological Complementarity', *PLA Notes*, 28, Sustainable Agriculture Programme, International Institute for Environment and Development, London, February

PLA Series: *RRA Notes* 1–21 (1988–94); *PLA Notes* 22–49 (1995–2004); *Participatory Learning and Action*, 50–57 continuing (2005–2008...), International Institute for Environment and Development, 3 Endsleigh Street, London WC1H 0DD

PLA (2006) 'Mapping for change: Practice, technologies and communication', *Participatory Learning and Action*, 54, April, IIED, London

PLA (2007) 'Immersions: Learning about poverty face-to-face', *Participatory Learning and Action*, 57, December, IIED, London

Pontius, J., Dilts, R. and Bartlett, A. (eds) (2002) *From Farmer Field School to Community IPM: Ten years of IPM training in Asia*, FAO Regional Office for Asia and the Pacific, Bangkok (copies from Meetings and Publications Officer, FAO Regional Office, Phra Athit Road, Bangkok 10200, Thailand)

Porter, M. E. (1990) *The Competitive Advantage of Nations*, Macmillan, Basingstoke

Potten, D. (1985) 'Rapid Rural Appraisal – emergence of a methodology and its application to irrigation: A bibliographical review', paper for the Review and Development Seminar on Selected Issues in Irrigation Management, International Irrigation Management Institute, Sri Lanka

Pottier, J. (1992) 'Agrarian change at the household level: Investigative styles in research on Mambwe agriculture', in P. Kaarsholm (ed) *Institutions, Culture and Change at Local Community Level*, International Development Studies Occasional Paper 3, Roskilde University Centre, Denmark, 61–74

Potts, L. (2001) 'Lies, damn lies and public protection: Corporate responsibility and breast cancer activism', *Journal of International Women's Studies*, 2.3: 1–11

PRA Team (1991) 'The Kyeamba Valley: Issues of concern to landholders and their families, identified in a participatory rural appraisal by members of the Kyeamba Valley Community', September 1991, compiled by a PRA Team with the following connections: Landcare, Department of Conservation and Land Management, New South Wales Agriculture, School of Agriculture, CSU-R, Centre for Conservation Farming, CSU-R, School of Crop Sciences, The University of Sydney and Wagga Wagga City Council

Prasad, C. S., Beumer, K. and Mohanty, D. (eds) (2007) *Towards a Learning Alliance: SRI in Orissa*, ICRISAT, Patancheru and Xavier Institute of Management, Bhubaneshwar (copies from WWF International- ICRISAT Dialogue Project, vgoud@cgiar.org)

Pratt, G. (2001) 'Practitioners' Critical Reflections on PRA and Participation in Nepal', *Working Paper 122*, Brighton: IDS, January

PRAXIS (2001) *The Politics of Poverty: A Tale of the Living Dead in Bolangir*, Books for Change, Bangalore

Pretty, J. N. (1990) 'Rapid Catchment Analysis for Extension Agents: Notes on the 1990 Kericho Training Workshop for the Ministry of Agriculture, Kenya', Sustainable Agriculture Programme, November, IIED, London

Pretty, J., Subramanian, S., Ananthakrishnan, D., Jayanthi, C., Muralikrishnasamy, S. and Renganayaki, K. (1992) 'Finding the poorest in a Tamil Nadu Village: A sequence of mapping and wealth ranking', *RRA Notes* 15: 39–42, IIED, London

PRGA (c. 2002) 'PRGA Program: Synthesis of Phase I (1997–2002)', Program on Participatory Research and Gender Analysis, CGIAR, www.prgaprogramme.org

Proctor, J. H. (ed) (1971) *Building Ujamaa Villages in Tanzania*, University of Dar es Salaam Department of Political Science, Studies in Political Science No 2, Tanzania Publishing House, Dar es Salaam

PTD (2005) Section on Participatory Technology Development, in Gonsalves et al (eds) *Participatory Research and Development...*, 157–199

Ramalingam, B., Jones, H., Reba, T. and Young, J. (2008) 'Exploring Complexity: Lessons from complexity science for development and humanitarian work', Working Paper, Overseas Development Institute, London

Rahman, A. Md. (ed) (1984) *Grassroots Participation and Self-reliance*, Oxford and IBH, New Delhi

Rahman, A. Md. (2008) 'Some trends in the praxis of participatory action research', in Reason, P. and Bradbury, H. (eds) *Action Research*, 49–62

Ramachandran, V. (1990) 'A Workshop on Participatory Learning Methods, 8–12 January 1990', MYRADA Talavadi Project, PRA/PALM Series No 1, MYRADA, Bangalore

Ramalingam, B. and Jones, H. with Reba, T. and Young, J. (2008a) 'Exploring the Science of Complexity: Ideas and implications for development and humanitarian efforts', Working Paper 285, Overseas Development Institute, London

Rambaldi, G. (2005) 'Barefoot Mapmakers and Participatory GIS', editorial, in *Participatory GIS, ICT Update*, 27, CTA Technical Centre for Agricultural and Rural Cooperation, Wageningen, September, http://ictupdate.cta.int

Rambaldi, G. and Callosa-Tarr, J. (2000) 'Manual on Participatory 3-Dimensional Modeling for Natural Resource Management', *Essentials of Protected Area Management in the Philippines*, 7, NIPAP, PAWB-DENR, Philippines

Rambaldi, G. and Callosa-Tarr, J. (2002) *Participatory 3-Dimensional Modelling: Guiding Principles and Applications*, ASEAN Regional Center for Biodiversity Conservation, Los Banos, Philippines

Rambaldi, G., Chambers, R., McCall, M. and Fox, J. (2006) 'Practical ethics for PGIS practitioners, facilitators, technology intermediaries and researchers', *Participatory Learning and Action*, 54: 106–113, April

Rambaldi, G., Kwaku Kiem, P. A., Mbile, P., McCall, M. and Weiner, D. (2005) 'Participatory Spatial Information Management and Communication in Developing Countries', paper for Mapping for Change International Conference, Nairobi, 7–10 September 2005

Ramisch, J., Keeley, J., Scoones, I. and Wolmer, W. (2002) 'Crop-livestock policy in Africa: What is to be done?', in I. Scoones and W. Wolmer (eds) *Pathways of Change in Africa*, 183–210

Rao, V. and Woolcock, M. (2007) 'Disciplinary Monopolies in Development Research: A response to the research evaluation process', World Bank, Washington DC, January

Reason, P. and Bradbury, H. (eds) (2001) *Handbook of Action Research: Participative Inquiry and Practice*, Sage Publications, New Delhi and Thousand Oaks, London

Reason, P. and Bradbury, H. (eds) (2008) *Action Research: Participative Inquiry and Practice*, Sage Handbook, 2nd edition, Sage Publications, Los Angeles, London, New Delhi, Singapore

Redd, B. (1993) 'Not Only the Well Off: PRA participatory rural appraisal', Report of a training workshop 4–22 October 1993, Chiredzi, Zimbabwe, Redd Barna Regional Office, Africa

Remenyi, J. (2007) 'Participatory village poverty reduction planning and index-based poverty mapping in China', in Brock and Petit (eds) *Springs of Participation*, 151–163

Resnick, M. (1994) *Turtles, Termites and Traffic Jams: Explorations in Massively Parallel Microworlds*, MIT Press, Cambridge, Mass., and London

Rhoades, R. (1982) 'The Art of the Informal Agricultural Survey', International Potato Center, Apartado 5969, Lima

Rhoades, R. (1987) 'Basic field techniques for RRA', *KKU*, 114–128

Rhoades, R. E. and Booth, R. (1982) 'Farmer-back-to-farmer: A model for generating acceptable agricultural technology', *Agricultural Administration*, 11: 127–137

Richards, P. (1978) 'Geography is a bottle of Heineken lager beer – how to be the most boring person in development planning and still get your facts wrong', *RRA 1*

Richards, P. (1985) *Indigenous Agricultural Revolution: Ecology and Food Production in West Africa*, Hutchinson, London and Westview Press, Colorado

Rietbergen-McCracken, J. and Narayan, D (1996) *The World Bank Participation Sourcebook*, Appendix 1, Methods and Tools, SARAR, World Bank, Washington DC

Robb, C. (2002) *Can the Poor Influence Policy? Participatory Poverty Assessments in the Developing World* (1st edition 1999), 2nd edition, World Bank 'Directions in Development', World Bank, Washington DC

Rocheleau, D., Wachira, K., Malaret, L. and Wanjohi, B. M. (1989) 'Local knowledge for agroforestry and Native Plants', in Chambers, R., Pacey, A. and Thrupp, L. R. (eds) *Farmer First*, 14–24

Rocheleau, D. E. (2005) 'Maps as power-tools: Locating "communities" in space or situating people and ecologies in place?', chapter 13 in Brosius, J. P., Lowenhaupt Tsing, A. and Zerner, C. (eds) (2005) *Communities and Conservation: Histories and Politics of Community-based Natural Resource Management*, Altamira Press

Rodriguez, F. (2007) 'Policymakers Beware: The use and misuse of progressions in explaining economic growth', *Policy Research Brief*, No 5, November, International Poverty Centre, Brasilia

Roe, D., Mayers, J., Grieg-Gran, M., Kothari, A., Fabricius, C. and Hughes, R. (2000) 'Evaluating Eden: Exploring the myths and realities of community-based wildlife management', Series Overview, IIED, London

RRA Notes 15 (1992) 'Special Issue on Applications of Wealth Ranking', IIED, London

RRA Notes, see PLA

RRA1 and RRA2 refer to the first and second workshops on Rapid Rural Appraisal held at the Institute of Development Studies, University of Sussex on 26–27 October 1978 and 4–7 December 1979. Details of the papers given at these workshops are available from the Secretary, Rural Group, Institute of Development Studies, University of Sussex, Brighton BN1 9RE

Russell, D. B. and Ison, R. L. (1991) 'The Research-Development Relationship in Rangelands: An opportunity for contextual science', Plenary Paper for Fourth International Rangelands Congress, Montpellier, France, 22–26 April

Sabarmatee, S. (2007) 'System of Rice Intensification: Enabling a joyful interaction with nature', in Prasad, S. C., Beumer, K. and Mohanty, D. (eds) *Towards a Learning Alliance*, 37–42

Sachs, W. (ed) (1992) *The Development Dictionary: A Guide to Knowledge as Power*, Zed Books, London and New Jersey

Saleque, M. A., Harun-Ar-Rashid, van Mele, P. and Bentley, J. W. (2005) 'Village soil fertility maps', in P. van Mele, A. Salahuddin and N. P. Magor (eds) *Innovations in Rural Extension*, 89–102

Sanaag CBO (1999) 'ActionAid Somaliland Programme Review', ActionAid, London, June

Sandford, D. (1989) 'A note on the use of aerial photographs for land use planning on a settlement site in Ethiopia', *RRA Notes* 6: 18–19

Savedoff, W. (2008) from a message to the Pelican Initiative Community, 11 January 2008. The archives of this community are available at www.dgroups.org/groups/pelican

Schön, D. A. (1983) *The Reflective Practitioner: How Professionals Think in Action*, Basic Books Inc., New York

Schön, D. A. (1987) *Educating the Reflective Practitioner*, Jossey-Bass Publishers, San Francisco

Scoones, I. (1988a) 'Patch Use by Cattle in a Dryland Environment: Farmer knowledge and ecological theory', paper for the workshop of Socioeconomic Determinants of Livestock Production in Zimbabwe's Communal Areas, Mazvingo, Zimbabwe, Centre for Applied Social Science, University of Zimbabwe.

Scoones, I. (1988b) 'Learning about wealth: An example from Zimbabwe', *RRA Notes* 2, London: IIED

Scoones, I. (ed) (2001) *Dynamics and Diversity: Soil Fertility and Farming Livelihoods in Africa*, Earthscan, London

Scoones, I. and Wolmer, W. (eds) (2002) *Pathways of Change in Africa: Crops, Livestock and Livelihoods in Mali, Ethiopia and Zimbabwe*, James Currey, Oxford and Heinemann, Portsmouth NH

Scott, J. (1998) *Seeing Like a State: How Well-Intentioned Efforts to Improve the Human Condition have Failed*, Yale University Press, New Haven

Scrimshaw, N. and Gleason, G. R. (1992) *Rapid Assessment Procedures: Qualitative Methodologies for Planning and Evaluation of Health Related Programmes*, International Nutrition Foundation for Developing Countries, Boston

Scrimshaw, S. and Hurtado, E. (1987) 'Rapid Assessment Procedures for Nutrition and Primary Health Care: Anthropological approaches for improving programme effectiveness', United Nations University, Tokyo; UNICEF/UN Children's Fund; and UCLA Latin American Center, Los Angeles

SDC (2003) 'Views of the Poor: The perspective of rural and urban poor in Tanzania as recounted through their stories and pictures', Swiss Agency for Development and Cooperation, Berne, May

Semler, R. (1989) 'Managing without managers', *Harvard Business Review*, September–October, 76–84

Senaratne, S. P. F. (1976) 'A Program of Micro-level Studies in rural Sri Lanka', mimeo, no source given, 12 pp

Shah, A. C. (1991) 'Shoulder tapping: A technique of training in participatory rural appraisal', *Forests, Trees and People Newsletter*, 14, October, 14–15

Shah, A. (2008) 'Gradual Awakenings – understanding the significance and potential of the Ubudehe social maps', unpublished manuscript

Shah, M. K. (2003) 'The road from Lathodara: Some reflections on PRA', in Cornwall and Pratt (eds) *Pathways to Participation*, 189–195

Shah, M. K., Kambou, S. D. and Monihan, B. (1999a) 'Embracing Participation in Development: Worldwide experience from CARE's reproductive health programs with a step-by-step field guide to participatory tools and techniques', CARE, Atlanta, October

Shah, M. K., Zambezi, R. and Simasuku, M. (1999b) *Listening to Young Voices: Facilitating Participatory Appraisals on Reproductive Health with Adolescents*, CARE International in Zambia

Shah, P. (1989) 'Concept of People's Participation in the Watershed Development – extension volunteer approach', mimeo, AKRSP, June

Shah, P. (1994) 'Participatory watershed management in India: The experience of the Aga Khan Rural Support Programme', in Scoones and Thompson (eds) *Beyond Farmer First*, 117–124

Shah, P., Bharadwaj, G. and Ambastha, R. (1991a) 'Farmers as analysts and facilitators in participatory rural appraisal and planning', *RRA Notes* 13: 84–94, IIED, London

Shah, P., Bharadwaj, G. and Ambastha, R. (1991b) 'Participatory impact monitoring of soil and water conservation programme by farmers, extension volunteers and AKRSP in Gujarat', Proceedings of the February 1991 Bangalore PRA Trainers Workshop, *RRA Notes* 13: 128–131

Shaner, W. W., Philipp, P. F. and Schmehl, W. R. (1982) *Farming Systems Research and Development: Guidelines for Developing Countries*, Boulder, Westview Press, Colorado

Sharp, K. (2005) 'Squaring the "Q"s? Methodological reflections on a study of destitution in Ethiopia', *Q-Squared Working Paper 7*, Centre for International Studies, University of Toronto, Canada, October, info@q-squared.ca, www.q-squared.ca/papers07.html (accessed 25 January 2008)

Sharp, K. (2007) 'Squaring the "Q"s? Methodological reflections on a study of destitution in Ethiopia', *World Development*, 35.2: 264–280

Sharp, K., Devereux, S. and Amare, Y. (2003) 'Destitution in Ethiopia's Northeastern Highlands (Amhara National Regional State)', IDS Sussex and Save the Children-UK Ethiopia, PO Box 7165, Addis Ababa, April

Sida (2007) 'Bangladesh Reality Check: A listening study, realities of people living in poverty concerning healthcare and primary education', Initial Report, Embassy of Sweden, Dhaka, September

Silverman, S. F. (1966) 'An ethnographic approach to social stratification: Prestige in a central Italian community', *American Anthropologist*, 68.4: 899–921 (quoted in Pelto, P. J. and Pelto, G. H. (1978) 82–84)

Simanowitz, A. and Nkuna, B. (1998) *Participatory Wealth Ranking Operational Manual*, Small Enterprise Foundation, Tzaneen

Singh, K. (2001) 'Handing over the stick: The global spread of participatory approaches to development', in M. Edwards and J. Gaventa (eds) *Global Citizen Action*, Lynne Rienner Publishers, Boulder, Colorado, 175–187

Sinha, A. (1989) 'Harvesting rain water in the tribal District of Singhbhum', *Wastelands News*, 5.2, November 1989 to January 1990, 2–7, Society for Promotion of Wastelands Development, New Delhi

Sitapathi, R. C., Sivamohan, M. V. K., Chandy, S. and Rao, R. S. (1989) 'Soil and Moisture Conservation Activities (a special study): Pilot project for watershed development in rainfed areas', Maheshwaram, Department of Agriculture, Government of Andhra Pradesh, Hyderabad, November

Soemarwoto, O. and Conway, G. (1989) 'The Javanese Homegarden', typescript, Institute of Ecology, Padjadjaran University, Bandung, Indonesia

SPR in Asia (1982) 'Participatory Research: An introduction', Society for Participatory Research in Asia, 45 Sainik Farm, Khanpur, New Delhi 110062

Srinivas, M. N. (1975) 'Village studies, participant observation and social science research in India', *Economic and Political Weekly*, 10, 33–36: 1387–1393

Srinivasan, L. (1990) *Tools for Community Participation*, PROWESS, UNDP, New York

Ssennyonga, J. W. (1976) 'The cultural dimensions of demographic trends', *Populi*, 3.2: 2–11

Stirling, C. M. and Witcombe, J. R. (eds) (2004) *Farmers and Plant Breeders in Partnership*, 2nd edition, Department for International Development and Plant Sciences Research Programme, Centre for Arid Zone Studies, Bangor, UK

Stocking, M. and Abel, N. (1979) 'Ecological and environmental indicators for the rapid appraisal of natural resources', *RRA* 2, Brighton: IDS

Sumberg, J. and Okali, C. (1989) 'Farmers, on-farm research, and new technology', in Chambers, R., Pacey, A. and Thrupp, L. R. (eds) *Farmer First*, 109–114

Swantz, M.-L. (2008) 'Participatory Action Research as practice', in Reason, P. and Bradbury, H. (eds) *Action Research*, 31–48

Swantz, M.-L., Ndedya, E. and Masaiganah, M. S. (2001) 'Participatory Action Research in Southern Tanzania, with special reference to women', in Reason, P. and Bradbury, H. (eds) *Handbook of Action Research*, 386–395

Swift, J. (1978) 'Notes on rapid rural appraisal in dry pastoral areas of West Africa', *RRA* 1

Swift, J. (1981) 'Rapid appraisal and cost-effective research in West Africa', *Agricultural Administration*, 8, 6 November, 485–492

Swift, J. and Umar, A. N. (1991) 'Participatory Pastoral Development in Isiolo District: Socio-economic research in the Isiolo Livestock Development Project, Isiolo Livestock Development Project', EMI ASAL Programme, Isiolo, Kenya

Taylor, J., Marais, D. and Kaplan, A. (1997) 'Action Learning for Development: Use your experience to improve your effectiveness', Juta and Co, PO Box 14373, Kenwyn, Cape Town in association with the Community Development Resource Association, 52–54 Francis Street, Woodstock, 7925, South Africa

Taylor, P. (2003) *How to Design a Training Course: A Guide to Participatory Curriculum Development*, Continuum, London, New York

The Inhabitants of Moikarakô, Pascale de Robert, P., Faure, J.-F. and Laques, A.-E. (2006) 'The power of maps: Cartography with indigenous people in the Brazilian Amazon', *Participatory Learning and Action*, 54: 74–78

Theis, J. and Grady, H. (1991) 'Participatory Rapid Appraisal for Community Development: A training manual based on experiences in the Middle East and North Africa', Save the Children and IIED, London

Thomas, A., Chataway, J. and Wuyts, M. (eds) (1998) *Finding Out Fast: Investigative Skills for Policy and Development*, Thousand Oaks, London and Sage Publications, New Delhi in association with the Open University

Thompson, K. (2007) 'Extract from immersion report: Funsi, Ghana', *Participatory Learning and Action*, 57, *Immersions: learning about poverty face-to-face*, 57–59

Thrusfield, M. (2005) *Veterinary Epidemiology*, 3rd edition (cited in Catley, 2007), Blackwell Science, Oxford

Tolley, E. and Bentley, M. E. (1992) 'Participatory methods for research on women's reproductive health', *RRA Notes* 16: 63–68, London: IIED

Turnbull, C. (1973) *The Mountain People*, Picador, Pan Books, London

Turnbull, D. (1989) *Maps are Territories: Science is an Atlas*, Deakin University Press, Geelong, Australia

Ubudehe Seminar (2006) *Creating Spaces for Citizen Participation in Self-Governance, Poverty Analysis, Local Problem Solving, Sector/District Planning*, Kigali, September

UNDP, Bangladesh (1996) *UNDP's 1996 Report on Human Development in Bangladesh*, vol 3, Poor People's Perspectives, UNDP Dhaka

UNHCR (2006) 'Facilitator's Guide for the Workshop on Participatory Assessment in Operations: Age, gender and diversity analysis', United Nations High Commissioner for Refugees, Geneva

Vaill, P. B. (1966) *Learning as a Way of Being: Strategies for Survival in a World of Permanent White Water*, Jossey Bass, San Francisco

van der Riet, M. (n.d.) 'Participatory research and the philosophy of social science: Beyond the moral imperative', forthcoming in *Qualitative Inquiry*, 14.3

van Mele, P. and Braun, A. R. (2005) 'Importance of methodological diversity in research and development innovation systems', in Gonsalves et al (eds) *Participatory Research and Development for Sustainable Agriculture and Natural Resource Management: A Sourcebook*, 151–156

van Mele, P., Salahuddin, A. and Magor, N. P. (eds) (2005) *Innovations in Rural Extension: Case Studies from Bangladesh*, CABI Publishing, Wallingford, UK and Cambridge, MA

van Steijn, T. (1991) 'Rapid Rural Appraisal in the Philippines: Report of a study on the application of RRA by Philippines NGOs, GOs and University Institutes', draft version for comment, Council for People's Development, 175B Kamias Road, Quezon City, Metro Manila, Philippines, July

van Wijk-Sijbesma, C. (2001) 'The Best of Two Worlds? Methodology for participatory assessment of community water services', Technical paper series 38, Delft, The Netherlands: IRC International Water and Sanitation Centre and World Bank Water and Sanitation Program, Washington DC

VeneKlasen, L. and Miller, V. (2002) *A New Weave of Power, People and Politics*, World Neighbours, Oklahoma City

Vernooy, R., Qiu, S. and Jianchu, X. (eds) (2003) *Voices for Change: Participatory Monitoring and Evaluation in China*, Yunnan Science and Technology Press, Kunming, International Development Research Centre, Ottawa

Viana, V. M. and Freire, R. (2001) 'Participatory Land Use Planning: Lessons learned for sustainable development in the Brazilian Amazon', unpublished manuscript, Sao Paulo, Brazil as adapted in Borrini-Feyerabend et al (2004) *Sharing Power*, 148–149

Voyce, M. et al (1989) 'The transfer of the family farm', *National Farmer* (Australia), 10 March 1989, 1–17

Wakeford, T., Singh, J., Murtuja, B., Bryant, P. and Pimbert, M. (2008) 'The jury is out: How far can participatory projects go towards reclaiming democracy?', in Reason, P. and Bradbury, H. (eds) *Action Research*, 333–349

Waldrop, M. M. (1994) *Complexity: The Emerging Science at the Edge of Order and Chaos*, Penguin Books, London

Walker, G. (1979) 'Notes on rapid appraisal of the utilization of rural health care services', *RRA* 2

Wallace, T. (2006) 'Evaluating Stepping Stones: A review of existing evaluations and ideas for future M and E work', ActionAid International, Johannesburg, www.actionaid.org

Wallace, T., Bornstein, L. and Chapman, J. (2006) *The Aid Chain*, Intermediate Technology Publications, Rugby

Watson, G. (1988) 'Settlement in the coastal wetlands of Indonesia: An argument for the use of local models in agricultural development', *Crosscurrents* (Rutgers University), 1: 18–32, September

Watson, K. (1994) 'Proportional piling in Turkana: A case study', *RRA Notes* 20: 131–132

WCED (1987) 'Food 2000: Global policies for sustainable agriculture', a report of the Advisory Panel on Food Security, Agriculture, Forestry and Environment to the

World Commission on Environment and Development, Zed Books, London and New Jersey

Welbourn, A. (1991) 'RRA and the analysis of difference', *RRA Notes* 14: 14–23, December, London: IIED

Welbourn, A. (1995) 'Stepping Stones: A training package on gender, HIV, communication and relationship skills', manual and video, Strategies for Hope, ActionAid, London

Welbourn, A. (2002) 'Gender, sex and HIV: How to address issues that no one wants to hear about', in Cornwall and Welbourn (eds) *Realizing Rights*, 99–112

Welbourn, A. (2007) 'HIV and AIDS, the global tsunami: The role of Stepping Stones as one participatory approach to diminish its onslaught', in Brock and Pettit (eds) *Springs of Participation*, 123–135

White, S. and Pettit, J. (2004) 'Participatory methods and the measurement of well-being', *Participatory Learning and Action*, 50: 88–96, October

Whyte, A.V.T. (1977) 'Guidelines for Field Studies in Environmental Perception', UNESCO, Paris

Whyte, W. F. (ed) (1991) *Participatory Action Research*, Sage Publications, Newbury Park, London, New Delhi

Wignaraja, P., Hussain, A., Sethi, H. and Wignaraja, G. (1991) *Participatory Development: Learning from South Asia*, United Nations University Press, Tokyo and Oxford University Press, Karachi

Wilken, G. C. (1987) *Good Farmers: Traditional Agricultural Resource Management in Mexico and Central America*, University of California Press, Berkeley, Los Angeles and London

Wilks, A. and Lefrançois, F. (2002) *Blinding with Science or Encouraging Debate? How World Bank Analysis Determines PRSP Policies*, Bretton Woods Project, London and World Vision International Monrovia, California

Willetts, J. and Crawford, P. (2007) 'The most significant lessons about the most significant change technique', *Development in Practice*, 17.3, June, 367–379

Wilson, K. B. (1989) 'Trees in Fields in southern Zimbabwe', *Journal of Southern African Studies*, 15.2, January, 369–383

Witcombe, J. R., Joshi. A. and Stharpit, B. R. (1996) 'Farmer participatory crop improvement: 1. Varietal selection and breeding methods and their impact on biodiversity', *Experimental Agriculture*, 32: 445–460

Witcombe, J. R., Joshi, K. D., Gyawali, S., Musa, A. M., Johansen, C., Virk, D. S. and Sthapit, B. R. (2005) 'Participatory plant breeding is better described as highly client-oriented plant breeding: 1. Four indicators of client-orientation in plant breeding', *Experimental Agriculture*, 41: 299–319

Wolmer, W., Sithole, B. and Mukamuri, B. (2002) 'Crops, livestock and livelihoods in Zimbabwe', in Scoones and Wolmer (eds) *Pathways of Change in Africa*, 137–181

Wood, G. (1979) 'The social and scientific context of RRA', *RRA* 2, Brighton: IDS

World Bank (1999) 'Consultations with the Poor: Process Guide for the 20 country study for the World Development Report 2000/01', Poverty Group, Poverty Reduction and Economic Management Network, World Bank, Washington DC, February

World Bank (2000) *World Development Report 2000/2001: Attacking Poverty*, Oxford University Press, New York for the World Bank

World Bank (n.d.) *The Poverty Experts*, World Bank video of the Tanzania PPA

Yearly, S., Cinderby, S., Forrester, J., Bailey, P. and Rosen, P. (2003) 'Participatory modelling and the local governance of the politics of UK air pollution: A three-city case study', *Environmental Values*, 12.2: 247–262

Index

security bias   45–46, 157
spatial biases   31–33, 42–43, 61, 157, 164
tarmac and roadside bias   31–33, 43
unperceived   39–41
urban bias   31, 33, 46, 52, 154–155, 156
urban research trap   26–29
user and adopter bias   36
Rwanda   113–114, 146, 155

San   134
SARAR   114
Save the Children Fund   113, 126
Savedoff, William   167
Scoones, Ian   61
Scotland   65n2
Scott, James   13, 143
SDC   159–160, 180, 184
seasonal bias   36–38, 44, 157
seasonal diagramming   133–134
security of tenure   59
self-organizing systems   174–176
semi-structured interviewing   78
Senegal   31
serendipity   14, 79, 153
Shah, Anil   90, 166n10
Shah, Meera Kaul   90, 153
Shah, Parmesh   90
sharing   85, 87–88, 101, 177
Sharp, Kay   110, 117
showpieces   34
Sida   159, 161, 180, 184
Sierra Leone   142
silt deposition fields   51, 53, 54, 55, 56, 58, 59
slime moulds   174
social anthropologists   9, 11, 27, 33, 36, 41, 68, 69, 70, 72–73, 73, 88, 106, 134
soil colour   75
soil sciences   63
Somalia   121, 171
SOSOTEC   176
South Africa   12, 62, 116, 137, 186
spatial information technologies   138–141, 143
specialization   39, 41
Spielberg, Stephen   1
Sri Lanka
experiences   68, 69
participatory research   115
roadside bias   32, 33
rural poverty   40–41
surveys   2–3, 13

Srinivas, M. N.   5
Ssennyonga, Joseph   32
STAR   178–179, 182
statisticians   6, 21–22, 153
statistics   8, 105, 122–124
Statistical Services Centre, Reading University   119, 131
Stepping Stones   95–96, 178–179, 180, 182, 184
stereotypes   52
structural adjustment   152, 161
Sudan   34, 38, 57, 90, 135
Sumberg, J.   153
surveys
See also questionnaire surveys
aerial surveys   78
participatory surveys   113–114
rural surveys   73
Sustainable Agriculture Programme   88
Swift, Jeremy   134
System of Rice Intensification   63–64, 66n10, 154

Tanzania
participatory mapping   137
participatory poverty assessment   114
participatory research   159–160, 171
refugees   31
RRAs   83n9
showpieces   34
team interaction   159
Taylor, Peter   171
teaching   184–186
team reality checks   159
teamwork   76, 80, 82
Thailand   79, 115, 146
theatre   169
Thomas, A.   26
Thomas, Tom   42
Thomson, Koy   64, 186
Thornton, Alec   62
time   163
timidity   38
Tinsley, Douglas   47n5
Training and Visit System   83
transect walks   63, 78, 88
transfer of technology   49–50
transport   157
traps   152–153, 154–156
triangulation   80, 99, 177
Turnbull, David   134